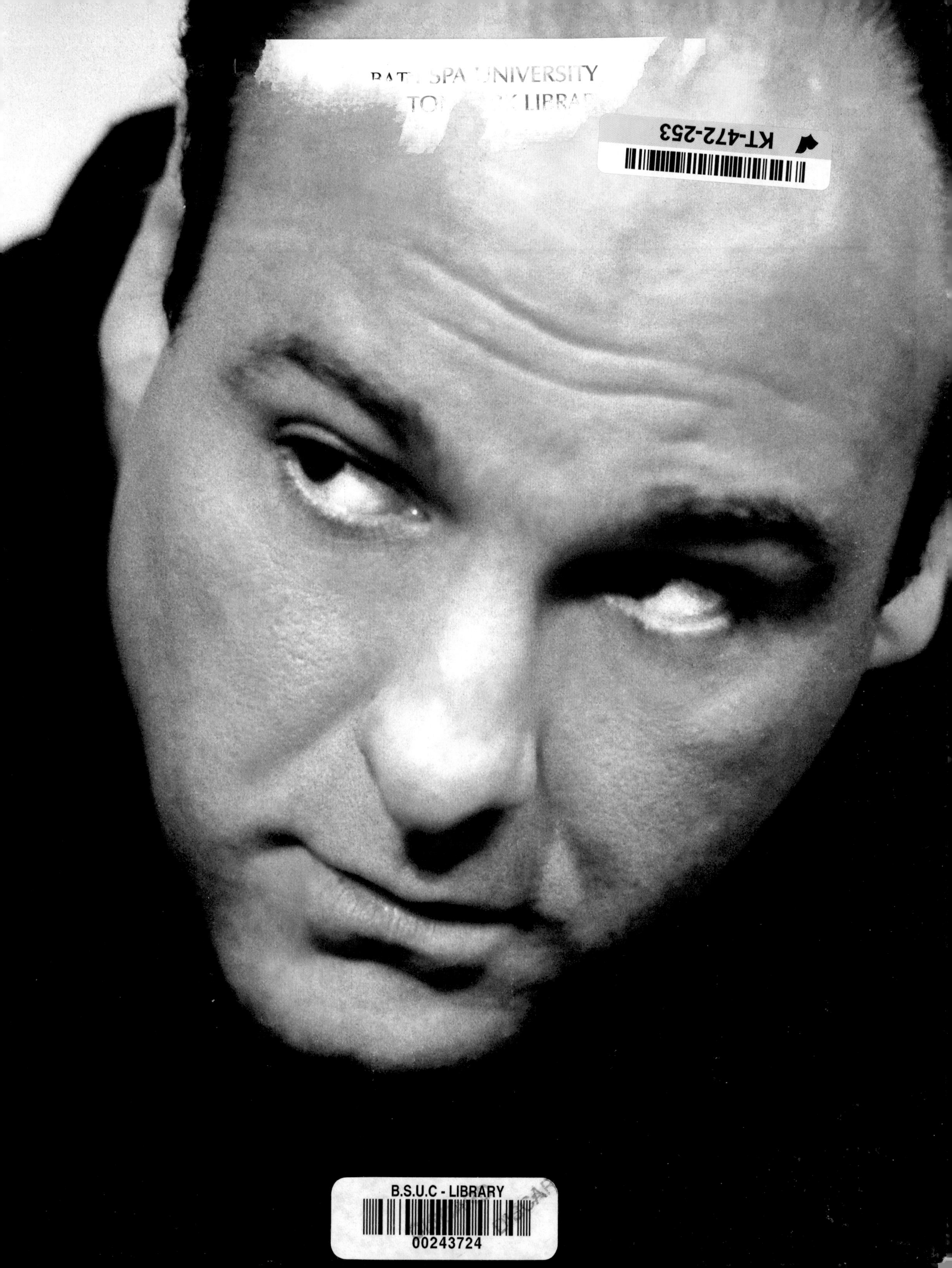

ACKNOWLEDGMENTS

Many thanks to many people, beginning with David Chase, of course, the Balzac of this enterprise; Emma Marriott, a superb editor, Dan Newman, a superb designer, and Charlie Carman; Louise Burke, Carolyn Nichols, Dan Slater, and Hillary Schupf; Dan Castleman; Robin Green, Mitchell Burgess, and all the brilliant writers of the show, with a special nod to Frank Renzulli; all the brilliant performers for their time and comments, with special help from Federico Castelluccio; Ilene Landress, Julie Ross, Chris Albrecht, Carolyn Strauss, Miranda Heller, Mike Garcia, Michael Lombardo, Carmi Zlotnik, Russell Schwartz, Bree Conover, Richard Oren, Peter Megler, Jami Attenberg, Nona Jones, Mark Kamine, and Jason Minter; Brad Grey, Susie Fitzgerald, Chris Newman, John Ferriter, Pauline Domyan, Eric Zohn, Michael Saraceno, Carl Lindahl, Joe and Sandra Consentino, and a man who taught me a lot about writing, Martin Mull. And, finally, the biggest thanks of all goes to Felicia Lipchik, who contributed monumentally to this effort. There would be no book without her.

David Chase wishes to thank Denise Chase and Michele Chase.

NEW AMERICAN LIBRARY
Published by New American Library, a division of Penguin Group (USA) Inc., 375 Hudson Street, New York, New York 10014, U.S.A.; Penguin Books Ltd, 80 Strand, London WC2R 0RL, England; Penguin Books Australia Ltd, 250 Camberwell Road, Camberwell, Victoria 3124, Australia; Penguin Books Canada Ltd, 10 Alcorn Avenue, Toronto, Ontario, Canada M4V 3B2; Penguin Books (N.Z.) Ltd, Cnr Rosedale and Airborne Roads, Albany, Auckland 1310, New Zealand

Penguin Books Ltd, Registered Offices: 80 Strand, London WC2R 0RL, England

Published by New American Library, a division of Penguin Group (USA) Inc.
This is an authorized reprint of a hardcover edition published by Channel 4 Books, an imprint of Macmillian Publishers Ltd, 25 Eccleston Place, London, SAW1W 9NF and Basingstoke

First New American Library Hardcover Printing, November 2000
First New American Library Trade Paperback Printing, September 2001
First New American Library Trade Paperback (Season 4 Update) Printing, September 2003

Printed in the United States of America
Designed by Dan Newman/Perfect Bound Ltd

Picture acknowledgments:
Cover photography: Annie Leibovitz
Gallery photography: Albert Watson
Unit/set photography: Seasons 1 & 2, Anthony Neste/HBO. Season 3, Barry Wetcher/HBO. Season 4, for "For All Debts Public and Private" through "Whoever Did This," Barry Wetcher/HBO. Season 4, for "The Strong, Silent Type" through "Whitecaps," Abbot Genser/HBO. Season 4, "Calling All Cars," 1st photo, Craig Blankenhorn/HBO.
Photograph of David Chase on pages 5, 128: Dana Lixenberg
Still life photography: Matthew May
Photograph on page 44 supplied by Corbis Images
Photograph on page 66 supplied by Vinmag Archive

PUBLISHER'S NOTE
This is a work of fiction. Names, characters, places, organizations, and incidents are either products of the author's imagination or used fictiously. Any resemblance to actual events, places, organizations, or persons, living or dead, is entirely coincidental.

THE SOPRANOS ℠

A Family History
Updated for the 4th Season

Allen Rucker

O

TWO: A SOPRANO

THREE

FOUR: THE SOPRA

F

SIX: TONY AND

Just a brief note on the genesis of this book: I had the good fortune, some time back, to be retained by the noted Mafia expert Jeffrey Wernick. My assignment was to sort through the voluminous research notes Mr. Wernick had compiled on the Soprano crime family. These "notes" filled three overstuffed file cabinets in Mr. Wernick's suburban garage. Shaping this material into a coherent narrative was no small task.

Jeffrey Wernick, for those unfamiliar with his work, is a veteran columnist and crime beat reporter, and author of a dozen books on organized crime in America. These include the classic *Mafia – America's Longest-Running Soap Opera*, plus *La Cosa Nostra: A Children's Guide To Our Thing*, *He's My F**king Brother – Kinship Patterns In Mafia Life*, and the upcoming *Mobspeak: How To Talk Like A Made Guy.*

Mr. Wernick has been building an archive on the Sopranos since early adulthood. His plan has always been to write an exhaustive, three-volume chronicle, the most definitive study of any Mafia family in the history of American letters. But, unfortunately, writing obligations, speaking engagements, and frequent appearances on cable talk shows have gotten in the way. The Wernick opus is still in the offing, but in the interim, we must settle for this humble pastiche.

Almost all the material included here was gathered by Mr. Wernick, a man with almost limitless access to FBI dossiers, public records, and a Rolodex full of informants. In addition, I interviewed Mr. Wernick on multiple occasions to drain his prodigious brain of details. I have also gone back to some interview sources to recheck pertinent facts. Compared to Mr. Wernick's Herculean efforts, this is little more than journalistic housecleaning.

The Soprano story is a long way from over. In a sense, this is only a preamble to the dramatic events unfolding as I write. Someday, though, the story will end – or at least the family will fade, as all mob families do – and then the full story

The people listed below are the principal named sources in this book. It is their recollections and opinions, in their own voices, that make up the body of the text. There are also innumerable unnamed sources who have made vital contributions. They will be identified (as much as possible) as they appear in the book.

THE CONTRIBUTORS

JEFFREY WERNICK nationally syndicated columnist, noted expert on the Mafia and in particular, the Sopranos, author of a dozen books on "the life."

VINCENT RIZZO ex-soldier in the Genovese crime family, currently in the Witness Protection Program. Author of his own life story, entitled, "It's A Killing Business, That's All It Is."

NATALIE DEL GRECO Senior Librarian, Reference Department, Newark Public Library. Specializes in local immigrant history.

CATHERINE DE LUCA high school English teacher, West Orange School District, retired. Tony Soprano's favorite teacher in high school.

BONNIE DICAPRIO M.S.W. Administrative Director, Green Grove Retirement Home, West Orange, NJ.

BEN KALISH high school principal, West Orange School District, retired. Currently serves on State Commission on The Future of New Jersey Education.

FRANK CUBITOSO Bureau Chief, Northern New Jersey, FBI. Federal Agent-In-Charge of the ongoing Soprano investigation.

FATHER PHILIP INTINTOLA Soprano family priest and spiritual adviser to Carmela Soprano.

DR. JOSEPH FUSCO, M.D. Internal Medicine and Emergency Room Medicine, Newark, NJ, retired. Also, longtime family friend of the Sopranos.

BEVERLY SCATINO WOODARD Las Vegas, NV. Second cousin of Davey Scatino, friend of Tony Soprano since high school.

CONNIE BLUNDETTO (maiden name), high school friend of Tony and Carmela Soprano, now married and living in undisclosed location "out West."

DWIGHT HARRIS field agent, FBI, Newark, NJ, assigned to cover the activities of the Soprano crime family.

AMY SAFIR Vice-President, Development, Favreau Moving Pictures and Entertainment Company, Burbank, CA.

NORMA CHARLES Psychiatric Social Worker, Green Grove Retirement Home, West Orange, NJ. Worked with Livia Soprano both in group and individual counseling.

PERRILYNN DIXON Newark, NJ, native of Trinidad, at-home geriatric caregiver. Employed by the Helping Hands Agency, Newark. For brief period, assigned to care duty for Livia Soprano.

INTRODUCTION

JEFFREY WERNICK

The Soprano family provides a unique chapter in the annals of American crime – and American *life* – and I am pleased to open my files to this query into their lives, their loves, and their sometimes-paradoxical relationship to the rest of us. As a lifelong chronicler of the nefarious, bloodstained culture of the Italian-American underworld, I have often asked myself: Why? Why are we so fascinated with the "mob" – we as people, as film and TV viewers, as a nation that pompously calls itself "the last best hope for humankind"? Why are we perpetually gaga over these remorseless, sociopathic deviants who defame the very ethnic banner they carry so high?

Before we delve into this, we must never forget: there are more than 35 million hard-working people out there who call themselves Italian-Americans. How many of those are associated in any conceivable way with the Mafia? By the best FBI estimates, maybe two or three thousand. Mario Cuomo is not in the Mafia. Neither are Rudolph Giuliani, Enrico Fermi, Tony Bennett (real name: Anthony Dominic Benedetto), Connie Francis (real name: Concetta Rosa Maria Franconero), Al Pacino, or Madonna Ciccone. And what about the millions of doctors, lawyers, corporate chieftains like Lee Iaccoca, and solid, Toyota-driving Italian-American men and women who still consider Joe DiMaggio the greatest ballplayer of all time?

Now think about how we non-Italians enlarge and amplify the aura of the Mafia. We don't go around making marquee movies about serial killers – but the Mafia are serial killers. Sammy Gravano proudly told Diane Sawyer that he personally "whacked" a slew of people. A single crew in Brooklyn in the 1970s – the Roy DeMeo crew – killed more people than all the Ted Bundys and Hannibal Lecters rolled into one.

A la *The Godfather*, we don't write bestsellers about the leader of a drug family in South Florida called *El Patron* – but the Mafia sells drugs, both directly and through third parties. And we don't tell our kids fables about the ski-masked punks who Uzi their way through the local Savings & Loan. But they all know about "Scarface" Al Capone and "The Dapper Don," both vicious killers. Go to the farthest reaches of the globe, say, the backwaters of Sri Lanka, and say "Al Capone." I'll bet you dollars to donuts some kid holds up a phantom machine gun and goes "rat-a-tat-tat." And then mutters, in a perfect Brooklyn accent, "Fuggedaboutit."

It's a sick thing, this love of all things Mafioso. I should know – I've been a party to it since I was a pimply-faced teen in the New York suburbs, pinning the full-page newspaper photo of the bloody corpse of Albert "Lord High Executioner of Murder, Inc." Anastasia to my bedroom wall. I, like most of you, can't get enough of this depraved world that we will never traverse, unless, God forbid, we are very unlucky at the crap table of life. Of course, as a reporter, I've seen a few of these guys up close. Their presence is chilling – I inevitably leave the room shaking in my penny loafers. Then I run back to the office and write reams about their dark charisma.

Why? Here's my own answer.

> *"A wiseguy always knows who he is, where he comes from, and whom he serves – the boss, the family, the Italian-American way of life."*

They're Italian

That's right, I'm pinning the ethnic tail right on the depraved donkey. Defenders of the good name of Italian-Americans, the anti-defamation crowd – and more power to them – will tell you that Mafia gangsters are just gangsters who happen to be Italian. Not for me. If they weren't Italian through and through, from the cut of their suit to the cut of their pasta, I wouldn't be interested. My guess is that without their Italian roots, they would have long ago been relegated to the dustbin of criminal history along with the old Irish and Jewish "mobs."

To me, Italians are cool. They have a terrific sense of humor (which is why you never see movies about German gangsters). Even the short ones ooze an aura of masculine power. They are hardy, stylish, sensual, food- and fun-loving embracers of life (which is why you never see movies about Swedish gangsters).

Intimidation works

The main tool of the Mafia trade is intimidation, and as a strategy for getting through life's many roadblocks and frustrations, big and small, intimidation undeniably works. My guess is that many a street corner wiseguy never has to lift a finger to get those timely protection payments. When he was 19, he busted a guy's face for parking in the wrong spot and made his reputation for life. If someone calls his bluff, he signals for an apprentice to step in. That's how he makes *his* reputation.

And though we flinch at the inevitable carnage, we all like the attitude. We all want to get done what we want to get done, now, with no questions asked. Imagine if your last name was "Genovese." Even Vern Genovese would do. Do you think that surly, pot-bellied plumber would charge you $400 for sticking a wire down a clogged drain? Not a chance. You'd say, "Here's a hundred dollar bill, have a nice day," and he'd say, "Thank you, Mr. Genovese, I'll give this money to your church, Mr. Genovese, if that's okay with you, Mr. Genovese."

In Mafia lore, it's called "respect." In fact, in the old days, the neighborhood Mafiosi were called "men of respect." I don't think this is respect as in, "We respect your right to plant a flamingo in your yard," but more like respect as in, "We respect your right to come into our store, take money out of our cash register, and tell us what to charge your in-laws for Portabello mushrooms."

You gotta serve somebody

The trouble with America today is that there are absolutely no obligations attached to living here. You have to work and pay taxes, but once you leave the job, you're entirely on your own. You don't have to go to church, get married, join a union, or be nice to your neighbor. Through 200 years of leaving home and "reinventing" ourselves, we've eliminated those shackles. As an American, your only duty is to "follow your bliss." We are a nation of "leave-me-aloners."

A mobster is a member of a great club. He is blessed with rich cultural heritage, usually an intact ethnic neighborhood, and a comfortably structured career and social life. His friends are his partners; his partners, friends. Going to work everyday with his buddies is a million laughs. Of course, to some, hanging out with the same bone-breakers for 30 or 40 years could get a little boring, but a wiseguy always knows who he is, where he comes from, and whom he serves – the boss, the family, the Italian-American way of life. For a mob guy, crime is what he does. Family is what he is.

Tony having a very bad day

That's the appeal, anyway. But is it the reality?

Enter the Sopranos. The Sopranos are out there, right now, living the life of your contemporary Mafia family. Of course, they'd prefer to remain anonymous. The sensible mob family of today loathes seeing its name in the newspaper or on *World News Tonight*. John Gotti made a spectacle out of himself and look what happened to him.

I myself first heard about the Soprano family in April of 1958. "Johnny Boy" Soprano, Tony's dad and a longtime figure in the bookmaking world of greater Newark, had been arrested on an extortion charge and it had made the lower right-hand corner of page 63 of the *New York Times*. I clipped the item for my boyhood Mafia scrapbook. I liked the name "Soprano" and since I didn't know much about the New Jersey mob at the time, I thought I'd learn a little by following this case. My interest rapidly evolved from hobby to addiction. Soon the Sopranos had their own scrapbook.

"Without their Italian roots, they would have long ago been relegated to the dustbin of criminal history."

What fascinated me, I think, and perhaps what fascinates us all, is that aside from their line of work, the Sopranos are not a whole heck of a lot different than you and me. They're a family with a secret, a big secret – Dad is a career criminal. So was Grandad. So is Uncle Junior. Doesn't your family have its own deep, dark, disgraceful secret? Maybe Mom is a three-bottle-a-day gin drinker or talks to the bathroom wall. Or Dad doesn't realize that Visa cards aren't free money. Or Mom and Dad haven't had sex since Gerald Ford was President. Or, God forbid, Dad once lost control and killed a guy.

On one page of my Soprano scrapbook is a newspaper photo of Corrado "Uncle Junior" Soprano on his way to court – known in police circles as "the perp walk" – after being arrested for mail fraud. On the next page is Tony's daughter, Meadow, proudly displaying her article on *The Melting Icecap* in the school paper. And so it goes, page after page – aberrant followed by normal; arguments ending in death followed by arguments ending in being grounded for a week; scenes from a real-life *Public Enemy* followed by scenes from a real-life *It's A Wonderful Life*. Such is the irony and complexity of the Sopranos' life. Just like our own lives, only bloodier.

Earlier I alluded to the fact that we love mobsters because they look like they have strong identities and the rest of us don't. Tony Soprano, from the shrouded profile we've been able to compose, seems to contradict this myth. He appears to be a brooding, self-questioning man, an anomaly in the Mafia world. He's apparently wrestling with some inner demons that even he can't intimidate into submission.

But that, and much more, will become clear in the following pages. Since the Sopranos haven't invited me, my associate, Mr. Rucker, the FBI or any other outsider into their luxurious suburban home to read their dream journals or go through their dirty laundry, this is largely a circumstantial portrait. It is a rich stew of public records, private wiretaps, and a healthy soupçon of undisclosed sources who, like all of us, wish to see their children graduate from college and will thus forever be relegated to Deep Throat anonymity.

A crime family, a real family, and in all ways an Italian-American family – welcome to the Sopranos.

"We're just like any other family."

Tony Soprano

When you talk about "the Sopranos," you are talking about a group of people where family lines, business lines, and generational lines constantly cross and merge. A current family portrait would include 25 to 30 people – some blood-related, some related by blood – whose individual actions have a ripple effect on others.

To get inside the Sopranos, Mr. Wernick engaged the services of some top-of-the-line Internet detectives. These people have the ability to retrieve Internet documents thought deleted or destroyed. (It's a mystery how they work and a little frightening to think they're out there retrieving your old emails as we speak.)

Here is a premium sample of their work – an exchange of unauthorized emails between two New Jersey-based FBI agents, talking at length about the Sopranos. Please note that the email addresses are not "@fbi.gov," the official FBI destination. The FBI does not allow agents to exchange vital information via official email channels.

To:	██████ ██████
From:	██████
Date:	██████
Subject:	The Sopranos

The Soprano home @ 100% (RGB)

100%   Doc: 195K/OK

Hey, ██████, since you just joined the team, I thought it might help if I filled you in on my own thoughts about the Soprano family. This is <u>not</u>, I repeat, <u>not</u> an official report and shouldn't be shared with <u>anyone</u> in the investigation and certainly not the assholes in New York. This is my own take on things. Much of it is guesswork.

I might as well admit this upfront – I've taken a lot of notes on the Sopranos because I'm thinking about writing a movie or TV show about them someday. I think it could be a big hit, maybe on cable. It's my ticket out of this hellhole.

First off, I like **Tony Soprano**. I genuinely like him. If he wasn't a professional thug, I think we could be friends. He's a guy that likes to be liked, so he goes out of his way to do favors for his friends, some of whom he's known since he was a kid. You can often judge a guy by his friends and Tony has a million of them.

He's got an intact family. Like President Clinton, Mr. Soprano has learned how to "compartmentalize" his life, i.e. the work is one thing, the family another. (And, just like Clinton and Monica Lewinsky, the "comare" is still another.) After you spend as much time tracking him as I have, you'll notice that after work, he usually goes home to his wife and the kids — eventually. Of course his "work" involves hanging out in a strip club for hours on end and coming and going whenever he damn well pleases. It sounds like a good life, doesn't it? How would you like to be able to abruptly walk out of your house at 8 o'clock on a Tuesday night, no questions asked, and come back three days later, handing your wife a wad of cash on the way to bed? Most married schlumps would die for that kind of freedom.

His family puts up with a lot, but I don't think it's necessarily because they're scared of him. I think it's because they love the guy. He's a real family man. They yell a lot, of course.

We've never been able to get a bug into his place, but you can hear many a family discussion from 200 yards. It sounds just like my house, e.g.:

"Don't say that. God forgive you."
"God? There is no God."
"Ey!"
"Where is this coming from?"
"They teaching you this crap at school?"
"They don't teach anything."

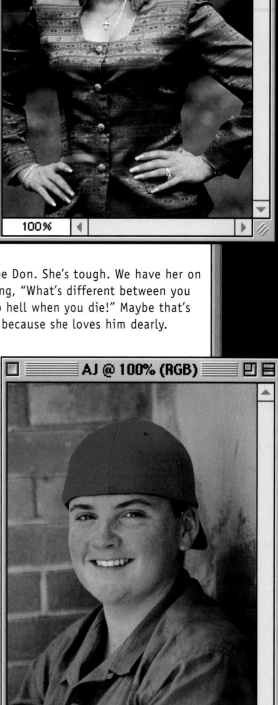

In my mind, his wife, **Carmela**, is a gem. She's very devoted to her kids, maybe smarter than Tony (she reads a lot of books), and doesn't take crap from nobody, not even the Don. She's tough. We have her on tape at a hospital shouting, "What's different between you and me is you're going to hell when you die!" Maybe that's her form of "tough love" because she loves him dearly.

Carmela could have married a lawyer or a chiropodist, I suppose, and had a terrific life, probably living in the same bushy neighborhood she lives in now. Whatever. She married a mob guy. She knew what she was getting into. And what does she get out of all of this? Drive by their house some time. She gets plenty.

The kids are pretty normal, too. The older girl, **Meadow**, is smart, athletic, and probably headed for an Ivy League school and a brilliant career as something. (That kills me – I can't afford to send my boy to Newark JC and this mobster's kid is off to Columbia, probably driving her own Lexus.) The boy, **Anthony, Jr.** (they call him AJ) is not Tony-in-training, I'm happy to report. He seems like a sweet kid, a little on the

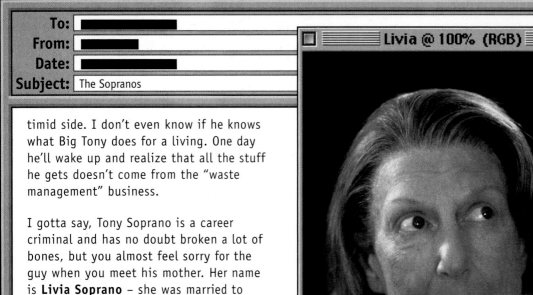

Livia @ 100% (RGB)

timid side. I don't even know if he knows what Big Tony does for a living. One day he'll wake up and realize that all the stuff he gets doesn't come from the "waste management" business.

I gotta say, Tony Soprano is a career criminal and has no doubt broken a lot of bones, but you almost feel sorry for the guy when you meet his mother. Her name is **Livia Soprano** – she was married to **"Johnny Boy" Soprano**, a captain in what was then called the DiMeo Family – and she is a piece of work. She lived for a while at the Green Grove Retirement Home over in West Orange, but now is back at her own place. She looks frail and acts like she's weak in the head but she's got Tony by the cajones. Maybe it's God's way of punishing him for being a gangster. Once you get to know her, you'll stay up nights wondering ... "What in the hell is her problem?"

100%   Doc: 217K/OK

Soprano has a couple of sisters, but they haven't been around all that much. Actually, one of them, **Janice**, a hippie-dippy type who changed her name to "Parvati" (don't ask) recently came back into the picture after

Barbara, Tony, Janice @ 100% (RGB)

something like a 20-year absence. We assume that she decided old boyfriend **Richie Aprile** and her momma's future inheritance was better than hanging around Pioneer Square in Seattle and going to Mudhoney concerts. When Richie disappeared, she disappeared. The other sister, **Barbara**, is married to a prop guy in the commercial business and lives up in Brewster. A depressed, taciturn woman. She got out, but not unscarred.

100%   Doc: 255K/OK

100%   Doc: 379K/OK

You've probably already been filled in about Soprano's close criminal pals, i.e., **Salvatore "Big Pussy" Bonpensiero**, **Peter "Paulie Walnuts" Gualtieri**, and **Silvio Dante**, the guy that owns the Bada Bing Strip Club over on Route 17. If not, check out their rap sheets. They're all sweethearts, as you can imagine. Anyone tell you about **Furio Giunta**, the latest Soprano import from Italy? I think he's part of a new Mafia exchange program or something. He's old school – smash your face into hamburger, then ask for the money.

100%

Except for Furio, these guys seem like guys you'd see at a Yankee game. Silvio does a bad impression of Michael Corleone from "The Godfather." You know the Bonpensiero story, I'm sure. Sad, sad business.

Then there's **Uncle Junior**, the aging patriarch and current boss of the Sopranos (we think). Junior's real name is Corrado Soprano, Jr. He spent most of his adult life as second banana to his younger brother, Johnny Boy Soprano (Tony's dad), so he's not too happy seeing Tony become the most respected guy on the block. He's got a chip on his shoulder like that poor sap Fredo from the movie. But Junior ain't Fredo – he's not stupid and he's still standing. Don't sell him short.

100%   Doc: 217K/OK

Christopher @ 100% (RGB)

100% Doc: 324K/0K

The other relative of the business is Carmela's distant something, **Christopher Moltisanti**. Tony calls him his nephew but it's muddled. He's got ambition. He wants to be something in life other than a mug from Nutley, which is too bad, because he's in too deep now to make a major career change. He likes to talk big and might be a good subject for a tap down the line. I heard he even wrote a screenplay about the life. If you hear about anyone getting their hands on it, let me know. I might want to "borrow" some of it for my own work.

Anyway, I'm just scratching the surface here. These people are rich. There is a lot more to learn about them. They are not cardboard Mafia cutouts from some bad TV-movie. With them, it never stops.

Hesh @ 100% (RGB)

100% Doc: 231K/0K

----------------- Original Message -----------------
From: ▮▮▮▮
To: ▮▮▮▮ ▮▮▮▮
Date: ▮▮▮▮
Subject: The Sopranos

Thanks for the info. But who's Hesh and who's Dr. Melfi? And can I be in your movie? Played by Jimmy Smits, ha, ha?

----------------- Original Message -----------------
From: ▮▮▮▮ ▮▮▮▮
To: ▮▮▮▮
Date: ▮▮▮▮
Subject: The Sopranos

Hesh is Herman "Hesh" Rabkin, a major New York/New Jersey shylock and a crooked Jewish

Dr. Melfi @ 100% (RGB)

record producer and family earner who was an advisor to Tony's dad, Johnny Boy, and now something of an advisor to Tony. If this guy had been born Italian, he'd have been a made guy. Since Tony can't trust his own Uncle Junior, he goes to the avuncular Hesh for counsel. Hesh probably knows Tony better than his own wife does.

Dr. Melfi is Dr. Jennifer Melfi, a psychiatrist with a private practice who we *think* is Tony's shrink. That's right, Tony Soprano has a shrink, or so it's rumored on the street. We can't subpoena her records, of course, given the confidentiality laws. Unless she has prior knowledge of a crime and doesn't report it. But how are you going to prove that? You know how wormy shrinks are. Christ, they'd be an expert witness for or against anybody.

That's about everyone out there right now, but new people pop up all the time, so keep asking questions.

-------------- Original Message --------------
From: ███████████
To: ███ ██████████
Date: ██████████
Subject: The Sopranos

How come Hollywood turns out such crap when this real stuff is right under their nose? Here's the opening scene of your movie:

Ellis Island, 1909, an Italian immigrant peasant named Soprano is getting his papers stamped.

"Soprano," the officer says. "What kind of name is Soprano?"

---------------- Original Message ---------------
From: ██████ ████████
To: ████████████
Date: ████████████
Subject: The Sopranos

Leave the writing to me, smartass.

Our guys @ 100% (RGB)

"You're born to this shit... You are what you are."

Tony Soprano is a second-generation Italian-American. He lives in the greater Newark, New Jersey area, only a few miles from Bloomfield Avenue, a major crime corridor, and only a few more miles from where his grandfather first landed as an immigrant in 1911. Tony has never lived anywhere else. His life is rooted here. He may be among the last generation of Italian-Americans – or Americans, period – where the past is more alive, and more defining, than the future.

Jeffrey Wernick's research on the Sopranos began in the Naples region of Italy. This brief oral family history looks at the lives of Tony's grandparents and the events that led to the marriage of his parents, Johnny Boy and Livia.

JEFFREY WERNICK: Corrado Soprano, Sr., Tony's paternal grandfather, grew up in a small Italian village called Ariano in the region of Naples. His wife, Mariangela D'Agostino, grew up in the same village and they married in the early 1900s. Shortly thereafter, they took off for a better life in the New World. Corrado was a skilled worker, a stone mason. His dream was to come back to his village a rich man, loaded down with presents for his family and friends. He never came back once, not even for his mother's funeral. And he was never rich.

NATALIE DEL GRECO, LIBRARIAN, NEWARK PUBLIC LIBRARY: Newark was a natural stopping-point for thousands of Italian immigrants arriving during that time and many of them were from the province of Avellino, near Naples. The community here was largely Neapolitan, more so than, say, Sicilian, and included members of the Camorra, the Neapolitan version of the Mafia. When the Sopranos arrived, there were familiar faces waiting for them here, people from the same village who spoke the same dialect, ate the same food, or shared the same economic struggle. My guess is that Corrado Soprano had a relative already here who took him in and helped him find a job. There are local census records with the name "Soprani" dating back to the 1890s.

CATHERINE DE LUCA, HIGH SCHOOL TEACHER, RETIRED: I was very fond of Tony Soprano. In my sophomore English class, he composed an ambitious history of his family during "Roots Appreciation Week." As I recall, his grandfather, of whom he was proud, was a stone mason of considerable repute and worked on some lasting edifices in this area. In fact, I believe that the Catholic church the Sopranos attend was built by his grandfather. Not in any design or oversight capacity, of course, but as one of many laborers. I don't know anything about his grandmother. I don't think she was even mentioned in the essay.

Napoli - Spiaggia di Mergellina

JEFFREY WERNICK: Corrado and Mariangela lived in a cold-water flat on Boston Street in Newark where they raised three boys. The oldest is Corrado, Jr., otherwise known as Junior. The second son, Ercoli, known as Eckley, was severely retarded. Until recently, no one except Junior and family friend Herman Rabkin even knew he existed.

Greetings from Napoli

NATALIE DEL GRECO:
According to hospital records, at a very early age, Ercoli, or Eckley, was put away in a state hospital in Glassboro. Those same records show that Eckley's father never came to visit him in the nearly 60 years he lived there. He died of a heart seizure in his sleep in 1985.

JEFFREY WERNICK:
The baby of the family was Giovanni or "Johnny Boy," Tony Soprano's father. Neither he nor older brother Junior had any interest in following their father into the stone mason trade. They both opted for less strenuous "indoor" work.

With both Johnny Boy and Eckley now dead, only Junior could tell us what really went on in Corrado, Sr.'s household. But given that two of his three boys turned into career criminals, it was probably pretty intense. Corrado, remember, came from the old country, where slapping your kids around was considered an acceptable child-rearing technique. My guess is that the old man was a prick – a loyal, hardworking prick, but a prick nonetheless. Junior has been heard to say that all the kids got at Christmas was an orange. Corrado, Sr. had a nasty temper and was subject to towering fits of rage. I'm sure he taught his boys the indelible lesson that the world is a hard place and you should kick the shit out of the other guy before he kicks the shit out of you.

CATHERINE DE LUCA: Tony's grandfather was a working man. Tony's father was a "businessman." Whatever else you might think, these people had no illusions about American equality or justice. They knew the lumpen proletariat were poorly paid lackeys, social "goombahs," to use the parlance – invisible, disposable, poorly paid. They knew they were dismissed by outsiders as stupid, uncouth "wops." How much does an abiding sense of social inferiority drive someone into the dirty business of crime? I'm just a teacher, mind you, not a sociologist, but my guess is, a lot.

GLASSBORO SECURE INSTITUTION, N.J.

Eckley's home

Uncle Junior, 1968

Teresa Pollio in Italy

Corrado Soprano Sr and
Mariangela holding baby Janice

Teresa and baby Livia, Providence,
Rhode Island

Tony, December 1959

Tony (foreground), age 4 and
Artie Bucco at Grandpa's
worksite, 1963

NEW YORK. STATUE OF LIBERTY

Two of Corrado's postcards to his
mother in Italy

mariangela (left) and friend

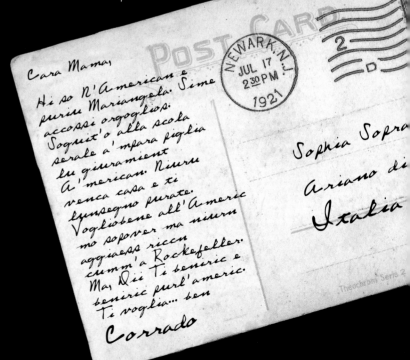

Cara Mama,

Hi so N'American e
purin Mariangela. Sime
accossi orgoglios.
Sognit'o alla scola
serale a' mpara figlia
tu giuramient
A'merican. Niuru
venca casa e ti
lynsegno purate.
Vogliobene all'Americ
mo sopover ma niurn
aggiaess ricca
cumm'a Rockefeller.
Ma, Dii Ti beniric e
beniric purl'americ.
Ti voglia... ben

Corrado

POST CARD

NEWARK, N.J.
JUL 17
2 30 PM
1921

Sophia Sopra

Ariano di

Italia

FRANK CUBITOSO, FBI: Italian kids don't go into the life because they feel marginalized by mainstream American culture. They do it because it's *easy*; a fast buck, a shiny new car. At heart, they're all conniving hustlers who want instant gratification and the easy way out in life. My father grew up in the same kind of neighborhood that Tony's father did – the same prick of an old man, the same torn curtains, the same hand-me-down shoes – and he didn't become a wiseguy. Ninety-nine per cent of kids from those areas don't turn into wiseguys. It takes a special kind of kid to do that. A remorseless punk.

VINCENT RIZZO: I have no idea why people become wiseguys. Hell, I don't know why the fuck *I* became one. I tell you this – it ain't an easy life. It's better than driving a fuckin' bus until you drop dead, but it ain't easy. It takes a tough guy with big *cazzis* to go into it.

JEFFREY WERNICK: God knows how Old Man Soprano felt when his two sons dropped out of high school and began hanging with the local social club, but he probably didn't lose too much sleep over it. Suddenly there was more money around and people on the street were very polite to his family. And remember, few people at that time actively spoke out against the mob. Corrado wasn't interested in someone else's definition of right and wrong. He was interested in survival and his boys were surviving fine.

NATALIE DEL GRECO: Records show that Livia Soprano, born Livia Pollio, was the sixth youngest child of Faustino and Teresa Pollio, both immigrants from Avellino, Italy. The Pollios arrived a few years later than the Sopranos and landed in another largely Neapolitan immigrant community

Teresa, later in life, Providence, Rhode Island. Faustino would not allow his photo to be taken.

in Providence, Rhode Island. The Pollios had a number of children – perhaps as many as eight – but one died in childbirth on the ship coming over and family records are in general very sketchy.

Livia has three siblings still living, two older and one younger, all sisters – Gemma, Quintina, and Settima, the baby of the family. Like Livia, they now live alone and they remain as close to her as anyone.

JEFFERY WERNICK: Livia's father, Faustino, called Augie, was not a hard-working laborer and that speaks volumes about her upbringing. He was a left-wing political activist, a Socialist/Anarchist in the style of Eugene V. Debs, the great American rabble-rouser. Faustino did odd jobs to pay the rent, peddling fish, working in jewelry factories, that kind of thing, but his heart was into the coming revolution that never came. Consequently, the family was dirt poor, I mean, shamefully poor.

Plus, you have to remember, this was the era of Sacco and Vanzetti and wild-eyed radicals like Faustino were not greatly appreciated in the working-class Italian community. In fact, they were generally scorned as seditious firebrands. Faustino stood up to their taunts. He had strong

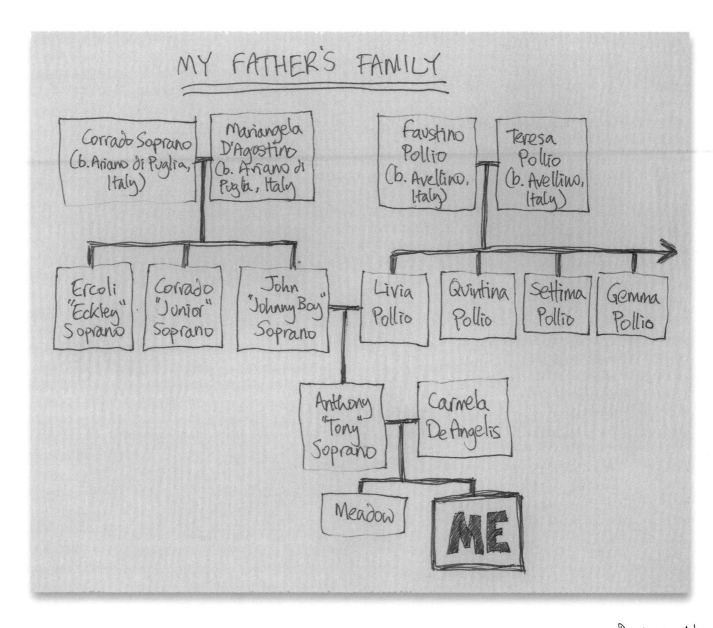

MY FATHER'S FAMILY

Corrado Soprano (b. Ariano di Puglia, Italy) — Mariangela D'Agostino (b. Ariano di Puglia, Italy)

Faustino Pollio (b. Avellino, Italy) — Teresa Pollio (b. Avellino, Italy)

Ercoli "Eckley" Soprano

Corrado "Junior" Soprano

John "Johnny Boy" Soprano

Livia Pollio

Quintina Pollio

Settima Pollio

Gemma Pollio

Anthony "Tony" Soprano — Carmela De Angelis

Meadow

ME

Drawn by A.J. Soprano, 1999

convictions and zero common sense. He was a proud man with his head in the clouds. He was there at the Massachusetts prison on August 23rd, 1927, the night Sacco and Vanzetti were executed. He was holding a placard reading "Electrocute Coolidge!" And he probably acted on those beliefs. He probably set bombs.

CATHERINE DE LUCA: In his "Roots" essay, Tony refers to his maternal grandfather as a "socialist jerk." I'm sure he got that inference from his mother, Livia, not the most congenial woman on earth. The family apparently moved from Providence to Newark when Livia was an adolescent – her father got an unpaid position as a union organizer in the soap factories. Can you imagine how hard that must have been for her – a new town, not enough money to buy a decent dress, and your family treated like pariahs? It's enough to give anyone a sour disposition.

FATHER PHILIP INTINTOLA: Livia rarely comes to our services, but one of her sisters, Quintina, is a very active member. Another sister, Gemma, lives in Tucson, I think. Anyway, "Quinn" and I have had long discussions about their upbringing and I don't think I'm revealing any confidences if I say

Johnny and
Livia

that Livia has always been troubled. Her mother was worn out and chronically ill from raising that many children on no money. Her father was a self-righteous tyrant. She was one of the youngest so the older children teased her mercilessly. Unlike her father, she had no intellectuality, but she did learn something from the old man – an almost constitutional distrust of others and a hatred for the status quo. She seemed to have few friends until Johnny Boy came along. According to Quinn, Johnny fell for her looks – tall, statuesque, very Loren-esque. Not a classically beautiful Italian woman, but beautiful nonetheless.

NORMA CHARLES, PSYCHIATRIC SOCIAL WORKER, GREEN GROVE RETIREMENT HOME: While she was a resident here, I held many informal chat sessions with Mrs. Soprano. She was very open with me and told me some details of her life, including the story of meeting her husband. It is still quite vivid in her memory. As she tells it, her husband was already a celebrity in the neighborhood by the time she met him as a teenager. It didn't bother him that she was poor and friendless. And he wasn't scared of her father. Given that both men were volatile types, I'm sure any disagreement probably came to blows on occasion, though Mrs. Soprano never said as much. She just said, "Johnny Boy told my father that if he ever hit me again, he'd kill him, and my father never hit me again."

Johnny was her protector and her friend, and probably the best friend she ever had, despite his betrayals with what she called his "puttanas."

DR. JOSEPH FUSCO, NEWARK PHYSICIAN AND FAMILY FRIEND: I first met Johnny Boy Soprano right after the war, around 1946–47. I was a resident in the Emergency Room at Martland Medical Center in Newark and he came in with a head injury after mysteriously blacking out.

Because of my love (then) for games of chance, we became friends. Gambling was very important to me and Johnny ran games. I liked him enormously. He was very quick, very funny, almost charismatic. I think he could have been a movie star, like Victor Mature, you know, if he had the ambition. Not that he wasn't doing all right in the retail meat business. It was shortly after we met that he maneuvered his way into Satriale's Pork Store over on Kearney Avenue because old man Satriale couldn't pay his gambling debts.

NORMA CHARLES: Mrs. Soprano can say some shocking things, you know. She once told me that the day her father died was one of the happiest days of her life. Can you imagine? Especially given the fact that her father died broke and discouraged. The Cold War, the McCarthy Hearings, the whole red-baiting thing must have broken his heart. That was no time to be a revolutionary. I'm not even sure Mrs. Soprano went to his funeral. I think she said she sent flowers, then got drunk. They apparently had a falling out over an incredibly small sum of money, and that was it for her. In her mind, he was already dead.

JEFFREY WERNICK: After the war it was a different world, even in the Down Neck or "Iron Bound" section of Newark. The Depression was long gone. People had money, even working people, and since gambling was a way of life back then, and still is, Johnny's gambling operations started booming. He set up floating card games, permanent card games, made books on every sport you could bet on, and then when the debts to him came due, he would loan the guy the money to pay him back at a huge interest. Johnny was a definite comer and good "earner" in the DiMeo family.

DR. FUSCO: Relative to others in their neighborhood, Johnny and his young bride, Livia, had money. They went to Yankee games, ate out a lot, since Livia was, by all accounts, a terrible cook, and took day trips to New York, where Livia

Johnny Boy

pursued her passion for Broadway shows. Livia loved this life and wanted to remain footloose forever. She was a peculiar party girl, Johnny's girl, admired by the very people who used to scorn her. But Johnny, like any good Italian, wanted kids. I'm convinced that Livia had those three kids solely because Johnny wanted them. She probably thought she could find someone to take care of them while she and Johnny lived the high life. It didn't work out that way. It never does.

Johnny and Janice

Sopranos at home, Sunday night with Ed Sullivan

"My dad was tough, he ran his own crew. A guy like that and my mother wore him down to a little nub."

Tony, Jersey shore, 1962

The story of Tony Soprano's upbringing comes to us from a variety of sources – neighborhood gossips, teachers, classmates, parole officers, and high school sweethearts. Most of these people wish to go unnamed, for obvious reasons. Tony's life is not ancient history – it's current events. Wernick's collection of interviews contains much pertinent information about the early life of Tony Soprano.

JEFFREY WERNICK: Anthony John Soprano was born August, 1959, the middle child of Johnny Boy and Livia Pollio Soprano. All the children came late because Livia had problems conceiving. Tony's older sister, Janice, was the only person in the family who ever stood up to the demanding Livia. Baby sister Barbara seemed to fade into the background. Tony was caught somewhere in the middle.

Tony and Janice (foreground), Jersey shore, 1960

NEXT-DOOR NEIGHBOR, NAME WITHHELD: They lived in a small three-bedroom row-house in the Ironbound section which Livia lorded over like Queen Elizabeth. The house was nuthin' to speak about, but they had nice things. I remember they were the first to put carpet in the bathroom. And Livia had a big stereo to play her Broadway musicals and Italian crooners at ten in the morning. She grew up poor, you know, and the insecurity of it really got to her. And Johnny brought home the cash.

CHILDHOOD FRIEND OF TONY, NAME WITHHELD: Tony was like any other Italian kid growing up in 60s and 70s "Down Neck" and later in West Orange. He played sports, in fact, was an ace baseball player, collected baseball cards, looked up girls' skirts, watched *The Ed Sullivan Show*, you know,

Johnny Boy and Livia in happier days

Tony as a runt

the regular stuff. The fact that his dad made the family paycheck from gambling and shit didn't seem to faze any of the kids and certainly not Tony. Tony liked his dad. Johnny was a good-looking guy, funny, smooth, hard not to like. But he had a temper and would knock Tony around. If Tony showed up late for dinner or talked back to his mother, the old man would slap him halfway across the room. It scared the shit out of him. Johnny would yell at the girls, but never hit them. Tony, he treated like a punching bag.

RETIRED NEWARK POLICE OFFICER, NAME WITHHELD:

Johnny Boy's connection to the meat business led him, eventually, into "buying into" the Pork Store over on Kearney Avenue, which could function as a legit enterprise. Buying in, of course, meant loaning the owner some money and then taking over the store when he couldn't pay up. A classic bust-out. He learned the trade – the crime trade, not the meat trade – from a legend in the neighborhood, Old Man DiMeo. DiMeo liked him. He was a smart kid. Smarter than Junior, by all accounts.

JEFFREY WERNICK: Down Neck was all working-class Italians at that time, and maybe a few Poles and Irish thrown in. There was no middle-class. Everyone was making the same lousy money working at the factory or driving a truck or laying cement. Then there were the mob guys. They had class. And if you lived next door to one, no one ever broke into your house. You could leave your doors wide open, it didn't matter. You were as safe as any rich guy in North Caldwell.

CLOSE FAMILY FRIEND, NAME WITHHELD: Livia was a terrible housekeeper, a

terrible cook – I think she made one baked ziti dish over and over – and not the world's greatest mother, either. I think she was ill-equipped for the responsibility of three kids and Johnny and everything. I don't think she had what you might call the mental stability to deal with it all. She was often agitated, focused on various crazy fears. She spent a lot more of her time pushing Johnny to get into this racket or that racket than she did helping the kids with their math assignment. She didn't care all that much if they did well in school. I think school reminded her of all those intellectual Eugene Debs types that used to sit around her father's house all night arguing about "the dictatorship of the proletariat" and crap like that. She saw where books got that crowd – nowhere.

Little Janice

NEXT-DOOR NEIGHBOR, NAME WITHHELD: Frankly I don't think anyone liked Livia much, except Johnny. Johnny was deeply and oddly attached to her. He knew that he was smart, but I think he thought she was smarter. She wanted to move up in the world, as did Johnny, but in her eyes he could seldom do anything right. You know what she calls him now, don't you? A saint. He was a saint because he pretty much did what she told him to do.

All I remember is that she hated our dog. She was so suspicious, paranoid, even, and she thought our dog, Googie, had it out for her. Hey, Googie growled at everybody, she was a good watchdog. So one day we come home to find Googie lying in her dog house with her throat slit from here to there. It was fuckin' awful. Remember that movie, *Rear Window*, where the little dog got killed and buried? Well, they didn't even bother to bury Googie. I don't think Livia herself did it, but she probably paid one of her husband's thugs $5 to do it. Everybody in the neighborhood knew about that woman – she was wacko.

GEMMA POLLIO, LIVIA'S SISTER: People say she killed that dog, but I don't think that's true. It really hurt her feelings, that story. When our goldfish would die, she always wanted to be the one to flush them down the john. But that doesn't mean anything.

LOCAL DOG DEATH LOOKS LIKE A PROFESSIONAL HIT
"Googie" was much loved pet
by EMMA TAIT

NEWARK—In a bizarre incident that has a three-block area of Down Neck up in arms, a German Shepherd was brutally killed early Monday morning in what authorities are calling "murder by contract."

"Googie," a three-year-old watchdog, was found outside of her doghouse with her throat slit from ear to ear. Animal care officials say her death occurred at approximately 5:30am. The dog's loving owner was too distraught to comment and was being comforted by relatives. Paramedics were called to administer narcotics to the woman.

Other neighbors, however, were quick to express their outrage. "It's an outrage," said one woman, afraid to give her name because of possible reprisals. "We have to stop these scumbags. Soon they'll be murdering our children for playing in the streets." Police are investigating.

```
FBI SURVEILLANCE TRANSCRIPT: 98/145652. SUBJECT: Junior Soprano.
--------------------------------------------------------------
I'll say one thing about Livia and then I'll shut up. You know how
everyone has this idea of the perfect Italian mother. She's usually
a tiny woman, usually the world's greatest cook, usually someone who
spoils her sons so rotten that they have a hard time finding a wife
to replace her.
   My sister-in-law is just the opposite. If anything, she's the anti-
Italian mother, more like a German type. She didn't spoil Tony, just
the opposite - she never let him off the mat. He was always trying
to please her but she couldn't care less. The girls helped her keep
things together and make sure Johnny got all the attention she didn't
feel like giving to him. But Tony? He was invisible.
```

NEXT-DOOR NEIGHBOR: The one girl, the older girl, got a little chubby, you know, while the younger girl stayed skinny as a rail. That says a lot, I think. Fat versus thin. Maybe the young one couldn't eat Livia's cooking, I don't know. I didn't like the older girl much. She had a big mouth like her mother. She'd yell, "Shut that dog up!" right through the window. Maybe she was the one who killed Googie.

RETIRED NEWARK POLICE OFFICER: What does any kid do? He takes after his dad. Tony was probably 10 or 11 when he realized why people on the street were always so cordial to Johnny. I'm sure he snuck around the corner one day and watched his dad and Uncle Junior kick the living shit out of some poor working sap who couldn't pay up on his numbers debt. Tony was small as a pre-teen but then began to beef up as a teen, so it probably wasn't much of a stretch for him to go back to Lincoln Junior High and mug a classmate and steal his lunch money. And the next day the classmate would give him the money before he even asked. That's the way it works. They're all bone-breakers.

```
FBI SURVEILLANCE TRANSCRIPT: 98/145652. SUBJECT: Junior Soprano.
--------------------------------------------------------------------------
My sister-in-law could fall into a fucking sewer and she'd come up holding a gold
watch in each hand. But all Livia does is piss and moan.
```

```
        PROBATION REPORT
        ------------------------------------------------------------------
            ESSEX COUNTY PROBATION OFFICE
            DATE: 9/26/72                      FILED 9/28/72
            OFFENDER: ANTHONY J. SOPRANO
            REF: EC70/2110
            AGE OF OFFENDER: 13
            OFFICER: ROMANO
        ------------------------------------------------------------------
COMMENTS:

Offender cont'ds to be surly, uncommunicative. Remains angry
that has to work Saturdays as bagboy to repay ██████████ for
unauthorized use/damage of vehicle. Sees as prank not crime.
Typical hatred of authority.  Spent 15 minutes making fun of my
crewcut, suit, etc.. Kept asking "how much they pay you to do
this shit?" These punks can get to you, you know?
Three more prob visits and he's gone. But he'll be back. Rec
turning up heat next offense. Looking at Johnny Boy, Jr. here.
Bad seed. Chance of rehab - nil.
        ------------------------------------------------------------------
```

Romano

Romano

Livia's home, West Orange (right)

CHILDHOOD FRIEND, NAME WITHHELD: Livia and Janice fought constantly. I think Tony was amazed at Janice for standing her ground while he would try to reason with his mother, which never worked. Barbara, the youngest, never took sides, as I remember. She was smart. She did anything to stay below Livia's radar. A depressed, quiet, strange girl.

HIGH SCHOOL CLASSMATE, NAME WITHHELD: The Sopranos moved from Down Neck to the North Ward and finally to West Orange. It was his mother's idea. She hated being poor and was fearful of the blacks who were moving into Newark. Johnny loved Newark, where he knew every street light and every monty game, but Livia wanted better. Even the North Ward wasn't good enough. Tony had to leave a lot of friends behind, including Jackie Aprile. Jackie and Tony were always close. Artie Bucco's family had known the Sopranos in Down Neck, then they moved to West Orange a couple of years ahead of them. That's when Tony and Artie became really good friends. They had something in common. They had come from the same place.

Tony, Artie and Davey are still friends (kind of)

BEVERLY SCATINO WOODARD, SECOND COUSIN OF DAVEY SCATINO: Davey was an Air Force brat and his father moved from Baden-Baden, Germany to West Orange,

New Jersey when Davey was a junior in high school. David was kind of a boy scout and had trouble fitting in. That's when he met Tony and Artie and the girl who later became Artie's wife, Charmaine. He kind of knew Tony's future wife then, too – Carmela De Angelis, her name was then. He didn't know her that well. I don't think Tony knew her that well then either. Charmaine was kind of a pistol, though, Davey once said that he thinks Tony liked Charmaine in high school. I don't know. I'm getting this third-hand, you know. Tony was a tough guy even then, no doubt about it. Lots of people were scared of him, even teachers. They knew what his dad did for a living and they knew he was cut of the same cloth, if you know what I mean.

BEN KALISH, HIGH SCHOOL PRINCIPAL, RETIRED: Anthony Soprano got into a lot of trouble in high school. In those days it was like a badge of honor with kids. If he got caught lighting a trash can on fire, everyone knew immediately and would congratulate him as he walked down the hall. "Way to go, Tony." "Hey, Ton', burn the whole place down, will ya?" Stuff like that. His grades were deplorable but he had plenty of friends, though, and they weren't all hoods.

BEVERLY SCATINO WOODARD: Tony wasn't the toughest guy in school. There were a lot of mean guys, wannabe wiseguys who would show you a gun in English class just so everyone would know and, you know, be scared of them. On Saturday night they cruised around in their daddies' Caddies and acted like hotshots. Tony apparently never brought a gun to school. He didn't have to. His father was a real gangster, and probably collected money from the fathers of the guys who pretended to be gangsters. People rarely crossed Tony. The ones who did realized right away that they had made a big mistake.

CATHERINE DE LUCA, HIGH SCHOOL TEACHER, RETIRED: In a teaching career spanning 35 years I saw literally thousands of kids come and go. Only a few make an indelible impression. Anthony Soprano was one of those few. If you walked down the hall and he was with his peer group, he was the life of the party. But if you caught him at his locker alone, late in the day, he was deep in thought, ruminating about something darker.

He had a definite sadness about him. I thought he had great potential. I wrote a couple of letters of support for him. I dare say one such letter helped him enter Seton Hall. He got in, but dropped out. I was sick when I heard that.

Trouble erupted around Tony after the game

HIGH SCHOOL FRIEND, NAME WITHHELD: In high school, Artie Bucco played trombone in the band and was the assistant editor of the yearbook. I was in the band, too. To him Tony was just another guy, big, friendly, up for anything. Sure, people were a little scared of him, but that didn't bother Artie. It meant they were a little scared of Artie, too, and he was a little shrimp, still is. And Tony was a great baseball player. He could hit the ball a mile and almost made All-City. I know Tony could've played college ball, if he wanted. And he had a lot of records. Journey. Deep Purple. "Hooked on a Feeling." But not Springsteen. You'd think it'd be natural for a Jersey guy to like Springsteen, but Tony didn't. Fuckin' depressing, he would say.

RETIRED WEST ORANGE POLICE OFFICER: Yeah, we busted the kid a few times in high school, stealing cars, mostly. He may have done a little time in juvie hall, but that's hard to check. Those records are sealed, you know. I remember taking the old man in on a big gambling bust, a high stakes game, many high rollers, like doctors, you know. They all got off with a slap, but Johnny did some time for that infraction. I remember talking to him then. He was upset. His wife was driving him nuts, he said, and his oldest daughter had just flown the coop and taken off to California to be a hippie. It was like his family was falling apart.

January 16, 1975

Dear Ben,

I am taking the unusual (and I dare say, precarious) step of bearing witness for one Anthony Soprano, a member of my sophomore comp class. I know that Anthony is presently "in hot water" over that hooliganism at Friday's game. He is a troubled lad, of that there is no doubt. But lurking beneath those turbulent, storm-tossed waves, there is a deep sea of humanity. The question is, how do we don our air tanks and "discover" this treasure without drowning ourselves?

Anthony has been raised in the perilous province of perfidy. His voracious Dionysian spirit wants to follow this larcenous path. "Apollo" Soprano, conversely, wants to climb Mount Olympus and commiserate with the gods. Like young Holden Caulfield, Anthony has "abnormal integrity." He suffers much because he feels much — the destiny of the thin-skinned.

How did I unearth this muse inside the malcontent? He wrote a fiery broadside for me, "Why An Italian-American Will Never Become President." I praised him mightily for his rough-hewed loquaciousness and we became instantly "simpatico." My afterschool hour was transformed into a salon of two and no subject was taboo, from Hamlet's hesitancy to the doorway of death.

Young, brave, confused, precocious Anthony has no ethical guide dog, Ben, to reach into my metaphorical grab bag, and therein lies this ensuing tragedy. My "teacher's intuition" is unambiguous – if we reach out with concern, he will respond in kind. It is my ardent wish that you allow Anthony to return to school so that we, his last best hope, can "work on him."

Let's give this thorn-covered rose the soil to bloom.

Sincerely,

Catherine De Luca

West Orange High School
273 North Matilda Drive, West Orange NJ 47038

Sarah: I received this from Mrs. De Luca today. She is concerned that Soprano is about to get expelled (and with damn good reason) for starting that terrible brawl in the bleachers at last week's basketball game. Can you file it in the boy's record, and see if the police will give us a copy of their report. When Soprano is back off suspension next week I need you to arrange an interview with him and Mrs De Luca. Maybe she can see some good in him . . . God knows I can't. Ben

Davey Scatino

CATHERINE DE LUCA: Believe it or not, I actually got a note from Anthony when I retired back in 1996. There was a party for me in the school library with lots of old students and friends. Anthony didn't come but a well-dressed young man named Christopher came to give me a note. It was very simple. It said, "Dear Mrs. De Luca, I hope you enjoy your retirement. You were the best teacher I ever had. I mean it. The *best*. Signed, Anthony Soprano." And there was a $500 bill included. I spent it right away. I had good reason since my daughter had what we thought at the time was lupus.

CONNIE BLUNDETTO, CLASSMATE, MARRIED NAME WITHHELD: I had a crush on Tony in high school and everybody knew. He was a sexy guy, a really sexy guy, both tough and nice at the same time, you know. I was never his girlfriend *per se*. He didn't really have girlfriends back then, just, you know, flings. He was dark and dangerous, you know, forbidden fruit, you might say, because of his dad. After high school, I married ▮▮▮▮▮ and we moved to ▮▮▮▮▮. But I never forgot Tony Soprano. Every time there's something about him in the paper, my mom sends it to me. I have a scrapbook of him. He's the only, I guess you'd call, celebrity I ever knew intimately. I mean, well.

BEVERLY SCATINO WOODARD: Artie and Davey didn't see a lot of Tony when he went to Seton Hall that year after high school. Artie was back from London where he'd been studying cookery. He had his own little place and Tony would come by and crash there occasionally, drink all night, that kind of thing. That's what Davey says. But Tony was kind of a loner during that period. He was trying to figure something out, I think. He hung out with himself and drank and listened to Zeppelin.

Artie Bucco

CLASSMATE, NAME WITHHELD: I went to high school with Tony and I went to Seton Hall, too, and I sometimes saw him there, you know, on the way to class. I even went out with him once, to get a drink, kind of a spur of the moment thing. It was weird. He hardly said anything the whole time and he was the life of the party in high school, so it was a little unsettling, you know. He had one friend, a kid named Joey. I remember I asked him what he wanted to do after college. He said he was thinking about brain surgery, then laughed. It was kind of a crazy laugh. I wanted to get away fast. I thought he should see the school psychologist, but I wasn't about to suggest that.

BEVERLY SCATINO WOODARD: His sister was a full-fledged hippie by then, but the later 70s version, you know, like the Manson Family out in California. I wonder if Tony thought about doing that, just shucking it all. Carmela probably talked him out of it.

Something happened to Tony at Seton Hall, I don't know what. Maybe he just wanted to go there to prove to his mother that he could do it. Or maybe he just hated that crowd. He quit, just like that. Tony's good at decisions. He's a natural born decision-maker, that I'll give him.

Seton Hall
Weds 15

Dear Carmela,

I know it seems kind of stupid to write you a letter like this when I could just call you up, but it's after midnight and I'm sitting here, drinking coffee from a fucking machine and trying to study for some fucking world history test and personally, I don't really give a fuck about the Babylonian justice system, you know what I mean? And I like history, you know, but not this shit. And it seems like everyone else in the class already knows it, because they're always asking questions about Eripades or someone, and I feel like an idiot the whole time. Maybe I shouldn't have slept so much in Crowley's class.

It was great seeing you at Davey's party. You were impressed that I was actually going to college, weren't you? You thought I was just another fucking long-haired goofball like Artie Bucco, right? Well, I'm here, but I don't feel like Joe College, I'll tell you that. I really don't know what I'm doing here, to tell you the truth. My parents don't give a flying fuck, that's for sure. I'm the very first person in either of their families to go to college. You'd think they'd be strutting around like peacocks. My dad is kind of proud, I think. He introduces me to the guys at the Pork Store as "my college boy." But if I quit tomorrow, he wouldn't care. And my mother would say "See, you're not smart enough to go to college." It's always good to have my Mom in your corner!!

[...] ...inking? That maybe I was going to be a doctor or lawyer or maybe a fucking stockbroker in a three-piece suit? There are plenty of paisans here but I don't talk to the little pricks. One guy I like. His name is Joey Urbisci. His dad knows Uncle Junior and the whole thing. He wrote an English paper for me. "Symbolism in Cat On A Hot Tin Roof." I got a B+.

Did you know the famous Greek philosopher Socrates killed himself by drinking some kind of poison? What a puss. Next comes the Romans. Fucking sandals. Maybe I'll call you this weekend. I should study but I got to get out of here. These fucking people make me nervous.

Love,

Tony.

REPUTED MOB FIGURE DIES OF LUNG CANCER: LIFETIME SMOKER— LONG POLICE RECORD

by our STAFF REPORTER

MARTLAND—John "Johnny Boy" Soprano, an alleged capo in the Domenico Ercoli "Dom" DiMeo crime family, died at Martland Medical Center Tuesday night of complications brought on by advanced cancer of the lungs. Soprano, 62, listed his profession as "retail meats," but police have long considered him a major operative in the DiMeo organization, active in gambling, loansharking, extortion, union racketeering, and possibly homicide. In the 1970's, Soprano spent five years at Rahway State Penitentiary on an extortion conviction and had many shorter sentences on his record.

"Hey, what can I tell you," one police source said, "I plan to send a thank you letter to the American Tobacco Company." Soprano was an inveterate smoker, which caused his lung cancer, according to his physician, Dr. Joseph Fusco, of North Caldwell. Soprano resided in West Orange, where he was well liked by neighbors and active in charitable causes like the United Way. His official place of business was Satriale's Pork Store on Kearney Avenue. His meats were reputed to be of the highest quality.

Soprano's survivors include one brother, Corrado Soprano, Jr., his wife of forty years, Livia, one son, Anthony John, two daughters, Parvati and Barbara, and one granddaughter, Meadow. Funeral services and interment details are pending.

FRANK CUBITOSO, FBI BUREAU CHIEF, NEWARK: As you probably know, the FBI began a wholesale assault on East Coast LCN (La Cosa Nostra) activities in the late 70s and early 80s. Our main weapon was the aggressive application of the Federal RICO statute. By the early 80s we already had a fat file on the DiMeo Family and had sent a few of them away for some sizable stretches on extortion or loansharking charges. By that point Tony Soprano had already started doing errands for his father, Johnny. It was only later that I found out that he had started college, then dropped out. Looking back, it's kind of sad, isn't it?

FAMILY FRIEND, NAME WITHHELD: Tony wasn't happy at college, but when he came back to his dad and his friends, with Carmela on his arm, he was happy. You can't tell people how to run their own lives, you know. You can't tell them what's "good" for them. At Seton Hall, Tony was a fish out of water. Back home, he was a fish in water. And he got instant respect.

BEVERLY SCATINO WOODARD: Tony was flying there after college. He and Carmela got married – it was a great wedding, I should know, me and Joey were actually invited – and then, boom, along comes their oldest kid, Meadow. He was bringing in money and spent a lot of time with his dad. They became friends, like guys in their 20s and their dads sometimes do.

JEFFREY WERNICK: Then Johnny died. It wasn't all that sudden, since it's well documented that he had had emphysema for years, but it was still a shock. Johnny smoked like a chimney and it just caught up with him. I always wondered if he sort of knew what was coming and that's why he spent so much time in those last days teaching Tony the ropes. But it also could have been because Johnny spent a lot of time in prison and just wanted to catch up with his son.

BEVERLY SCATINO WOODARD: Artie and Charmaine Bucco were around the whole time, since Charmaine was close with Carmela and Artie was close with Tony. Livia was a complete basket case, of course. After the funeral, she wouldn't come out of her room for days on end. Tony felt guilty because he couldn't help his father with the cancer and his mother with her grief. Janice came back and stayed for about five minutes. Junior was heartbroken, of course – he'd just lost his only brother. On the other hand, he had his old crew back. It was like Tony's place to take charge, to arrange everything, to talk to the lawyers and the priest, and he did so without blinking. Of course, a few years later, he took charge of everything.

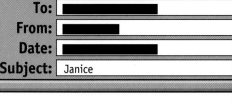

Janice 1 @ 100% (RGB)

100%   Doc: 276K/OK

This should help you with the Richie Aprile end of the investigation. I got this from friends, a couple of twisted arms, public records, etc. These are the "missing years," I guess you'd say.

Okay, Janice is the oldest, and never got along with dear sweet Mama. The minute she graduated from high school, she was gone. (She had already run away a couple of times before that.) First she landed in San Francisco, probably for the weed, but since the Summer of Love had crashed and burned a few years before, she moved on to LA.

Apparently she had a spiritual awakening on the way down the coast and ended up in an ashram/commune kind of deal in Tujunga, a working class sub of LA. LA authorities tell me there were a lot of these groups in those days. They usually gathered in a run-down house in a bad part of town, furnished with old mattresses and a blacklight. When they weren't worshipping an Indian cow or eating bean sprouts, they were having "holy sex" or passing the hookah around. My source said they were mostly Jewish guys with Buddhist names who didn't know what to do after the anti-war rallies stopped. He called them "gurunoids." I guess getting a job was out of the question.

Actually Janice did work during this period. She was a mover for the Starving Students Moving Company in Santa Monica, CA, work records show. Probably gave all the money to the guru.

At some point she wrote home to announce that she had changed her name to "Parvati Wasatch." Rolls right off the tongue, doesn't it? "Parvati" is a big time Hindu goddess and "Wasatch" is the mountain range in Utah. I'm thinking of naming my next kid Swami Appalachia.

Seriously, I got curious about the name Parvati, so I looked it up on Yahoo. She was apparently the consort of Lord Shiva, who is kind of the Hindu Godfather. Parvati is known for "affection for and

obedience to the elders, loyalty to tradition, and determination," among other things. Does that fit Janice? Read on.

Parvati a.k.a. Janice came back to NJ for her father's funeral and even spent the night with her old flame, Richie, but after all of 26 hours, according to a source, she split again.

The ashram broke up shortly thereafter and the trail gets a little cold. She apparently waited tables for cash, then took off for Europe, Italy, for sure, and India. Her sister, Barbara, has postcards marked Pradesh, India, probably another ashram. (There apparently was a side trip to a Mexican acid sex commune in there somewhere, I'm not sure.) I know she lived in Amsterdam for a stretch where she met a French-Canadian guy, first name, Eugene, and they got married. They had a kid and gave him the name, "Harpo." He's got to be about 13–14 by now. He apparently changed his own name to Hal, probably after getting the shit kicked out of him at school. Dad and son now live in Montreal, doing what, I don't know. As soon as I find a birth certificate or a last name, I'll have Montreal police look into them.

Anyway, "Parvati" moved back to LA at some point and went to work for the welfare office as a family caseload trainee. She didn't last long, according to official records. She developed the mysterious Epstein-Barr disease and applied for disability and got it. It was a great scam. They can't treat this stuff so they don't know when it's been cured.

Then she left LA and resettled in Seattle. She immediately got into grunge – a 43-year-old Nirvana groupie. Smart girl that she is, she weaseled her way into another disability scam. She came down

Janice & Livia @ 100% (RGB)

100%   Doc: 276K/OK

with Carpal Tunnel Syndrome from working the steamed milk machine in a coffee bar. I'm not kidding. I have the official disability app if you want to see it. According to friends back here, she was very lonely up there. She was getting up in years and running out of options.

Then someone from here called her, probably her sister, and reported that Livia and Tony were having a little "problem." So Parvati the prodigal daughter moved back home, crystals and all. She started being Mother

Janice & Richie @ 100% (RGB)

100%   Doc: 276K/OK

Teresa to her mom (remember "affection for the elders") and she hooked up with Richie Aprile again.

As you know, they were engaged to be married until his untimely disappearance. Twenty-four hours later, she was on a bus back to Seattle. I wonder if disability pays for a broken heart?

Should we stay on her case? She might know something about Richie's vanishing act. Please advise.

"My father was in it, my uncle was in it. Maybe I was too lazy to think for myself."

Tony and the guys at the Pork Store

Tony Soprano's biological family can be traced back to 19th-century Naples. The same could be said of his crime family. His forefathers weren't criminals, but there is a 200-year-old criminal tradition that travelled with them to America at the turn of the last century. To tell this part of the Soprano story, we turn to public officials and public records, not to mention a few ex-wiseguys who decided their lives were more important than the sacred vow of "Omerta," or silence.

The Soprano crime family has been active in the area of Essex County and Port Newark, New Jersey since the 1930s. In FBI records, it is formally known as the DiMeo family because of the longtime leadership of boss Domenico Ercoli "Dom" DiMeo, currently serving concurrent life sentences for murder, conspiracy, extortion, income tax evasion, and jury-tampering. Since the death of Mr. DiMeo's hand-picked successor, acting boss Jackie Aprile, in 1999, Corrado ("Junior") Soprano has been elevated to boss, at least in title.

FRANK CUBITOSO, FBI BUREAU CHIEF, NORTHERN NEW JERSEY: From what we know, the DiMeo/Soprano family is an anomaly in LCN activity in New Jersey. They are a free-standing, semi-autonomous organization with probably some ad hoc partnership with one or two of the five families. The Sopranos have more independence than most. Their contacts with New York are sketchy at best. Of course, if they want to kill someone of importance, like a soldier in another family or even in their own family, they have to go to New York for permission. As everyone has done since 1939, when Lucky Luciano set up the five families.

VINCENT RIZZO: I knew Johnny Boy Soprano in the 50s and 60s, but the family was established long before that. I ain't no historian, but my guess is they first got together around bootlegging. Bootlegging was the best fuckin' thing that ever happened to the mob. That and the fact that that candyass J. Edgar Hoover spent his time chasing commies and left us alone. Local guys worked out a deal with New York guys. First there was a guy named Alfano, I think, followed by old man DiMeo, a real ballbreaker, you know what I mean? As long as someone in New York was getting a slice, no one cared. On their own turf, they could do whatever the fuck they wanted.

JEFFREY WERNICK: This is very important. The DiMeo/Sopranos are mostly Neapolitan, not Sicilian. Many of them come from Naples, or their grandfathers did. They are an outgrowth of the Camorra, the Neapolitan crime society dating back to the early 1800s. Many of the rituals we have come to know as *Mafia* rituals, like the initiation rites, are identical to those of the 19th-Century Camorra. The Camorrista in America got subsumed by the Sicilian Mafia in the 1920s, but Neapolitans maintained a proud ethnic identity to this day. They are not Sicilians. They are a breed apart. Less organized, but more vicious than Sicilians.

VINCENT RIZZO: Junior Soprano had his own crew in the DiMeo family when I met Johnny and he was a bigshot. The brothers were in different crews but they were into everything that they're still in now. Sports betting was big – remember, this was before all of the legit betting outlets. Johnny was a terrific book-maker, one of the best.

Family ties

NEWARK POLICE OFFICER, RETIRED, NAME WITHHELD: We arrested Johnny maybe a dozen times and made a few things stick. He did some serious time. Many of his associates, like Paulie Walnuts, a young kid back then, did hard time for bookmaking, numbers, extortion, robbery, what have you. Junior got off a little easier.

Johnny gets pinched

VINCENT RIZZO: What happened, see, sometime in there, is that old man DiMeo began to take a special liking to Johnny, began to treat him like a fuckin' son, you know what I mean? I think if Johnny had lived, he would have taken over when DiMeo got pinched. Anyway, DiMeo decided to give Johnny his own crew, and most of his crew members wanted to go with Johnny anyway. Johnny's crew also earned better than Junior's.

```
RESPONDED TO:
DATE    01-01-80      STATE OF NEW JERSEY      TR. NO  PR2044
TIME    0918       DIVISION OF CRIMINAL JUSTICE  PAGE   1 OF 1
FAX NO --                                        B#     B8342010
CONFIDENTIAL TO:          NEWARK PD              DOB    05-11-24
KEYED BY: DN/3453                                RAC    WHITE
                                                 SEX    MALE
                                                 HGT    5-11
-----------------------------                    SOC    099-99-9999
NAME   JOHN VITO SOPRANO                          FBI    9003300
-----------------------------                    PRB    10934532
```

                        NAMES USED BY SUBJECT

JOHNNY BOY SOPRANO

                     ----CRIMINAL HISTORY----

ARREST INFORMATION   DISPOSITION AND RELATED DATA

ARREST INFORMATION		DISPOSITION AND RELATED DATA
Juvenile Record		SEALED BY COURT ORDER
04-08-46	ARR: NK463498	SUSPENDED SENTENCE: 6 MONTHS
Grand auto		
11-22-46	ARR: NK469343	NO CONVICTION
Grand theft		only witness killed
12-13-46	ARR: NK469810	SUSPENDED SENTENCE: 9 MONTHS + FINE
Illegal gambling		served in full
03-03-48	ARR: NK48598	SUSPENDED SENTENCE: 1 YEAR + FINE
Illegal gambling		served in full
05-16-50	ARR: NK502035	SENTENCE: 90 DAYS
Illegal gambling		served in full
01-26-51	ARR: NK51106	NO CONVICTION
Check fraud		insufficient evidence
08-19-51	ARR: NK514592	NO CONVICTION
Union racketeering		insufficient evidence
09-04-52	ARR: NK526823	NO CONVICTION
Conspiracy Murder One		hung jury
05-30-54	ARR: NK542930	SENTENCE: 18 MONTHS
Illegal gambling, loansharking, extortion		served in full
04-26-56	ARR: NK562917	NO CONVICTION
Attempted Murder One		hung jury
06-05-59	ARR: NK595862	NO CONVICTION.
Income Tax Evasion		
11-16-65	ARR: NK658337	SENTENCE: 2-3 YEARS
Illegal gambling, loansharking, extortion, mail fraud		served: 2 years, 1 month.
02-20-70	ARR: NK701928	NO CONVICTION
Union racketeering, extortion, conspiracy to incite riot		hung jury
09-26-73	ARR: NK736642	SENTENCE: 5-7 YEARS
Extortion, loansharking, trafficking of controlled substances, attempted Murder One, evading arrest		served: 5 years, 4 months
07-17-79	ARR: NK796224	NO CONVICTION
Murder One		hung jury

JEFFREY WERNICK: One other thing about Johnny. According to the most confidential sources I have, he had some kind of nervous condition that kept popping up. You'll find this alluded to in police reports dating back to the 60s and 70s. That probably bothered everyone around him and may have undermined his ability to reach the top. He had a severely retarded brother, you know. Maybe mental illness runs in the family.

VINCENT RIZZO: Here's what I think. Johnny and Junior were brothers, you know, but they were probably fuckin' pitbulls when it came to business. So Johnny teaches Tony the ropes, then dies. Junior goes, "Good, now I'll rule and as soon as I figure out what to do with fuckin' Jackie Aprile, I'll be boss." But then all of Johnny's old crew stayed loyal to Tony. That must have pissed Junior off big time.

BIG PUSSY: CW16

Salvatore "Big Pussy" Bonpensiero is one of Tony Soprano's oldest friends, longest associates, and as close to a blood relative as a non-blood relative could be. Becoming an informant must have been among the most excruciating decisions any man could have to make. The eventual discovery of his betrayal, which we're pretty sure happened, must have been a crushing blow to Tony, Paulie, and the others.

CW16 is the son of Lino Bonpensiero. He is married to Angie Bonpensiero, his wife of 25 years, and has three kids. That's how we ended up cornering him. Desperate to pay the bills, including all that college tuition, he got involved in heroin trafficking and walked right into a trap. Why he didn't go to Tony for help, we don't know. Given CW16's friendship with Tony's father, Johnny, it would have been a logical move. But he didn't, and might have paid for it with his life.

Ask Special Agent Lipari - CW16 is not a bad guy, more like a big, friendly family man with a bad back, caught up in circumstances he could not escape. What a dirty business. and one act of cold-blooded "justice" could potentially change a lot around the Sopranos.

WEAKNESSES: We know the answer to this - misplaced loyalty, to providing for his kids and to Tony.

PAULIE WALNUTS

Peter Paul ("Paulie Walnuts") Gualtieri has no known legitimate occupation — he puts "professional investor" on his 1040 form — and no known family except for an aging mother in Tom's River that he visits twice a month. Records show that he is an only child. His father, Gennaro Gualtieri, has a substantial criminal record. There are also numerous filings of local police visits to the Gualtieri home because of domestic disputes. The senior Mr. Gualtieri apparently used his fists to settle arguments, which is probably why Paulie is almost preternaturally violent.

Paulie has been in trouble since he was nine. Juvenile records show that at that age he deformed a schoolmate with a 32" Louisville Slugger. Apparently the victim made an Italian-American slur. Paulie's been in and out of jail ever since. He dropped out of Barringer High School at age 17 and hooked up with Johnny Boy Soprano's crew. Even at that age, he quickly became the family enforcer.

Paulie spent two years in the military and was then "Sectioned 8." His longest stretch behind bars was a nine-year stint at Rahway on a murder conspiracy conviction. Prison reports show that he spent his time reading library books and pumping up. Rumor has it that he killed an adversary by breaking his neck in the shower, but officials couldn't make the charge stick.

He's very proud of his Neapolitan heritage and very loyal to Tony. Without the crime family, he'd be lost. It's his whole world.

WEAKNESSES: His violent, impulsive temperament, fed by chronic paranoia. He's a superstitious man. You could see him bringing the house down by annihilating the wrong guy at the wrong time.

JEFFREY WERNICK: There's an FBI transcript somewhere where Pussy tells Tony that when Johnny died, he made Pussy and Hesh and Jackie Aprile swear on a Bible to watch out for Tony. They all loved Johnny. Sometimes loyalty actually exists in the Mafia.

VINCENT RIZZO: Now, Hesh the Jew shylocked with Johnny and would have been a capo if he had been Italian. Also, he and Johnny made a fuckin' bundle in the music business back in the 50s before big corporations stepped in and cleaned it up. Hesh found these mulignan singin' groups, signed them to lifelong contracts, took over all their music rights, then got radio stations to make them big hits. Hesh wrote a few hit songs himself, or so he says, but it's bullshit. Now he's got fuckin' horses. He's still got his hand in the business – loans, bootlegging, doing things for Tony, the usual shit.

FRANK CUBITOSO: Ours is an ongoing investigation, mind you, so I am prohibited by law to talk about any details of pending indictments, but I can say that Tony Soprano is known to be a close friend of Silvio Dante, Peter "Paulie Walnuts" Gualtieri, Salvatore "Big Pussy" Bonpensiero, and Christopher Moltisanti. For the purposes of our investigation this is his "crew," and yes, at least Paulie and Pussy were associated with his father, Johnny Soprano.

JEFFREY WERNICK: There are six known crews in the family, the biggest and most powerful being the one run by Tony Soprano. Some crews specialize in one thing, like labor racketeering, medical fraud, etc., but others do a little of everything. Almost no one does anything without checking with Tony. Junior Soprano has his minions – like Robert "Bacala" Baccilieri, the late Mikey Palmice, and the late Phillip "Spoons" Parisi. But other crew bosses often fail to enlighten Junior of their activities. He usually finds out second-hand. In a lot of ways, it's his own fault. He's a hands-off Don.

Christopher and his guys Sean Gismonte and Matt Bevilaqua do business

FRANK CUBITOSO: We consider Junior the boss, but in that world, titles are often illusionary. It all comes down to exercising power.

JEFFREY WERNICK: The FBI has hard evidence that Junior and Tony's mother, Livia, decided to have him killed. They have it on tape – it's devastating. Plus there was a rumor circulating that Richie Aprile, upset that Tony was cramping his act, was moving against Tony, but his sudden vanishing act put the kibosh on that. There's no evidence that Tony had anything to do with Richie's disappearance. The problem is that Richie may be in the Witness Protection Program.

VINCENT RIZZO: Hey, wiseguys complain – that's their fuckin' lot in life. I'm sure guys bitch when Tony won't let them sell crack to school kids or when they have to pay Junior money for jack shit. You know why Paul Castellano got whacked? Because the average Gambino street soldier thought he was greedy. But with Tony around, no one will ever clip Junior. Do you get the irony of this? Junior tries to kill Tony but Tony *protects* Junior. It's hard to explain.

JEFFREY WERNICK: They all have their jobs. Paulie collects money and cracks bones. Christopher, the kid, breaks into vaults and whatever else Tony tells him to. Silvio looks good, runs a great front joint and can talk to the mulignans. It's a full-service operation.

FRANK CUBITOSO: The recent arrival from Italy, Furio Giunta, is even more dangerous than Paulie, who's as dangerous as they come. Killing and maiming and watching a guy defecate in his pants is fun for him.

Date of transcription _____

CONVERSATION CONTINUES:

JUNIOR: Livia, open up, it's Junior!

LIVIA: Come on in, it's open!

JUNIOR: What's going on? My Dominican girl
          said you called me.

LIVIA: Well...he sold the house.

JUNIOR: Uh, don't people have names any
          more? Who's "he?"

LIVIA: Anthony. He sold my house! The home
          my husband and I made!

JUNIOR: What else were they gonna do with
          it?

LIVIA: (DISGUSTED) You too!

JUNIOR: Hey!

LIVIA: I suppose he would have found it
          harder to have his meetings at my
          house, than in this nursing home.

JUNIOR: What are you talking about,
          meetings?

LIVIA: Don't think I'll ever see any of
          that money, either.

JUNIOR   (MORE INSISTENT): What meetings?

LIVIA: Raymond, Larry! That sneak from
          Manhattan.

JUNIOR: Johnny Sack? Johnny Sack was here?

LIVIA: With his mohair suits and his shoe
          lifts.

JUNIOR: Suits, pleurisy? More than once he
          was here? Why didn't I know about
          this?

CONVERSATION CONTINUES:

LIVIA: Well, maybe it was you they were
          talking about, who knows? I just
          don't like being put in the middle of
          things!

          I shoulda known something was strange
          when, when suddenly Larry Boy's
          mother moved in here.

          And then Jimmy Altieri's mother.

JUNIOR: Three of my capos have their mothers
          in this place?

LIVIA: Instead of living in normal homes
          with their sons, like human beings.

JUNIOR: (TO HIMSELF) This must be some kind
          of fuckin' end move. What do they
          think, I'm stupid? We'll see!

LIVIA: Now, wait a minute!
          I don't like that kind of talk! Now
          just stop it, it upsets me!

          Or I won't tell you anything any
          more.

JUNIOR: (FUMING) If this is true, Livia, you
          know what, I, I mean...I'm the boss
          for Chrissake! if I don't act, blood
          or no...

          I have to.

LIVIA: Oh God! What, what did I say now?
          (SNIFFS)

          I suppose I shoulda just kept my
          mouth shut, like a mute. And then
          everyone would have been happy.

Investigation on _____ at _____

FURIO GIUNTA

We know very little about Furio Giunta. He's an import from Naples, around the same area where the Sopranos themselves come from. My Italian contacts, who aren't all that cooperative, tell me that over there he was part of a Camorra gang run by a legendary old "Guappo" named Zio Vittorio, i.e. Uncle Victor. The acting boss is one Mauro Zucca, married to the old man's daughter, Annalisa. He's in jail for life. The person in charge, they say, is the daughter.

Apparently, the Sopranos and the Camorra of that area have been in business together since importing heroin in the 1960s. We now speculate that they are in the stolen luxury car business. Unfortunately, we have no hard evidence to back this up but we think The Sopranos send Vittorio's people hot Mercedes and they pay as much as $50-100,000 a car. Tony went over there a while back and Furio came back shortly thereafter.

This guy is a predator. The Neapolitan gangs are notoriously violent which is probably why he's here — to instill fear and get results.

JEFFREY WERNICK: Tony's grooming of Christopher Moltisanti fits right in with contemporary mob practices. They need a business heir and if it isn't a son, hopefully it's a close in-law, like a nephew or cousin. After all, they have an investment to protect. Someone's got to take over some day and it might as well be a blood relative.

AGENT HARRIS: Christopher Moltisanti is the logical candidate to take over DiMeo/Soprano crime operations at some distant point in the new millennium. He is, you might say, the future of the mob or at least the mob in Essex County, which is not exactly good news. He's probably the first generation of wiseguys who've gotten their entire

CHRISTOPHER MOLTISANTI

Christopher Moltisanti is the son of the late Richard "Dickie" Moltisanti, a longtime street thug who was gunned down in a pizza place on Bloomfield Avenue in Belleville. Dickie was Carmela's cousin and a mentor of Tony Soprano, i.e. the connection. To our knowledge, Moltisanti is not a made guy, only an associate, but there is little doubt that he is being groomed for made status. Until recently, Moltisanti worked as a stockbroker at an East Rutherford firm called Pitzer & Koolhoven. The office was shut down after a fraudulent "pump & dump" scheme was discovered around a stock called Webistics. We're sure Moltisanti was in the middle of it, but have no hard evidence. That's just the kind of business he could excel in — he's smart, presentable, and not afraid to shoot a guy in the foot to make him jump.

He also goes to acting classes, recording sessions, knows Hollywood types, and dresses his girlfriend in high fashion. Wait until the media finds him.

WEAKNESSES: Hot headed, impulsive, opinionated, wants to call his own shots. Also, it's said that he constantly second guesses Tony's decisions. That will either get him respect or get him killed.

view of the world strictly from mob movies. Tony had his father, remember. I don't think the real world moves fast enough for Moltisanti. So what does he do? He writes a screenplay.

AMY SAFIR, DEVELOPMENT EXECUTIVE, HOLLYWOOD: Please don't call me again about this. I have a job to protect.

UNDISCLOSED LCN SOURCE: The best thing that Chris has going for him, other than Tony covering his ass, is his girlfriend, Adriana La Cerva. They're engaged, which means it's time for the Feds to get out their rent-a-tuxes. Adriana is hot, a real snappy dresser, designer labels and all, and Christopher's biggest cheerleader. And she knows the life. Jackie and Richie Aprile were her uncles. But I'm sure she's like every other mob queen. She's on a rescue mission. She knows Chris kills people, but that's not the "real" Chris, Chris the dreamer, Chris the guy who's going to discover another career

CUT TO: EXT. ROOF - A BLACK NIGHT
Rocco has just fucked the brians out of two Asian hookers,
"Asia" and "Tokyo Slit" and goes up on the roof to smoke a
joint. Frankie sneaks up behind him. He's got a Glock Nine.
He's going to shoot his sorry ass. Rocco turns around.

> ROCCO
> Holy fuck!

> FRANKIE
> Didn't you hear my taps, fuckstick?

> ROCCO
> It was an accident, I swear Frankie. How did I know
> she was fuckin going to...

> FRANKIE
> Fuck me, man. At this point in my life I don't know
> wether to shit or go blind.

> ROCCO (TRYING TO BE FUNNY)
> Can I hold your gun while you shit?

> FRANKIE
> A va napola, you lousy fuck!
> BLAM! to his stomack. BLAM! to his crotch. BLAM! to
> his ugly fucking head.

DISSOLVE TO:
INT. APARTMENT - SAME NIGHT.
Frankie's blind as a bat old man is on the cuoch, reading the
"Racing Forum." Frankie walks in.

> FRANKIE'S OLD MAN
> Hey, d'you hear about Rocco?

> FRANKIE
> Why don't you shut the fuck up?

> FRANKIE'S OLD MAN
> Hey, what's that I smell?

> FRANKIE
> I give up. The piss you're sitting in?

> FRANKIE'S OLD MAN
> No, its tar. Like on that roof where Rocco got it.
> You killed Rocco, didn't you, you fucking stroonz.

> FRANKIE
> Yeah and now I'm going to kill you, Mr. Magoo!
> BLAM! to his stomach! BLAM! to his crotch. BLAM! to his blind
> face. Frankie smiles.

> FRANKIE (DESOTO VOCO)
> Two fucks down, a fucking millon to go.
CUT TO:

SILVIO DANTE

Silvio owns the Bada Bing strip club on Route 17, a major gathering place and front for Soprano operations. He is married to Gabriella Dante and has one daughter, Heather. She's very athletic, soccer star, mediocre student. She thinks the topless business is "disgusting." She doesn't know the half of it.

Dante is the son of Joseph "Beppy" Dante, a mob soldier gunned down in 1959. Silvio's ambition, like many Italian Romeos of that era, was to be the next Frank Sinatra. He didn't have the talent so he went into another branch of show business – topless dancing.

Dante fancies himself a player in the world of entertainment, having owned many clubs in Asbury Park. He dresses carefully, has an encyclopedic knowledge of movies, and is always on the lookout for fresh, young talent that he can "nurture." He moves young girls from his strip club into the showrooms (or backrooms) of Atlantic City and Las Vegas and takes a big cut of their income.

His role in the crime family seems to be bookmaking, collecting loanshark receipts, and helping Tony negotiate deals and mediate disputes. He is now acting consigliere since Tony's ascension to street boss. He is very engaging and gets along with everyone. He has excellent people skills, a valuable asset in an age of multi-ethnic organized crime.

WEAKNESSES: Believing his own press. In many ways, the man's delusional. His pretensions of class are a defense against low self-esteem. But he will never flip on Tony. He's loyal to the core.

and blow out of town in a Mercedes S-500 convertible, his middle finger held high. Is she that naïve? Hey, love can addle your brain.

NEIGHBOR, ADRIANA'S FAMILY HOME, NAME WITHHELD: Her mother hates that boy. He's a hood, everybody knows that. But these girls never listen. I went out with a mob guy many years ago, I know what it's like. You feel like a queen. Other girls back away when you want to check your makeup in the bathroom. Of course if your guy gets killed or sent to jail for life, you don't feel like a queen no more. You feel like a schmuck.

JEFFREY WERNICK: You wonder why a smart young man like Christopher doesn't get out and stay out? Because he wants it all now. He's just like the rest of them, only younger. They're all about the emotional age of a 15-year-old.

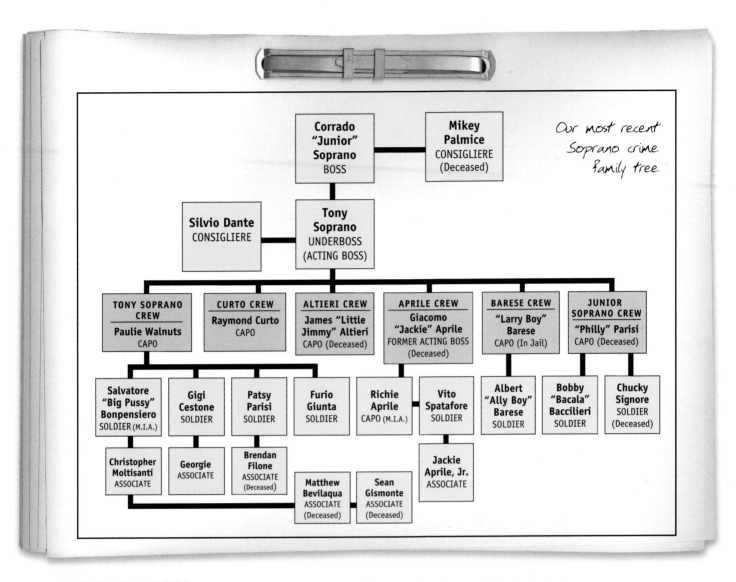

Our most recent Soprano crime family tree

Corrado "Junior" Soprano — BOSS

Mikey Palmice — CONSIGLIERE (Deceased)

Silvio Dante — CONSIGLIERE

Tony Soprano — UNDERBOSS (ACTING BOSS)

TONY SOPRANO CREW
Paulie Walnuts — CAPO

CURTO CREW
Raymond Curto — CAPO

ALTIERI CREW
James "Little Jimmy" Altieri — CAPO (Deceased)

APRILE CREW
Giacomo "Jackie" Aprile — FORMER ACTING BOSS (Deceased)

BARESE CREW
"Larry Boy" Barese — CAPO (In Jail)

JUNIOR SOPRANO CREW
"Philly" Parisi — CAPO (Deceased)

Salvatore "Big Pussy" Bonpensiero — SOLDIER (M.I.A.)

Gigi Cestone — SOLDIER

Patsy Parisi — SOLDIER

Furio Giunta — SOLDIER

Richie Aprile — CAPO (M.I.A.)

Vito Spatafore — SOLDIER

Albert "Ally Boy" Barese — SOLDIER

Bobby "Bacala" Baccilieri — SOLDIER

Chucky Signore — SOLDIER (Deceased)

Christopher Moltisanti — ASSOCIATE

Georgie — ASSOCIATE

Brendan Filone — ASSOCIATE (Deceased)

Matthew Bevilaqua — ASSOCIATE (Deceased)

Sean Gismonte — ASSOCIATE (Deceased)

Jackie Aprile, Jr. — ASSOCIATE

FRANK CUBITOSO: Years of hard investigative work are starting to pay off vis-à-vis the Soprano crime organization. I mean, we have put in literally thousands of hours building cases against those guys – a Herculean effort, if I may say so. Corrado Junior Soprano is now under house arrest awaiting trial on Federal racketeering charges. Tony Soprano barely escaped a murder charge in the death of one Matthew Bevilaqua, a kid who must have stepped over the line. An eyewitness to the Bevilaqua killing changed his testimony at the eleventh hour. But, as you know, Mr. Soprano is currently under indictment for mail fraud and wire fraud in conjunction with the illegal purchasing and distribution of airline tickets.

JEFFREY WERNICK: If Tony Soprano goes to prison, the authorities will be very happy. If they can get him in a situation like John Gotti, where only blood relatives can come visit him and they can tape every visit, they'd be ecstatic. As it stands, if Tony did time for this mail fraud charge, he would still be able to make policy decisions from jail, but he would be crippled. He tends to be a hands-on, face-to-face kind of boss. Paulie Walnuts or Chris Moltisanti or the others do not have the same power of persuasion. They can do the heavy lifting, but they don't have the executive skills. Without Tony's presence, believe me, things wouldn't get less bloody. They'd get *more* bloody.

"An almost **mystical** ability to wreak havoc..."

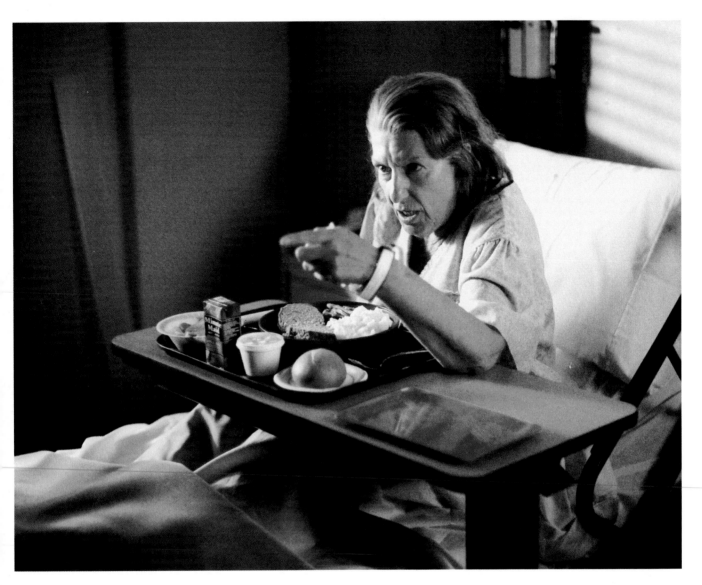

"He can go shit in his hat."

Jeffrey Wernick stumbled upon a treasure trove the day a disgruntled ex-employee of the Green Grove Retirement Home handed him a thick file marked "Livia Soprano." Apparently the ex-employee, now living out of the country, had a falling out with Green Grove owner Frederick "Freddie" Capuano and made ample use of the Xerox machine on the way out the door. His financial arrangement with Mr. Wernick is undisclosed.

Livia Soprano is arguably the most important person in Tony Soprano's life. And unlike the standard mob cliché about women, she is far from powerless. You never heard Mrs. Vito Corleone utter an opinion or weigh in on a business decision, but Mrs. John "Johnny Boy" Soprano exercises power at every turn. She is the embodiment of "the tyranny of the weak."

JEFFREY WERNICK: Livia Soprano was always a tough cookie, but maybe part of her abiding frustration was that she never really got to put her brain to use. In the same sense that wiseguys use the term, she never got *respect*.

Green Grove

ADMISSION SUMMARY

Name __LIVIA POLLIO SOPRANO__   Medical Record# _'23455/345_

Admission Date__see cover__   Room Allocation ___916-B___

Admission Diagnosis __Mild cognitive impairment__

Comments

Mrs. Soprano comes to us from her family home in West Orange. A kitchen fire (SEE official report) was the catalyst for transferring her from independent living into an assisted living environment. She was, needless to say, very attached to her home and very resentful about having to be thrown into this "glue factory"(her own words).

Her immediate family support system includes her son, Tony, his wife, Carmela, their two children, Meadow and Anthony, Jr, her brother-in-law, Corrado "Junior" Soprano, and an occasional friend from the old neighborhood. Less frequent visitors include a daughter, Barbara Giglione, an elderly sister, Quintina, or "Quinn" Pollio, and Father Philip Intintola.

Room assignment: Since she has a decidedly downbeat demeanor, initially assigned to a bright, sunny corner room with a lovely view of the woods. Her initial impression was not positive. Smelled like "rotting dead bodies," she said. Pine-scented plug-in air freshener on order.

Norma Charles assigned to background interviews. All family members listed above refused to be interviewed. Considered it an invasion of privacy. Outside interview process ongoing.

Notes to caregivers

Favorite food: orzo with chicken soup, mushrooms, Lorna Doons, baked ziti, macaroons, biscotti with sesame seeds, i.e. nothing on our menu.

Favorite clothing: One tattered housedress and one pair of leather buckled shoes. Do __not__ attempt to take these items away from her.

Favorite TV shows: "Wheel of Fortune", "The New Jersey Lottery", "The Weather Channel", "Rikki Lake."

Favorite music: Mario Lanza, Ezio Penza, the De Castro Sisters, Connie Francis and old Broadway musicals - "The Pajama Game", "Most Happy Fellow", "Kiss Me, Kate."

Favorite reading material: Obituaries, newspaper stories about bizarre and unforeseen human tragedies, e.g. people electrocuted by hairdryers or eaten by pitbulls.

Religion: Catholic by tradition, but not important. If cajoled, will attend chapel services.

Signature __Bonnie DiCaprio__   Date ▮▮▮▮▮▮▮

Green Grove

1500 Pleasant Valley Way, West Orange, New Jersey 07052

DR. JOSEPH FUSCO, M.D. – LONGTIME SOPRANO FAMILY FRIEND

Q: How long have you known Mrs. Soprano?

DR. FUSCO: For well over 50 years. Actually I knew her husband much better than I knew Livia. I was there, however, at the birth of her three children. All were difficult births. She conceived late in life, you know.

Q: Do you like Mrs. Soprano?

DR. FUSCO: "Like" may be too strong a word, but I often enjoy her company. She's perversely funny, though not aware of it herself. Even when she's on the attack, you want to laugh. As long as it's not directed toward you, of course.

Q: She refers to her late husband as a "saint". Did they have a happy marriage?

DR. FUSCO: Who's to say? I do know about one incident that I think affected their marriage greatly. Do you have time?

Q: Absolutely.

DR. FUSCO: In the middle 1960s, before the family moved to West Orange from Newark, Johnny wanted out. He wanted to go to Reno, Nevada and start over. As he himself explained it to me, the plan was to do whatever came along, then move into the nightclub business and go legit.

Q: And how did Livia feel about this move?

DR. FUSCO: She loathed the idea. To her, leaving her family and the neighborhood meant the possibility of failure and a return to poverty.

Signature _____ Date _____

Q: Why was this incident so important?

DR. FUSCO: Because going to Reno was Johnny's dream and Livia took it away. That argument about Reno is when Livia lost all respect for Johnny. The idea was so insane, so threatening to her that she resented him for it.

Q: Why didn't she leave him?

DR. FUSCO: Oh, come on, in those days, divorce was not an option, and anyway, why should she leave? She ran the show. They went on to move to West Orange and Johnny kept earning, but Livia never let him off the hook after that. He started getting ill about this point. The more she chipped away at his self-esteem, the more erratic he became, sometimes blacking out in the middle of a poker game. Just like that. All over the table.

Q: He had black-outs?

DR. FUSCO: I don't really know and certainly won't speculate. Ask someone who knows, like Hesh Rabkin. There was one other, smaller incident that Johnny talked about. One night after the

Reno incident, he couldn't take it any more so he moved into the Breaker's Hotel in Mantaloking with some whore but came back after two weeks. To Livia, this was a capital crime – he had left her high and dry with three hungry mouths to feed. He had "abandoned" her. I'm sure she clubbed him to death with that.

Q: How did Mr. Soprano die?

DR. FUSCO: The man smoked all the time which, of course, she used as another club to beat him with. She smoked, too – filterless Lucky Strikes – but that didn't keep her from nailing him. She said, "If I die, who cares."

Q: So he died of lung cancer.

DR. FUSCO: Yeah, and it broke her heart. That's where the saint thing comes from. She realized her need for him *after* he died. Livia's greatest fear was that Johnny was going to die and leave her alone in the world. And right on cue, that's exactly what he did.

Q: Anything else you want to add about Mrs. Soprano?

DR. FUSCO: One more thing. I'm a lot older than Livia and I think I know what she's going through. All old people hate being forced into a nursing home, but they're not as bullheaded as that mother. Hatred burns in that woman's heart. The thing about old people is that age tends to bring out their *worst* qualities, not their best. Livia always wanted the world to revolve around her. Now she wants the universe.

Signature _Bonnie DiCaprio_

THIS SPACE FOR WRITING MESSAGES

PUBLISHED BY THE PHOTO AND ART POSTAL CARD CO.

Hey, Johnny Boy, get your ass out here! They're fucking handing out money and the pussy is free! Beppie is here, so is Ball-Less Charlie Venturi. "Financial services" needed, maybe a tittie club in your future.

Rocco

119780

POST CARD

QUALITY

THIS SPACE FO

Johnny
Soprano
1142 Nor
Newark
NJ 10

Green Grove

1500 Pleasant Valley Way, West Orange, New Jersey 07052

PERRILYN DIXON – AT-HOME CAREGIVER

Q: Mrs. Dixon, how long did you attend to Mrs. Soprano?

MRS. DIXON: Too long. She was a trip, that lady. She was like a witch or something.

Q: Please explain.

MRS. DIXON: See, they brought me in to take care of her after she went and almost burnt down her house. She didn't like me coming through the door. She didn't wet her bed or forget to bathe, like most of them do, but she was mean. Mean mean, you know what I'm saying? First of all, she didn't like black people. She called us *"bruschetta."* She thought I was stealing her blind. Every time I come over, she'd start yelling… "Where's my silver brooch?"

Q: And you weren't stealing, of course.

MRS. DIXON: I'll let that one go, lady. Actually, what it was, was that she gave all of her best jewelry away to some relative named Josephine Pollio just to keep it away from the son, you know, the big one.

Q: Other than the accusations of theft, was she difficult?

MRS. DIXON. Like I said, she wasn't a soiler, thank God, but when I tried to help her take a bath, she must've thought I was trying to molest her or something, because she would swing at me like a boxer. I quit one time, but the son bribed me into coming back. He had a lot of money, that son, and I don't think he wanted to be giving her no bath. Then I quit. She vexed me one too many times.

Q: Is there anything nice you have to say about Mrs. Soprano?

MRS. DIXON: She liked her music. Whenever she got way out of control, which was a lot, I would put on one of her old Mario Lanza records and she would stop and listen. She loved one song by Elvis Presley, which I thought was strange, you know. It was called "Surrender." She called it "Sorrento." I kind of liked that one, too.

Q: Anything else you liked about her?

MRS. DIXON: Nope.

DiCaprio　　Date ▮▮▮▮▮▮▮▮

Mario Lanza

Green Grove

1500 Pleasant Valley Way, West Orange, New Jersey 07052

RESIDENT: Livia Pollio Soprano   **ROOM:** 916-B   **AGE:** 70   **RESIDENT FOR:** 4 months, 9 days

GENERAL HEALTH: Physical health, good. Mental health, poor.

The staff evaluation committee assigned to Mrs. Soprano is in unanimous agreement that she continues to be a difficult resident. She is moody, standoffish, and is extremely reluctant to participate in group activities. Many of the other residents are afraid of her and there are many staff complaints, especially from African-American staff.

DIAGNOSTIC IMPRESSIONS: In a word, unpredictable. Orderly K.L. reports that Mrs. Soprano threatened him with a letter opener when he came to change her sheets. Recreational Staff Member P.R. reports that Mrs. Soprano kicked resident Seamus Kelly in the testes during ballroom dancing class after accusing him of intentionally and repeatedly touching her buttocks. (See resident complaint #639.) Mr. Kelly threatened lawsuit. Kitchen staff talked him out of it with extra serving of ice cream at evening meal.

NUTRITIONAL COMPLIANCE: Nutritionist D.N. reports that Mrs. Soprano continues to be a poor eater. Refers to food as "institutional dog s**t." Often refuses to join others in dining room for meals. Her weight has dropped precipitously since arrival. She often takes her meals in bed and then hides the food in the mattress rather than being spoon-fed. When Orderly E.M. finally changed her sheets on Wednesday, he found week-old lasagna covered with mold. We all must check daily for rancid food products like this. The State Board of Health could jerk our license for just one such infraction.

PRECIPITATING FACTORS: According to all observers, Mrs. Soprano has little social interaction. Her children and grandchildren come at least once a week but seldom stay long. Primary social outlet is her brother-in-law, Mr. Corrado Soprano. They sit for hours talking about the family, especially her late husband, Johnny, and her son, Tony. They don't seem to like Tony. Other residents complain about coarse language that Mr. Soprano uses in public. (See resident complaint #653.)

MENTAL STATUS OBSERVATION: Is she depressed? Staff psychologist Dr. W.D. thinks yes. She sits for hours in the hospitality room, alone, staring out the window. Any attempt to engage her in conversation, cards, bingo, or aerobics is received with tears or a litany of woe and abuse.

MEDICATION COMPLIANCE: Zero. With the written permission of her son, Anthony – who claims to have power of attorney over her affairs – Dr. A.C. prescribed common psychotropic Xanax and anti-depressant Celebrex, to no avail. Her MO is to take the dosage, hold it in her mouth, then spit it out when nurse on duty leaves the room. She told nurse A.N. that we're trying to poison her at her son's instruction and split her inheritance!

PHYSICAL STATUS OBSERVATION: No observable symptoms of pain, discomfort, or illness. Her manner suggests the early presentation of Alzheimer's but the staff is not buying it. Comments include: "She's faking it." "It's a cry for sympathy or maybe she did something she'd really like to forget." "She's never forgotten Mr. Kelly stepping on her foot." She repeats to anyone who'll listen, "I wish the Lord would take me now." Is this a true suicidal ideation?

CONCLUSIONS: Mrs. Soprano has repeatedly expressed the desire to leave "this glue factory," as she calls it. She is deeply unhappy and her behavior belies the view that this is just an act. If she could find a friend here, she might come out of hostile shell. Most staff members agreed that they would like to help her, even some she has repeatedly insulted. Dr. A.S. volunteered to draw up a list of suggestions for our next evaluation. Further efforts required.

Signature _____*Bonnie DiCaprio*_____   Date _____

Green Grove

1500 Pleasant Valley Way, West Orange, New Jersey 07052

FATHER PHILIP INTINTOLA – SOPRANO FAMILY PRIEST

Q: Does Mrs. Soprano believe in God?

FATHER PHIL: Absolutely. I like to think that she simply hasn't found her own way of communicating with God.

Q: Or anyone else, apparently.

FATHER PHIL: Or they haven't learned to communicate with her. I think, with Mrs. Soprano, you have to be attuned to hearing what she is saying beneath what she actually says.

Q: Is her son good at communicating with her?

FATHER PHIL: Join them at lunch and find out for yourself. Let's face it, Tony and his wonderful, caring wife, Carmela, were left holding the bag. It's traditionally a daughter's job to look after an aging parent, but not in this case. Barbara only lives a hundred miles away, but she might as well be in another time zone. Livia refuses to cross the Hudson River. Janice is Janice. She was back for a while, acting like a saint, but then she split again. So the burden falls on Tony, which means Carmela, whom Livia distrusts and belittles. I guess they're just like a lot of middle-aged people out there. The sandwich generation. The kids are the ham and the aging parent is the cheese.

Q: Excuse me?

FATHER PHIL: The "sandwich" generation. You know, Baby Boomers who have to take care of aging parents and raging teens at the same time. *Newsweek* did a cover story on it.

Q: And how would you describe her relationship with her brother-in-law, Junior?

FATHER PHIL: Odd. It's like they need each other but don't particularly like each other. He must remind her of Johnny. I think he confides in her, probably issues the rest of us don't need to know about. Sometimes they'd be arguing, sometimes smiling. I thought it was kind of sweet. Wouldn't it be nice if they fell in love and got married? It would be Junior's first.

Q: One last question – do you think that Mrs. Soprano and her son will ever reach some kind of rapprochement?

FATHER PHIL: I'm not sure. I do think there is some mutual respect there. I can see Tony turning to his mother for advice, even business advice. And it will probably be the right, or should I say, the strategic, thing to do. In her kind of "Did I say that?" way, she'll talk and he'll listen. And after all the rest have stumbled and fallen, she'll still be standing. It's her special gift to survive by exercising power through powerlessness.

INITIAL REPORT/WEST ORANGE FIRE DEPARTMENT

INCIDENT: HOUSEHOLD FIRE
LOCATION: 55 BENEDEK AVENUE, WEST ORANGE, NJ 07052
VICTIMS: 1 (ONE) - uninjured
DATE: SEE DUTY LOG
NUMBER OF ALARMS: One
DESCRIPTION OF OCCUPANT(S): MRS. LIVIA SOPRANO,
elderly woman, living alone, a known figure to the
department because of many previous visits to
residence
CALLED IN BY: Anthony Soprano, North Caldwell, son

CAUSE OF FIRE: Burnt mushrooms
EXTENT OF FIRE: Interior damage to kitchen area, smoke damage to walls. Fire burned
freely for approximately 10 minutes but contained to kitchen. Appliances charred but
still functioning. Threat of gas explosion avoided.
COMMENTS: According to testimony by Mrs. Soprano, in the presence of her daughter-in-
law, the blame for the fire rests with her son, who called her at the wrong time, and
a passing African-American postal worker, who she felt was "stealing something across
the street." Records show that on three other occasions units were called to residence
after neighbors reported smoke coming from kitchen. On two of these occasions, Mrs.
Soprano would not let firefighters in the door. She apparently thought we were coming
to take her to "the nut house."
ACTION REQUIRED: Require responsible relatives to install hair-trigger alarm system
with signal directly to station house.

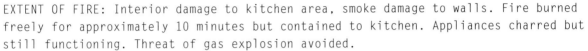

Green Grove

RESIDENT COMPLAINT FORM

RECEIVED BY BC: 4/27
ACTIONED: BC

Filed by___MR. SEAMUS KELLY_____   Complaint # ____639_____

Details:

Mr. Kelly reported to the front desk that during last Thursday's
"Parisian Nights" ballroom dancing class, Mrs. Livia Soprano attacked
him for no reason. According to witnesses, i.e., the whole class, Mrs.
Soprano accused Mr. Kelly of intentionally and repeatedly touching her
buttocks during the complicated twists and turns of the elementary
tango. His response was somewhere along the lines of "You're crazy,
lady." She then apparently called him some unprintable names, then
kicked him hard in the testes. He required immediate medical attention,
dance class had to be stopped, and Mr. Kelly was confined to a
wheelchair for a week. According to witness Mrs. Ida Samuelson,
Mrs. Soprano had to be restrained by dance staff from inflicting
further damage on Mr. Kelly.

ACTION TAKEN: Mrs. Soprano barred from the dance class for a month.
This report passed on to Norma Charles for review and possible therapy.

Green Grove

RESIDENT COMPLAINT FORM

Filed by __MRS. ESTHER PIETROWICZ__   Complaint # ___653___

Details:

This complaint was phoned in by Mrs. Pietrowicz's daughter, Mrs. Alexis Sabato, from Clifton. Mrs. Pietrowicz apparently called her night before last in an hysterical state. She had witnessed an argument between Mrs. Livia Soprano and her son Anthony in which he spoke harshly and obscenely to his mother. Mrs. Pietrowicz's description of the language was "abusive."

  Mrs. Pietrowicz claimed she was in the act of moving away from this unsettling argument when Mrs. Soprano decided to include her in the discussion. She physically held her by the arm and repeated in detail everything her son had just said. Mrs. Soprano kept pleading with Mrs. Pietrowicz to give her all of her sleeping pills so that Mrs. Soprano could take them in the presence of her son and "put him out of his misery." When Mrs. Pietrowicz started whimpering quietly, Mrs. Soprano let go. Mrs. Pietrowicz sustained a bruise on her right upper arm.

ACTION TAKEN: Staff talked to Mrs. Soprano about her son's language. Her response was that she had never cussed a day in her life. Bonnie contemplating directly writing Mr. Soprano explaining the center's client behavior policy.

Interoffice Memo
From: ███████ ████████
To: BONNIE DICAPRIO
Subject: LIVIA SOPRANO

Bonnie - I know you probably think I'm crazy to do this, but I love what often comes out of Mrs. Soprano's mouth so much I started running back to the staff room and writing it down! Have you ever heard her around her grandchildren? They don't have a lifetime of issues with her like her son does. To them she is just crazy Grandma who dumps on their parents, which kids always like.

I really want to be a writer someday, and maybe I'll create a character like Mrs. Soprano. Hey, you never know!

I've done this on my home computer in my own time, don't worry. I'm still doing my job properly!

The World According to Livia

In conversation with her grandson, Anthony, Jr., on the purpose of life:

LIVIA: *Just in the paper the other day, a bunch of teenagers from The Delaware Water Gap, they overcrowded their car and it hit a tree and incinerated. They were all trapped, people heard them screaming, they couldn't get out. The safety belts did it. Buckled them in.*

ANTHONY, JR.: *See? That's what I mean. What's the purpose?*

LIVIA: *Of what?*

ANTHONY, JR.: *Being. Here on our planet. Earth. Those kids, they're dead meat. What's the use? What's the purpose?*

LIVIA: *Who says everything has a purpose? The world's a jungle. You want my advice. Anthony, don't expect happiness. You won't get it. People let you down. I won't mention any names. But, in the end, you die in your own arms.*

ANTHONY, JR.: *You mean … alone?*

LIVIA: *It's all a big nothing. What makes you think you're so special?*

Livia on child-rearing:

LIVIA: *I wasn't always perfect. But I did the best I could. You didn't like it – any of you – that I tried to tell you what to do. But little babies are animals. They're no different from dogs. Unless someone teaches them right from wrong. I was your mother. Who else was going to do it? And if you ask me, I did a pretty darn good job.*

Livia on the state of the world:

LIVIA: *The whole world's gone crazy. A woman in Pennsylvania shot her three children and set the house on fire.*

— — — — — — — —

LIVIA: *I read in the paper last week about a family in San Luis Obispo, California who died from trichinosis. Undercooked pork.*

TONY: *That was last year. That same family.*

LIVIA: *Listen to him, he knows everything.*

— — — — — — — —

LIVIA: *I don't drive when they're predicting rain.*

In conversation with her grandson, AJ:

LIVIA: *They sent you to a psychiatrist?*

ANTHONY, JR.: *Uh-huh.*

LIVIA: *That's crazy. It's all nonsense. It's nothing but a racket for the Jews.*

ANTHONY, JR.: *Dad goes.*

LIVIA: *He does not.*

ANTHONY, JR.: *Yes, he does.*

LIVIA: *To a psychiatrist?*

ANTHONY, JR.: *Yeah.*

LIVIA: *He does not.*

ANTHONY, JR.: *Does so.*

LIVIA: *Why do you say that? That's ridiculous!*

ANTHONY, JR.: *'Cause it's true. I heard him and Mom talk about it.*

LIVIA: *Your father goes to a psychiatrist? What does he need a psychiatrist for?*

ANTHONY, JR.: *Is it okay if I take this pear, Gramma?*

LIVIA: *Hah. He's talking about his mother, that's what he's doing. Sure, he talks about me and complains. I did this, I did that. (CRYING) I handed over my life to my children on a silver platter. And this is how he repays me.*

In other conversations:

LIVIA: *What's he got to be depressed about? Nobody dumped him in the glue factory and sold his house out from underneath him.*

Livia, in conversation with her daughter-in-law, Carmela, on her greatest skill:

CARMELA: *What am I talking about? I'm talking about this. This poor mother, nobody cares about me, victim crap. It's textbook manipulation and I hate seeing Tony so upset over it.*

LIVIA: *I know how to talk to people.*

CARMELA: *I'm a mother, too, don't forget. You know the power you have and you use it like a pro.*

LIVIA: *What power do I have? I'm a shut-in.*

CARMELA: *Livia, you're bigger than life. You are his mother. And I don't think for one second that you don't know what you're doing to him.*

LIVIA: *What? Me? What'd I do?*

"Carmela, you're not just in my life. You $\frac{are}{my\ life.}$"

Tony Soprano

Carmela De Angelis Soprano, Tony's wife of 18 years, knows the cardinal rule of survival: Keep Your Mouth Shut. That's the easy part. The hard part is raising two kids and pursuing a "normal" life with a husband who's edgy, depressed, violent, and one step away from 20 to life. It's hard on her nerves and it's hard on her conscience. Unlike many people in Tony's life, she actually has one.

Again, a single, well-placed source has opened the door on this Soprano life. A female FBI undercover agent donned a tight-fitting tank top and became a regular at Carmela's health club. What follows are excerpts from her daily surveillance reports, transcribed from tape, along with gossip and insights from neighbors and friends.

JEFFREY WERNICK: Carmela Soprano wasn't an innocent babe in the criminal woods when she met and married Tony. She grew up in the same Italian-American world that he did. Her father, Hugh De Angelis, is in the building trade but as a youth he was a numbers runner, as were many kids in that neighborhood back then. Even young girls were told to pick up a bag and take it from here to there without knowing there was money in it.

```
Surveillance Transcript: 073-991012. Subject: CS.Location ref: NJ-4510 (gym).
----------------------------------------------------------------------------
CS arrived as usual around 9:15am and immediately did 20 minutes of heavy
cycling before speaking to anyone. Complained about TV tuned to "nauseating"
Regis & Kathy Lee, attendant changed to CNBC. Bad mood. Finally calmed down,
moved to treadmill, next to ███████████. Complaints about family.
   Daughter only drinks cranberry juice for breakfast. Son addicted to diet of
pop tarts and is flunking out of school. TS on another "emergency business trip"
for third day in a row. CS and ███████████ had a good laugh over that one.
"Where is he this time?" asked ███████████. "Signing a peace treaty with the
Russians?" (TS has a hot Russian mistress, name: Irina Peltsin.) Then CS broke
down in tears, stopped treadmill, gulped Evian. She hates the goomar thing:
"humiliating. Degrading. And he might get a disease, God forbid." "Or a little
Ruskie," said ███████████. Painful scene.
   I got into a tiff with a tubbo over the rowing machine and missed a few
minutes. CS seemed relieved to cry...this place is her therapy. Mine, too.
Outlined rest of day to ███████████. Georgette Klingers for massage and
facial. shopping for new glass-topped coffee table at Ethan Allen, son's swim
meet at Verbum Dei at 4, rush home to watch Emeril on Food Channel. Big night
- priest for dinner.
   CS showered - in excellent shape - left at 10:26am, in much better mood,
driving Mercedes.
```

JEFFREY WERNICK: Carmela's mother, Mary, is a tough lady and professes to hate the mob. She reportedly won't be in the same room with Tony's mother, Livia. On top of Livia's sparkling personality, Mary is Sicilian and Livia's a *Napoletan'*. Carmela's real mob connection is this – Hugh's sister, Lena, married Joseph Moltisanti, not the most reputable guy in the neighborhood, and they reared a son named Richard Moltisanti. To Tony and Carmela, Richard was "Cousin Dickie." He was a thug who was killed in broad daylight right out on Ampere Parkway in 1983, not long before Johnny Boy Soprano succumbed to lung disease. So Dickie was Carmela's older cousin and she had a crush on him. Dickie had a son, Christopher Moltisanti, who later became one of Tony's main guys. That would make Christopher Carmela's second cousin or maybe first cousin once removed. But you get the idea. To avoid confusion, Tony calls him his nephew.

CONNIE BLUNDETTO, CLASSMATE, MARRIED NAME WITHHELD: In high school Carmela was very popular. Her group was one of the best and she was involved in everything – student council, the United Nations club, the Catholic Youth Organization, you name it. Tony was an outsider – he drove around in his souped-up Trans Am, high on pot, playing the Doobie Brothers at full blast. You could never see them together in a million years. But I think Carmela had her eye on him the whole time. She's a smart girl. Always was.

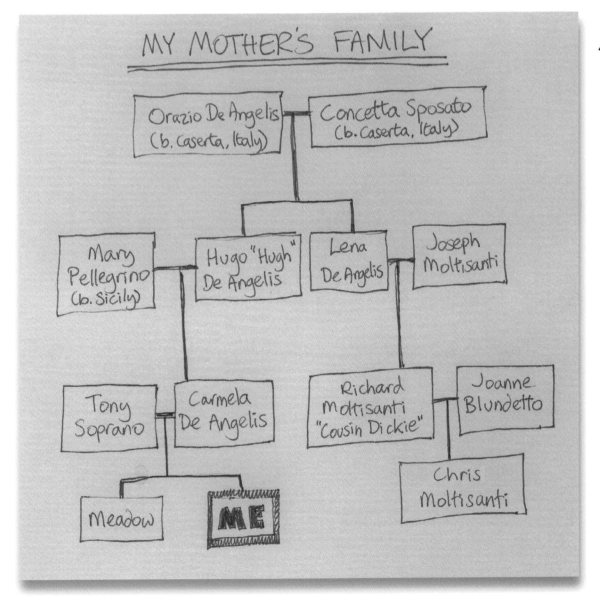

Drawn by AJ at school, 1999

Surveillance Transcript: 073-991015. Subject: CS. Location ref: NJ-510 (gym).

Another day, CS in another black mood. I sat in foggy steam room listening to CS
bitch about TS to ███████████. Fascinating. "Why did I marry him?" she wonders
out loud. "Sex?" says ███████████. They laugh. CS lists reasons: she loves him,
best prospect at the time, a rock, a life of comfort, gives her confidence, always
good for a laugh, etc. "Face out of a Giovanetti painting." CS laughs. "I guess
we'll both burn in hell..."

     They went into whispering, very hard to hear. CS said something like "she's a
woman...why couldn't he tell me?" ███████████ made sign - right index finger
into circle of left index finger & thumb. CS shrugged. I think they noticed me
watching, had to leave. Turning into prune anyway.

     In CS's open locker, I saw the following items. Two books: "The Religions of
Man," Houston Smith and "Women Who Run With The Wolves," by something Estes.
Blockbuster video rentals: "Casablanca," "When A Man Loves A Woman," "Groundhog
Day." A cashmere sweater from Ann Taylor, to be returned is my guess.
     Dinner plans: Take-out Chinese.

Charmaine and
Artie Bucco

CLOSE FRIEND, NAME WITHHELD:
Mary De Angelis did not like the idea of Carmela
marrying Anthony Soprano one bit. Cousin Dickie
was still alive then and Mary kept announcing that
Tony was "Dickie-in-training." Mary and Hugh
strictly forbade Carmela from associating with Tony
but she did it anyway. And there wasn't a damn
thing they could do about it.

CONNIE BLUNDETTO: Carmela was tight
with Artie Bucco and Charmaine Cifaretto in high
school. She and Charmaine were in fact the best of
friends, but I heard they had a falling out later on. It
probably had to do with the fact that Carmela is now
rich and Charmaine is, you know, married to Artie.
Anyway, Carmela went off to Montclair State
University, and soon dropped out like Tony. Two peas
in a pod, I guess.

Surveillance Transcript: 073-991018. Subject: CS. Location ref: NJ-4510 (gym).

CS late - 9:40am - but very upbeat, chatty. Came in patting stomach, said she "ate
a ton" last night at barbeque at Randy and Barb Wagner's. Huffing and puffing on
treadmill, named every person and every food item there: the Cusamanos, the Krims,
delicious barbequed sausage, etc. Liked the non-mob company, it was apparent, and
said TS fit right in. Passed along a stock tip from party to ███████████:
American Biotics. (Check it out - could be TS scam).

     Later. CS in long locker room chat with ███████████. All about this college
and that college, etc. Pouring over US News' annual college issue. So proud of daughter making National Honor Society. Says "She's going to have a much better life than
I've had, thank the Lord." Lectured ███████████ on the pros and cons of Columbia's
pre-law program. Complained about cost. TS told her not to worry. I bet.

From the desk of Carmela Soprano

Dear Mario,

I'm writing in response to your invitation to have our house photographed for an exclusive "At Home" spread in "New Jersey Today" magazine. I know you are very proud of the redecorating you did and we love it, too. But, unfortunately, a big magazine story is out of the question.

My husband has a very sensitive job. Suffice it to say, it has to do with the very hush-hush field of non-putrescable waste management and environmental clean-up. On top 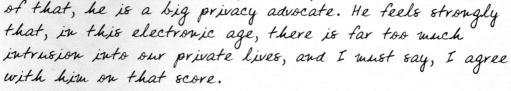 of that, he is a big privacy advocate. He feels strongly that, in this electronic age, there is far too much intrusion into our private lives, and I must say, I agree with him on that score.

I know you only met him that one time when he refused to let you throw out his favorite easy chair. He didn't mean to call you that name and this is not about that, I promise. It's about media exposure.

Again, thank you for all your hard work on the interiors. The color choices of taupe and heavy cream were perfect, the Murano glass is perfect, the sconces are perfect, and the kitchen is an absolute dream. In fact I better get busy with dinner right now!

Sorry about the article. You might try the Cusamanos next door. You did a great job with their house, too, and Jeannie would love the attention!

Sincerely

Carmela Soprano

Stuffed Calamari — (Big Nanna's recipe)

9 Calamari- cleaned, with cartilage, wings & ink removed (save wings)
1 Loaf of Italian bread- soaked in water, crust peeled off
3 Anchovies- cut up
1 Egg- beaten
1/4 cup grated cheese
1 tsp. Parsley
Black pepper - a dash

(Cousin Miriam leaves crusts on)

Directions: Mix all above ingredients together except bread. Add enough olive oil to hold together. Squeeze the Italian bread into a ball and break it up and put it in with the above mixture. This stuffing should be rather dry. Put a teaspoon of stuffing in each fish (no more or the fish will explode). Thread with toothpick to close opening. Drop the stuffed calamari with saved wings into prepared marinara sauce and cook until pink, (20-30 minutes). Serve over pasta.

CLOSE FRIEND: There was a time when life was really fun for Carmela, but not so much anymore. Things used to be easier because Tony was very successful but he wasn't the main guy, the guy that everybody brought their problems to. There's a lot to be said for being middle-management, you know. You don't have to call the shots – literally.

FATHER PHIL: Carmela is a wonderful mother. Many of the other mothers in the parish look askance at her because of all the gossip, but I think they're a little jealous, frankly. She doesn't talk about "family values," she practices them. She keeps her head up and focused on the family's needs no matter how many officials come knocking at the door. She worries about her kids' emotional as well as intellectual progress and never misses one of their school functions. She invests much of her life in those children. And I'm sure Tony appreciates it, especially since he's often off in another world. He's got to appreciate it. All he has to do is look at his own mother to see the flip side.

Surveillance Transcript: 073-991023. Subject: CS. Location ref: NJ-4510 (gym).

CS missed personal trainer session with "Michelangelo" on Wednesday, drags in Thursday at 11am complaining about her "weird life." Describes to ███████████ an all-night session with Father Phil, her "spiritual mentor." (TS calls him "Monsignor Jughead"). He almost became her "carnal mentor," she announces. ██████████ gave out an "Eeeek!", jumped off ergometer, ran over for details. CS clams up. Something about lonely, too much Chianti, eats like a horse, etc. Drop it, she said.
   The good father came up again in jacuzzi. This time praise all around. Rosalie Aprile there, said he's only man who listens to her, gave her a book on "When Bad Things Happen To Good People," very helpful. CS agreed that he was always challenging her. She said she wouldn't even know the name "Merchant Ivory" without him. Many blank looks re that reference. ██████████ asked, "Is he gay?" Long discussion. Consensus: split vote. Carmela held the crowd from leaving while she went to car and retrieved a brand new addition to her angel collection. Beautiful little ceramic seraphim, "very Italian." All were impressed.

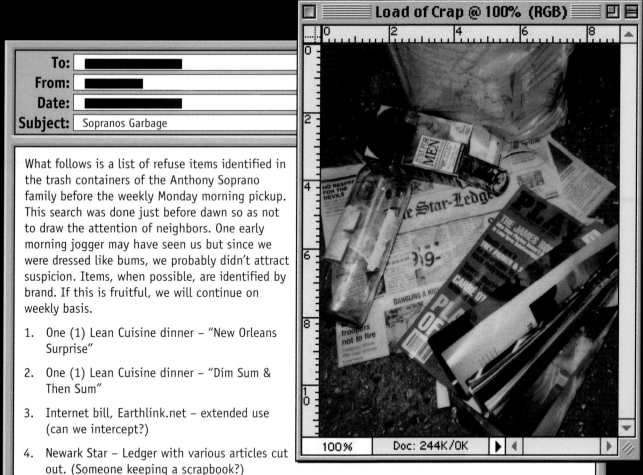

Load of Crap @ 100% (RGB)

What follows is a list of refuse items identified in the trash containers of the Anthony Soprano family before the weekly Monday morning pickup. This search was done just before dawn so as not to draw the attention of neighbors. One early morning jogger may have seen us but since we were dressed like bums, we probably didn't attract suspicion. Items, when possible, are identified by brand. If this is fruitful, we will continue on weekly basis.

1. One (1) Lean Cuisine dinner – "New Orleans Surprise"

2. One (1) Lean Cuisine dinner – "Dim Sum & Then Sum"

3. Internet bill, Earthlink.net – extended use (can we intercept?)

4. Newark Star – Ledger with various articles cut out. (Someone keeping a scrapbook?)

5. Three (3) prescription medication bottles – labels scraped off.

6. One (1) bottle, "Just For Men" hair coloring, dark brown.

7. Promotional flyer, "Movie Of The Month" Club, subscription form removed.

8. One (1) Playboy magazine, well-thumbed.

9. One (1) half-eaten home-produced baked ziti casserole with refrigerator mold.

10. Three (3) clothing boxes with perfume smell, probably from someplace in the Willowbrook Mall.

11. Six (6) bottles, Italian red wine, labels scraped off (Why?)

12. Nine (9) college promotional brochures, some application forms removed. Colleges id'ed: Colby, Bates, Bowdoin, Bard, University of California – Berkeley, Georgetown, NYU, Washington University, St. Louis, Emory.

13. Small bag, duck feed (?)

14. Notebook marked "Dream Journal," all pages ripped out

15. Three (3) gallon containers, empty, Neapolitan Ice Cream, generic brand.

16. Large stack, Pamela Anderson Lee cutouts (the boy, I'm sure).

17. Brochure for package tour, Lourdes, France.

18. Assorted pork products – chops, bacon, sausage – rancid.

19. A scrunched-up copy of "Waste News." Lead stories: "Used Oil - Ten Steps to Better Disposal Practices." "End Uses of Recovered Aluminum." "New Rates for Densities of Bulk Recyclables." "New Miss Recycled Plastic Named."

20. Soup cans, egg cartons, old cottage cheese.

Father Phil administers to Carmela

CLOSE FRIEND: What sustains Carmela is her faith. Don't ask me how she reconciles a belief in God's grace and the awful things her husband has been accused of doing. Ask Father Phil. He listens to her confessions. I guess that's between him, her, and God. The argument going on inside her head must be brutal. Maybe she's in so deep by now that God is the only way out, for both of them. Carmela once told me she thought Tony was a very spiritual person. I almost spit coffee in her face, but she was serious. She must see a spiritual side to him, a spiritual thirst, you might say, that I doubt if anyone in the "waste management" business has ever seen.

FATHER PHIL: I know it's a cliché, but faith can indeed move mountains and faith can bring the unrighteous into righteousness. Remember that scene in *The Godfather* when Michael is attending the baptism of his son while his henchmen are eliminating all of his enemies? Such is the irony of Carmela's life.

```
Surveillance Transcript: 073-991027. Subject: CS. Location ref: NJ-4510 (gym).
----------------------------------------------------------------------------
Like a mob wives' convention at gym today. They were all there, lined up side
by side on treadmills: Rosalie Aprile, Angie Bonpensiero, Helen Barone,
Gabriella Dante. Jabber, jabber, jabber. Next week's book at their book club
is "A Man In Full," by Tom Wolfe. Angie complains that it has too many pages,
suggests new "Far Side" anthology. Angie then breaks down, announces she's
leaving "Fatso." He's uncaring, distracted, spends hours in the bathroom doing
something, probably drugs. After much deliberation, all agree this is not a
good idea, no matter how distant he is. "This is the life we choose," said
Gabriella, solemnly, which I think is a line from Hyman Roth in "Godfather
II." Carmela: "Marriage is holy, Angie, a vow for life. None of us are
perfect."
    Pertinent mob information learned: zip. These gals are trained to keep quiet.
```

CONNIE BLUNDETTO: It's a terrible life for her, I think. She has to censor every word that comes out of her mouth. It's like your husband is a child molester and you can't talk about it to anyone.

Carmela discusses the issues of the day with Rosalie and Angie

CLOSE FRIEND, NAME WITHHELD: When I stand back and look at Carmela's life, it seems to me that it is all one big complicated game of denial. She has to deny that Tony's a gangster. He has to deny to her that a) he kills people and b) that he has girlfriends. The girlfriend has to deny that he isn't going to abandon her someday. If all of this came out in one big group therapy session, they'd all explode into a million pieces. I mean, how long can you pretend that your life isn't what it is?

```
Surveillance Transcript: 073-991029. Subject:
CS. Location ref: NJ-4510 (gym).
------------------------------------------------
CS didn't show up all week. ███████ told
personal trainer "Michelangelo" that "the family
is under a lot of stress." He said, "Yeah, I
know, I read the papers, Grandma got busted with
a bad ducat." He told ███████████ to tell
Carmela she should come in for two-hour Shiatsu
massage. On the house. Makes any problem disap-
pear, he says, even "visiting day at Rahway."
What an idiot.
    By the way, I've lost 14 pounds and 2 inches
off my waist. Thanks for the assignment.
```

Scenes from a marriage

"Gary Cooper... He wasn't 'in touch' with his feelings. He just did what he had to do."

There is no concrete evidence to support the assertion that Tony Soprano sees a psychiatrist on a regular basis. The FBI's official response is "no comment." According to an inside source, the closest they've come to a direct reference is a wiretap comment from Paulie Walnuts to the effect that he "too" once saw a shrink because of "poor coping skills."

Jeffrey Wernick, not bound by legal strictures, takes a different view. He believes that ongoing psychotherapy is a central fact in Tony's life and he has plenty of hearsay evidence to back up his claim.

JEFFREY WERNICK: Tony's psychiatrist, named Dr. Jennifer Melfi, MD, MA, CFT, is in her early 40s and lives in Essex Fells, New Jersey. She grew up in Bloomfield, New Jersey, the only daughter of Joseph and Aida Melfi. She graduated Phi Beta Kappa with a BA in Psychology from Rutgers University, received a MD from the Tufts University Medical School, and interned in Psychiatry at the Baylor University Hospitals in Houston. She has been in private practice for seven years, specializing in family therapy, sexual dysfunction, and post-Freudian childhood trauma analysis.

Dr. Melfi is divorced from Richard La Penna, formerly a psychiatrist in private practice, now an advisor to HMO's and a physician broker, ie, a middleman who recommends doctors to patients and vice-versa. She has one son, Jason, an art history major at Bard College. Dr. Melfi herself sees a personal psychiatrist, Dr. Elliot Kupferberg, and she, her ex-husband and her son see a family therapist, Dr. Samuel Reis.

OLD MELFI FAMILY FRIEND, NAME WITHHELD: Jennifer's parents, Joseph and Aida, are lovely people and they are so proud of their little girl. They moved from Brooklyn to the New Jersey suburbs to give her all the advantages and she didn't disappoint. 3.9 at Rutgers. Elected to the medical honors society, AOA, her junior year at Tufts Medical. Even learned competitive archery in her spare time. She has always been a high achiever. Personally, I think she's a little like Hillary Clinton. She wants to stand on her own but keeps falling for the wrong guy, you know what I mean? Richard was certainly the wrong guy.

FRIEND OF RICHARD LA PENNA, NAME WITHHELD: Listen, I am not Jennifer's biggest fan. She said some pretty nasty things about Dick when they got divorced. She called him uncaring, a womanizer, and a "psychological abuser." One minute, she said, he was berating her, the next calling her "mama." Richard showed me the court transcript. It was pretty brutal. His reply was that he had simply fallen out of love with her and felt she had some "self-esteem issues" to deal with. Richard was her mentor, I think, and she outgrew him, or at least thought she did. What's amazing is that they've remained friends. Maybe there's an unwritten code among shrinks that you can't stay mad. Or maybe they are just playing nice for the sake of the boy.

JEFFREY WERNICK:
Despite her personal problems, she has a very good practice. If you hang out in the hallway outside her office, as I have, you see some very well-dressed men and women going in. Whatever their problems, they're well hidden. The day Tony waltzed in must have been a real shock.

Tony loved those ducks

FBI SOURCE, NAME WITHHELD: We know Tony's routine pretty well, but once a week he goes into the Montclair Physician Suites, stays an hour or so, then leaves. Why, we don't know. Could be another mistress, I guess, but why hide that? Could be some private dealings with a rival family. Or, being that it's a physician's building, he could be going in for something like cancer treatment, which wouldn't be too good for business. It's a mystery.

FRIEND OF JEANNIE CUSAMANO, NAME WITHHELD: Jeannie told me the whole story, in strictest confidence. Apparently Mr. Wiseguy has nervous attacks and no one knows why. Jeannie used the word "ideopathic." Nervous attacks of ideopathic origin. In other words, Mr. Wiseguy is a little looney.

VINCENT RIZZO: This is not good. A made guy seeing a fuckin' shrink. Once you start doubting what you have to do in that business, it's all over. Pretty soon they're going to have 12-step programs for, you know, recovering bonebreakers. WA. Wiseguys Fuckin' Anonymous.

JEFFREY WERNICK: Tony is not far from the model of the people in that area who would see a psychiatrist. Affluent, upper-middle-class, a high-stress occupation. These are people with "issues." You know, high-powered business execs who can't get it up (an intimacy "issue") or maybe a rich housewife with the self-respect of a go-go dancer (ie, a dependence "issue"). The only difference is that Tony doesn't run Citibank – he runs his own bank.

FBI SOURCE: A neighbor who has since relocated tells us he observed Soprano in and around his backyard, grilling burgers or watching his kids swim. But then these two ducks showed up to mate in his pool or something, and they became a family with three or four little duckies, as I recall. They'd come and go, you'd turn around and there they were, and Soprano got the biggest kick out of that. He loved those ducks. He fed them, would drag his family out to see them, and stare at them for hours. They gave him the kind of delight they would give a little boy. It was the strangest thing. Maybe he missed his calling. Maybe he should've been a vet.

9: Jack Gallino, aka diaper guy. He's-ssss back! Recurrence of fixation with loss of control, bladder and emotional. Must go through whole toilet training ritual again!! Maybe Elliot wants to do this?

10: Tom Amberson. Fifth visit, first at motel, then with wife here twice, no progress. Re sex, he's ED, she's not interested. Passive aggressive, needs to get it out and deal with it. Boofers!

11: Catherine Chinksy. Standing - same drinking prob. Who am I to help someone with a drinking problem? AA's better at this than I am but C. is shy, afraid of public speaking. Role-play AA?!

12: Lunch with Nils - Romano's - why?

1: Randall Curtin. One visit only. Hear him out then send to Elliot or Morty. I'm not good with OCD. Continues to have nightmares, fantasies about being "taken out" on street. Tell him the truth? No.

2: TS!!! I'm scared. Explain mother's borderline personality disorder. Also, her nihilism. Make him stay with sadness, heartbreak, psychic injuries, get it out. Massive character armor. Don't be intimidated!

3:
Leave open NO APPTS!

4:

5: Elliot. Drinking. Fear. Obsession. Train wreck image. Elliot doesn't have a clue - get another opinion? Hell, I don't have a clue either.

6: Liquor store.

6.45pm - Dinner with Jason - El Cholo

Page cut from Jennifer Melfi's diary, found in garbage

NICK GARRISON, FBI PROFILER, WASHINGTON, DC: I've studied LCN figures for years, though I don't know the Soprano case or New Jersey families in general. I specialize in unsolved cases in heavy caseload areas like Bensonhurst and East New York. I've found that there is a generic type – they all come from the same milieu and have very similar socio-psychological profiles. It's part arrested emotional development, part poor impulse control, part distorted cognitive self-imaging, and part narcissistic disturbance. But I still have no idea what those ducks mean.

CONSULTING NEW YORK PSYCHIATRIST, NAME WITHHELD: You cannot analyze a patient from hearsay and gossip. I refuse to do it. Having said that, it's my opinion that your alleged crime boss criminal figure with those alleged symptoms is suffering from acute mood shifts bordering on bipolar disorder, uncontrollable rage, hyperventilation syndrome, and perhaps adult-onset ADD, all stemming from severe childhood emotional deprivation brought on by a distracted mother figure, possibly one with borderline personality disorder. It's just a stab in the dark.

JEFFREY WERNICK: One psychiatrist told me that Tony suffered from a condition called alexithymia. He described it as the need for certain people "at odds with society" to crave constant action to avoid coming to terms with the consequences of their actions. When a serial killer goes on a non-stop rampage, that's what he's doing. Apparently, when they stop, they can't handle thinking about what they've done. If you're always moving from one crisis to another, you never have to think.

FRIEND OF JEANNIE CUSAMANO: It's obvious why a thug needs a psychiatrist – he's clearly all screwed up, full of guilt and anger and afraid of getting shot at any minute. But my question is, why would a psychiatrist see a gangster? What is that, masochism? A "save a heel" complex? The lure of the darkside? We're in Roman Polanski territory here. Someone should look into that woman. She's the one that needs help.

NICK GARRISON, FBI: Why would a psychiatrist see a wiseguy? It's simple. One, excitement. Have you ever sat through 50 minutes of a mousy housewife whining about her life? It's like having the

Jennifer Melfi and her mother

soles of your feet toasted. Two, intellectual curiosity. For someone in the field of human psychology, you couldn't find a better psyche to plumb, could you? It's a psycho-socio-cultural gold mine. And three, testing your limits. Are you really good at this work? Do you have enough courage and stamina to push difficult people to the brink of change? Well, here's a tough nut, sweetie. Go crack it.

LAURA O'CONNELL, YOUNGER SISTER OF JEANNIE CUSAMANO: Maybe it's about mothering. Maybe it's her maternal instinct talking here. This mob guy never had much of a mother, I'm told. My sister has met the madre on numerous social occasions. She calls her "the mother from hell." So maybe the doctor is his surrogate mother or something twisted like that.

MELFI FAMILY FRIEND: Did it ever dawn on you that maybe she continues to see him because she genuinely cares about him and wants to help him? The minute a man and a woman strike up a relationship, everyone immediately thinks it's either sexual or weird. Maybe it's neither – maybe it's human.

JEFFREY WERNICK: The idea of a mobster seeing a psychiatrist is not without precedent. One of the most famous mobsters of them all, the dapper Frank Costello, saw one for two years. His name was Dr. Richard H. Hoffman, a Manhattan doctor with a very uptown clientele. The tabloids found out about it and Hoffman came clean. Wouldn't you have liked to have been the fly on the wall at those sessions? "Hey, doc, I'm feeling bad about that Canary Kid Twist Reles getting pitched out of that sixth story window in Coney Island. And happy at the same time. How do I deal with these conflicting feelings?..." I'm sure Hoffman's practice quadrupled after that.

FRIEND OF RICHARD LA PENNA: So work with me here. Jennifer Melfi is a psychiatrist. Ostensibly, she helps people and knows what she is doing. But then she herself sees a psychiatrist to help her with her problems. And then she and Richard see another psychiatrist to help them with their problems. Remember, Richard's a certified psychiatrist, too. Doesn't this seem a little strange? I mean, when does she have time to have a life that needs analyzing?

MELFI FAMILY FRIEND: Poor Jen has no life. Not unlike a million career women out there, she is extremely lonely. She has her son, of course, but he's in his third year at Bard and I doubt if hanging out with his mother is his first priority. She dates a little but that is such an awful grind in this day and age. Her boyfriends tend to be professional types like her, an estate

Jennifer and her ex, Richard La Penna

lawyer here, an endocrinologist there, and they don't last very long. She's 40-whatever and like they say, the good ones are all taken. I think she thinks she needs more than, you know, a French garden, a Mercedes SL500, and a husband winging off to another AMA conference in Orlando. God knows she doesn't need anyone else with problems. She'd probably be happier with a working-class WWF fan who drags her to Jimmy Buffet concerts on the weekend.

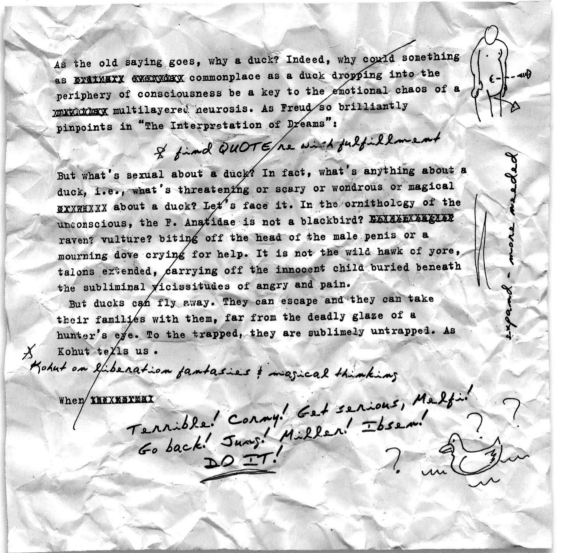

As the old saying goes, why a duck? Indeed, why could something as ~~ordinary~~ ~~everyday~~ commonplace as a duck dropping into the periphery of consciousness be a key to the emotional chaos of a ~~particular~~ multilayered neurosis. As Freud so brilliantly pinpoints in "The Interpretation of Dreams":

I find QUOTE re wish fulfillment

But what's sexual about a duck? In fact, what's anything about a duck, i.e., what's threatening or scary or wondrous or magical ~~XXXWXXX~~ about a duck? Let's face it. In the ornithology of the unconscious, the F. Anatidae is not a blackbird? ~~XXIXXXXXXXXX~~ raven? vulture? biting off the head of the male penis or a mourning dove crying for help. It is not the wild hawk of yore, talons extended, carrying off the innocent child buried beneath the subliminal vicissitudes of angry and pain.
    But ducks can fly away. They can escape and they can take their families with them, far from the deadly glaze of a hunter's eye. To the trapped, they are sublimely untrapped. As Kohut tells us.

Kohut on liberation fantasies & magical thinking

When/ ~~XXXXXXXXXX~~

Terrible! Corny! Get serious, Melfi! Go back! Jung! Miller! Ibsen! DO IT!

expand – more needed

LAURA O'CONNELL: She drinks like a fish but you didn't get it from me.

MELFI FAMILY FRIEND: I think that's way overblown. Now you're just gossiping, defaming a perfectly decent person. I've been to Aida's house many times with Jennifer and she has never been the slightest bit tipsy.

NICK GARRISON, FBI: She's got to be afraid of the guy. I mean, jeez. I'm sure he tells her constantly that she's different, that he would never hurt her, that he may be gruff but he really appreciates her insights into his "unusual" behavior. Hey, I've seen perfectly normal people attack a therapist when their deeply-repressed buttons are finally pushed. Here you have a guy with zero impulse control, a guy who, in the final analysis (no pun intended), has no friends. She should be thankful she's a woman. If she were a male shrink with a Van Dyke goatee and a well-rehearsed spiel about "homoerotic undercurrents," she'd be landfill by now. Even so, what with the train wreck he calls a life, he could decide that she knows too much. What then? It's against the code, but, hey, codes change.

FRIEND OF RICHARD LA PENNA: It disturbs Richard no end, that Jennifer is seeing this "monster." Honestly, I think he feels threatened. I think he has a private fantasy that she's going to marry

Jason

the guy and when they drop by for some pasta, Soprano is going to blink and Richard is going to soil himself. Or maybe he's afraid it's going to make her famous and every time he turns on CNBC, she'll be wagging about the state of maleness in America.

MELFI FAMILY FRIEND: To me, personally, it has all the markings of a bad love affair or maybe that's too sexual – maybe it's more like a ill-fated friendship. From what Aida tells me, there is some kind of push-pull going on that is very much like your daughter falling for someone from the wrong side of the tracks and not being able to extract herself from the relationship. Those things usually end in tragedy, you know. I think Jennifer is sincere, but I think she's swimming in some deep, shark-infested waters. If she actually does help the poor man, she's the future of psychiatry. If she doesn't, all she gets out of it is maybe a best-selling book and stories to tell her grandkids. Or worse.

To:	████████████
From:	████████
Date:	████████████
Subject:	Mom's Lost It

Kit, I just had to tell someone what happened today. You won't frickin' believe it. I was having a rare lunch with my mother, you know, "how do you like your lit teacher?," that kind of bullshit. Anyway, she's moving through a bottle of San Giovese red in record time and this lady at the next table starts blowing smoke her way. It was nothing – please, we're in New Jersey. But Ma Barker, two and a half sheets to the wind, goes off on this lady bigtime! Pesters her, then shouts "Could you move the fucking thing?" I mean, my mother turned into a fuckin' wisegal! I was like blowing it, ready to crawl under the table, and then Mom hauls off and whacks the lady in the face with her napkin!!! Un-fucking-believable! Have you ever seen your mother get into a cat fight? It doesn't get much more humiliating than this. And the woman wasn't backing down. Called mother a bitch and started after her, but thank god the restaurant guy showed up in the knick of time and kicked mother out. I don't know what happened after that. I was three blocks away, my heart pounding like a jackhammer.

Should I tell my dad? Should I call Bellevue? Maybe I should just sign up for Alanon now, beat the family rush. This is turning into a bad TV-movie. "The Days of Wine and Broken Noses." I think I need a drink.

NOT ADMISSABLE

CONVERSATION CONTINUES:

DR. MELFI:	Thank you. How was your college trip with your daughter?
UNIDENTIFIED MALE:	I'll tell you, my life is like an episode of "Provoloney-something."
DR. MELFI:	What's going on?
UNIDENTIFIED MALE:	My wife. All we do is fight. Can you believe it, she's jealous of you.
DR. MELFI:	Is this something that you feel or has there been some discussion with Carmela?
UNIDENTIFIED MALE:	She didn't know you were a girl ... you know, a woman. Excuse me, a doctor. Woman doctor.
DR. MELFI:	Why did it take you so long to tell her?
UNIDENTIFIED MALE:	I didn't tell her. You spilled the beans when you called to change my appointment.
DR. MELFI:	Let me ask you a different question. Why a female? Why a female doctor?
UNIDENTIFIED MALE:	You know, she asked the same friggin' question and I sometimes wonder myself.
DR. MELFI:	And...
UNIDENTIFIED MALE:	I'll tell you what I told her, Cusamano gave me a choice between two Jewish guys and a paisan like me. So I picked the paisan.
DR. MELFI:	What's one thing that every woman, your mother, wife and daughter, have in common?
UNIDENTIFIED MALE:	They all break my balls.
	No, I know what you mean. They're all Italian. So what?
DR. MELFI:	So, maybe by coming clean with me you're dialoguing with them.
UNIDENTIFIED MALE:	Let me ask you a question. Why do you have me as a patient? Most legit people I know they'd go a hundred miles out of their way not to make eye contact. But you, you didn't flinch.

NOT ADMISSABLE

"It's business... we're soldiers. We follow codes."

Tony Soprano

FRESH
BLOOD
$6.00 GAL.
$1.00 PT.

What do wiseguys really do? How do they earn their money and how much money do they earn? These are questions the movies rarely address. They are the mundane business realities of an American enterprise that has prospered for almost a hundred years. And it's what Tony Soprano thinks about all day, every day.

JEFFREY WERNICK: A crime family like the Sopranos works from a business model that might be called "trickle up" economics. Money trickles up the chain of command from street associate to boss. The boss's power to settle disputes and enforce rules trickles back down accordingly. It is in no way Easy Street. The workload is constant and often exasperating – much of it bill-collecting – the hours are brutal, and the rules keep shifting. Plus, your co-workers are all crooks.

FRANK CUBITOSO: These guys like to see themselves as businessmen. They're in it for the money, just like your stock broker or car dealer. They like the lifestyle, too, like never having to punch a clock, but the money is the real lure. And the way they do business avoids many of the pitfalls associated with legitimate commerce. There are no pension or health plans to administer, no audits, and no taxes. Record keeping is nil and they never have to go to court to settle a dispute.

VINCENT RIZZO: The businesses that wiseguys are in tend to be the ones their father or uncles were in or, you know, their family. With the Sopranos, they're heavily into organized labor, but their main thing is gambling – sports gambling, mainly, and cards. That's their bread and butter. See, long before there were legal ways to gamble, like OTB [off-track betting] or going to Vegas, people still liked to gamble, you know. So they went to the neighbor bookie, a guy they've known their whole fuckin' life, to bet on the Yankees or whatever. It was easy and no one gave a fuck.

JEFFREY WERNICK: A lot of what the mob excels at is ongoing, day-to-day extortion. The mob's ability to invade a person's life or business is gradual and insidious and usually begins with that person making the first move, like placing a "surefire" bet on the Green Bay Packers.

Let's place that bet with Benny, the neighborhood bookmaker – say for $1000 – and see what happens. First, no money changes hands between bookmaker and customer. It's all done on the "honor" system. You settle up at the end of the week, depending on how good a customer you are. If you're into the bookie for a lot of losses, let's say, you probably settle up daily.

The bookie "writes" you this "action" on the Packers. He takes in, say, a hundred bets on this particular Packer game. If he has too many people betting on the Packers on that particular game, and not enough betting on the opponent, say, the Giants, he "lays off" some of his Packer bets to another bookie who has too many Giants bets. The bookie's primary goal is to break even at the end of the game. He wants to pay out the amount of winnings exactly equal to the losses he collects. He makes his money on the "vig," short for vigorish – his fee for placing the bet. A typical vig is two points, or 2%. On your $1000 bet, he'd get $20 for his efforts.

VINCENT RIZZO: Why, you might ask, do I go to a bookie instead of placing a bet with a friend in Vegas? A, it's easier, the guy's two blocks away, and you know his kids, and B, there're no fuckin' taxes! Even OTB bets get taxed. Good service, tax-free. That's the main thing.

JEFFREY WERNICK: Back to our Packers fan. As long as he wins, everything is peachy and the bookie is his best friend. But most likely the guy is a problem gambler and sooner or later he's going to lose and probably lose big. So he borrows from his brother or hocks his wife's jewelry to pay his losses and the vig. He knows all he needs is one good bet and he'll be flush. The bookie, of course, encourages this. Is this immoral? Tell that to Donald Trump or the people at Caesar's Palace.

Paulie using his considerable powers of persuasion

THE PYRAMID OF MONEY

The following demonstrates how street income gets distributed up the Soprano family food chain. The example used here is sports gambling or bookmaking, but it could also serve as an economic model for other street activities like loansharking, numbers, drug trafficking, the bootlegging of cigarettes, or a score of similar cash-based enterprises.

STEP ONE: Paulie Walnuts, a soldier in the Soprano crew of the DiMeo/Soprano crime family, has three bookmaking associates out in the neighborhood, taking bets on sports events and distributing winnings and losses. Paulie goes to his bookies on a given Friday and collects $5000.

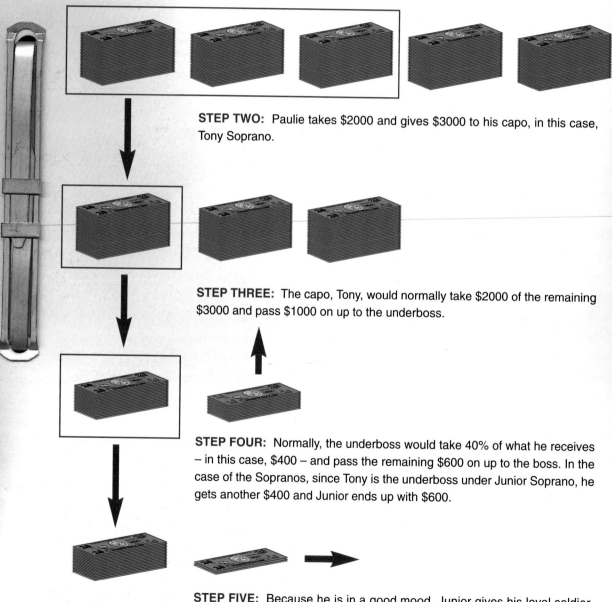

STEP TWO: Paulie takes $2000 and gives $3000 to his capo, in this case, Tony Soprano.

STEP THREE: The capo, Tony, would normally take $2000 of the remaining $3000 and pass $1000 on up to the underboss.

STEP FOUR: Normally, the underboss would take 40% of what he receives – in this case, $400 – and pass the remaining $600 on up to the boss. In the case of the Sopranos, since Tony is the underboss under Junior Soprano, he gets another $400 and Junior ends up with $600.

STEP FIVE: Because he is in a good mood, Junior gives his loyal soldier, Bobby "Bacala" Baccilieri, $100 for picking up the money from Tony or Paulie.

FRANK CUBITOSO: A street soldier like Paulie Walnuts has a series of bookies he controls. He's their bank, their enforcement service, their bill collector. One bookie could have a hundred regular accounts or more. Those customers often don't know what they're in for until it's too late and they're in trouble.

VINCENT RIZZO: Here's the bottom line – you never see a bookmaking operation without a loansharking operation attached. That's it. It's the same business. The bookie brings the clients in the door, the loanshark keeps them.

JEFFREY WERNICK: Our gambling friend has exhausted his outside resources and after a string of desperate longshots, now owes Benny the bookie a whopping $10,000. It's easy to do, like running up a credit card bill. He tells Benny, "Listen, I need your help." At that point he has effectively taken out a loan of $10,000 from Benny's colleague, Paulie Walnuts, who reports to Tony Soprano, who reports to Junior Soprano. Our gambler friend has just been invited into the Soprano family.

Paulie takes over the account. He charges the gambler five points, or 5%, a week in interest, payable every Friday. That's $500 a *week*. Paulie wants his five bills every week and he doesn't give a rat's ass where it comes from. If you have to put your wife out on the streets, that's fine with him. If you can't make a payment, well, that's a problem, isn't it? The missed interest payment ($500) gets tacked on to the principal, so you now owe Paulie $10,500, or interest of $525 a week. It's a good business, loansharking. The weekly take generally gets bigger and bigger.

VINCENT RIZZO: Of course your wiseguy loan officer, you might call him, makes up all the rules. Say, you promise to pay the debt back in a certain time frame and then don't deliver. Well, if I was the guy in charge, your interest rate would go up a point or two. I had a schlump once, a dentist with a love of the horses, he was paying me $5000 a year on a $10,000 debt. That's a lot. It's like a 500% interest rate. Better than fuckin' Visa.

Paulie at the office

FRANK CUBITOSO: Most states have usury laws. In New York, for instance, it's a crime to charge someone more than 25% a year in interest. A Mafia loanshark would find that rate demeaning, like you were trying to run him out of business.

JEFFREY WERNICK: So let's move on to stage three of wiseguys ruining your life – the point where you will *never* be able to pay them back and they must look for alternative ways of collecting their money. I interviewed a very bright capo who explained it to me in almost business-school terms. He said that, in this situation, you first had to "analyze your customer base." Then you get "pro-active" and take advantage of that base depending on what marketable goods and services you can "grow." In other words, you bleed the guy dry.

Davey flirts with the opt-out clause

Jeffrey Wernick is the Samuel Johnson of mob talk. He has studied formal Italian, street Italian, and all the hybrids in-between, as well as recording the oral tradition of wiseguys for 30 years.

What follows is an abridged dictionary of Northeastern regional mob patois. Learn this language, and the accent and attitude that goes along with it, and you can sit down in front of the Pork Store and complain about the ways of the world with the best of them. Just say you're Paulie's second cousin from Bensonhurst.

A friend of ours: mob shorthand for introducing one made guy to another made guy. "A friend of mine" is just another jamook on the street.

A trippa di zianita: "Your aunt's tripe."

Action: a bet that a bookie "writes" and for which you pay him his "vig."

Agita: anxiety, edginess, an upset stomach. Tony's constant condition.

Anti-Trust Violations: what authorities call the mob practice of carving out exclusive territories. Wiseguys call them "mine."

Associate: someone who works with the family but is not a made guy.

Buon' anima: salutation meaning rest his soul.

Bust Out: a forced bankruptcy of a merchant who can't pay his debts. Using him as a cover, you steal everything you can get your hands on and leave him to deal with the creditors. Few businessmen recover from a full-blown bust out.

Buttlegging: bootlegging untaxed cigarettes.

Cafone: a peasant or lower-class. How Livia feels about the other half of the family.

Capice: the last word in a conversation with a wiseguy, meaning, "You understand, fuckface?"

Capo: the leader of a crew, or captain.

Cazzis: *see* Stugots.

Che bruta: how ugly you are.

Che peccato: what a pity, what a shame.

Chiacchierone: chatterbox.

Col tempo la foglia di gelso diventa seta: old Italian saying meaning, "Time and patience change the mulberry leaf to satin."

Comare (also **goomah, goomar,** or **gomatta**): slang for girlfriend or mistress. No self-respecting wiseguy is without one.

Come Heavy: to walk in carrying a loaded gun. You shouldn't have lunch with a Russian drug dealer unless you "come heavy."

Compare: the connection between two Italians. Tony and Melfi are "compare."

Consigliere: a trusted family advisor, always consulted before important decisions. See Tom Hagen in *The Godfather*.

Cugine: young soldier trying to get himself made.

CW: FBI shorthand for Co-operating Witness. Big Pussy is known as "CW16."

Executive Game: a special-event card game for celebrities and other high-rollers.

"Facia bruta": ugly face, something Livia likes to call anyone she doesn't like.

Fanook, or Finook: derived from "finucchiu," or fennel, a derogatory term for homosexual or gay, i.e., people that wiseguys feel nervous around. A "mezzofinook" is half gay, sissy, bi.

Forbidden Fruit: the lure of a wiseguy to a nice Italian girl from the neighborhood.

Fuckface-itis: a disorder suffered by Mikey Palmice before his unfortunate demise while jogging in the woods.

Gabagool: (capo cuoll) something to eat

"Gira diment": going crazy.

Googoots: Cucuzz – squash, pumpkin, i.e. stupid person.

Goombah: a guy who hangs around and does things for you, like order take-out Chinese or buy hockey tickets. Bobby Bacala functions as Junior's goombah.

Guests of the state or **Guests of the government:** going to prison, doing time.

In the wind: <u>after</u> you leave the Witness Protection Program, you are "in the wind," meaning you're on your own somewhere out there.

Jamook: idiot, loser, lamebrained, you know, a jamook.

Large: a thousand dollars, a grand, a G.

LCN: FBI talk for La Casa Nostra, or, translated, "Our Thing."

Made guy: To be initiated into the brotherhood of the Mafia by secret ceremony. Essentially, you pledge your allegiance to the boss and the family for life. To even qualify, your mother has to be Italian.

Madonn': Madonna, common expression meaning holy smoke, holy cow, holy shit.

Mannagge: darn, damn.

Meddigan: *see* Wonder Bread Wops.

Mezza morta: half-dead.

Mobbed up: involved with the mob. The carting industry in New Jersey is allegedly "mobbed up."

Moe Green Special: Getting killed with a shot in the eye, like the character, Moe Green, in *The Godfather*. One form of "sending a message."

Mortadella: derived from the Italian sausage, meaning a loser. As in: "Guy's a fuckin' mortadella."

Mulignan: literal translation: eggplant. Another word for African-Americans. Also called "mooleys".

Musciata: mushy.

OC: FBI talk for Organized Crime.

Omerta: the much-vaulted Mafia vow of silence. In other words: don't rat on your friends. Transgression is punishable by death.

Oobatz: u'pazzu – crazy.

Piacere: "Pleasure to meet you."

Pootsie: Paulie's childhood word for "shit," as in "[Americans] ate pootsie until we gave them the gift of our cuisine." From "che puzzo," "what a stink."

Poverett: poor person.

Predicates: an offense which the Justice Department can choose to "fold into" a RICO statute. As in, "This charge could be tough. It could have predicates."

Pucchiacha: cunt.

Pump and dump: standard practice for unethical stockbrokers. First drive up the price of a small stock by "encouraging" investors to buy it ("pump") and then sell your own shares ("dump") for a tidy profit.

Puttana: whore.

RICO: stands for Racketeer-Influenced and Corrupt Organization Act. A Federal statute, enacted in 1970, which allows prosecutors to throw a mob boss in prison if they can prove a connection to a criminal "enterprise" or criminal "commission," even if he has no direct link to a particular crime. In theory, once a criminal conspiracy has been proven, every member of a family could be prosecuted and every ill-gotten asset seized. RICO keeps wiseguys up at night. (Dr. Melfi thought "RICO" was Tony's brother.)

Schamozz': a schamorza, a smoked mozzarella cheese. As in: "Does this guy even know his own ass from a schamozz'?"

Schifosa: ugly woman.

Sfogliatelle: an Italian pastry.

Strunz: strunzo – piece of shit.

Stugots – from stu cazzo or u'cazzu, the testicles. Tony's boat is *The Stugots*.

Taste: a percentage of the take. Tony gets a big taste from bookmaking or racketeering, but a little taste from medical fraud.

Tizzun: Neapolitan derogatory term for black person.

Va fa napole: "Go to Naples" i.e., "Go to hell."

Vig: short for vigorish. The payment to a bookie for placing a bet. Usually two points, or 2%.

Wearing it: showing off one's status in the organization by dressing the part. "Wearing it" usually involves an Italian suit, a pinky ring, a hankie in the breast pocket, gold cufflinks, and other ornamentation. Silvio has his own inimitable way of wearing it.

Whack: to kill, exterminate, eliminate with extreme prejudice.

Wonder Bread Wop (also known as **Mayonnaiser** and **Meddigan**): an Italian-American who has totally assimilated into suburban culture. The Cusamanos next door fit the description.

VINCENT RIZZO: This is the creative part of business. Say you got a stockbroker client who has too high an opinion of the Dallas Cowboys. You need the money and he doesn't get it. You could break his arms, of course, but that doesn't always work. If you kill him, then he's, well … dead. So, you suggest that he starts giving you inside stock tips, the more inside the better. Soon you're making money off the tips and he still owes you the full balance of the debt.

If he's a druggist, he supplies you Percodan. If he's a trucker, he tells you when a big shipment of Sub Zero refrigerators are coming in and conveniently turns off the alarm. Then he collects insurance on the stolen goods and you get a piece of that, too. See? It's highly fuckin' entrepreneurial.

FRANK CUBITOSO: Any time the mob loans you money, for whatever reason, they in essence own you. Often they will assume ownership of your restaurant or body shop and you work for them. Or they bankrupt you on purpose – a "bust out." They use your good credit to buy everything they can get their hands on that's fenceable and then when the creditors begin to beat down your door, you file for bankruptcy. That's how we recently indicted Mr. Soprano. He got some airline tickets during a bust out operation at Ramsey Sporting Goods and gave one of those tickets to his mother. Unlike most items, airline tickets leave a paper trail.

JEFFREY WERNICK: Tony Soprano is in the carting business – legitimately. Or kind of legitimately. For all we know, it could have been something his father or old man DiMeo or maybe Jackie Aprile acquired as part of a loan gone bad. But it gives Tony a great cover and a handsome income. Carting is Tony's big-ticket item.

FRANK CUBITOSO: The Mafia's biggest income producer is, without a doubt, industry-wide corruption activities. I can't talk about an ongoing case like Tony Soprano's, but I can give you a general picture. The mob likes to take over a discrete segment of a whole industry, like all the delivery trucks in the garment district or all product distribution in the Newark fish industry. Imagine you make dresses and need to get them to stores in time for the spring season. You argue with the guy who controls every truck and they get there in September. This is not good. Whatever he charges, you pay.

Let's apply this to the carting, or garbage, business. A mob-run carting company usually has a set number of customers that no competitor touches. This is his "territory." It's not geographical, it's client-based, and clients are passed on from one generation to another. Since I have an exclusive arrangement with that business, I can charge whatever I want. He can't go to my competitor. There is no competitor. So, I jack up the price to just

The Bada Bing,
by daylight

that point where it's not going to drive my customer out of business. In real costs, it may cost $1000 a month to pick up wet garbage from a restaurant. I charge $3000. That's a 200% overcharge. Any business would flourish with that kind of pricing structure.

JEFFREY WERNICK: They also control the local carting trade association, which can settle disputes among mob-controlled carters. In Tony's territory it's called Garden State Carting Association. This is a real source of power, a genuine cartel. And they control the local carting drivers *union*, so they keep the labor peace. If a non-mob operation tries to move in, it'll have a tough time picking up the garbage without any drivers. They got you coming and going.

VINCENT RIZZO: See, the thing is, you want to be in a business that no one gives a shit about. Businesses that fall under the radar. Drugs and prostitution are right in the middle of the radar. They're glamorous. Garbage pickup or commercial maintenance or gravel delivery are way off the screen. If you don't shoot anybody or charge too much, no one complains and everybody makes money. I mean, who wants to start trouble with cold-blooded killers over a garbage bill? It's just the cost of doing business.

JEFFREY WERNICK: A guy like Tony Soprano makes his big paycheck from "waste management," but he has money coming in from all kinds of scams. Mob guys are criminals of opportunity. They see an opportunity, they move. Untaxed cigarettes, for instance, otherwise known as "buttlegging." Probably every liquor store in Essex County has taxed cigarettes for Joe Lunchpail and untaxed ones in back for the cognoscenti. And he got them from Tony. Calling card scams are big right now.

The mob used to control all these blackmarket operations – porno, videocassettes, etc. – but now they have to compete with other ethnic gangs and an army of street hustlers. Which doesn't mean they don't do business with other ethnics. They do. That's where a guy like Hesh or maybe Silvio comes in.

Tony's crew negotiate a peaceful settlement with protesting jointfitters

They can talk to blacks, Greeks, Hispanics, what have you, and do deals. The notion that there are only a few hundred made guys out there is deceiving. Add up all the multi-ethnic associates out there and you're talking thousands. Actually, tens of thousands.

VINCENT RIZZO: How much does a guy like Tony make? A fuck of a lot. It's cash in, cash out, no records. He probably makes somewhere in the ballpark of $1.5 million a year, some years more, some years less. Tax free, remember, plus the perks are great – free furs off the truck, a free condo in Florida acquired from a deadbeat gambler, that kind of thing.

Now Paulie Walnuts, a made guy for 20–25 years, probably makes $60 to 100K a year, which is not bad for a guy who would otherwise be pounding nails and paying Uncle Sam his third. But it's very uneven, you know. There are definite dry spells.

FRANK CUBITOSO: You know when you see in movies a bunch of wiseguys pull into their social club and empty a garbage bag full of cash on the pool table? That's pretty much how it is. Money comes in Hefty bags.

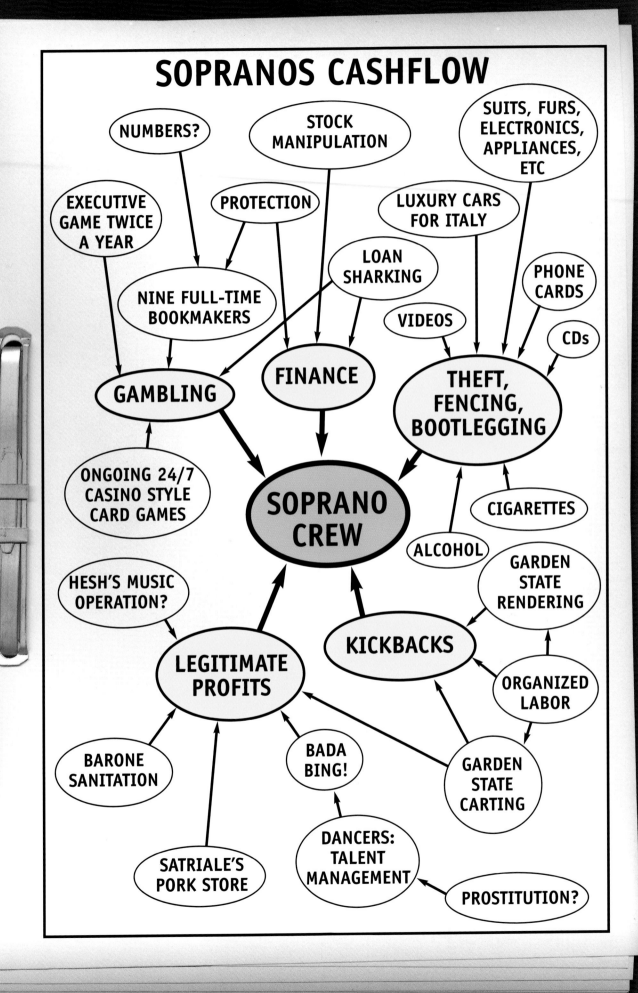

Ton' on The
Stugots with
the goomar,
Irina

JEFFREY WERNICK: Wiseguys notoriously get it and spend it, usually on themselves, their goomars, their coke habits, etc. They are not great savers. But who really knows? There are Mafiosi who have done very well in the stock market, but that's probably not Paulie or Silvio. They don't strike me as Wall Street Wizards.

VINCENT RIZZO: Of course people get killed. There are sanctioned killings, unsanctioned killings, like dissing the wrong girlfriend at the bar, accidental killings, you name it. Does it go on all the time? Not these days. But it happens.

JEFFREY WERNICK: Killing is bad for business. It causes friction among crews and brings down the heat. Most of the problems in a mob operation, internal and external, are managerial problems. You know, one guy stole a shipment of DVDs and didn't give his capo his cut, or two different families are loan-sharking the same poor deadbeat, so they have to decide who gets to burn his appliance store down. No press, no violence. That's the lesson of John Gotti and Sammy "the Bull" Gravano. When was the last time you heard about a "mob war"? Those days are gone.

Sean Gismonte and Matt Bevilaqua, aka Chip and Dale

FBI SOURCE, NAME WITHHELD: Everybody cheats and everybody knows that everybody cheats. The soldier cheats the capo, the capo cheats the underboss, and all the way up. As long as times are good, no one complains. The minute times turn bad, the boss is counting every shekel.

VINCENT RIZZO: Hey, it's a shaky fuckin' business. Why do you think I got the fuck out? The government offered me a better deal, that's why. Better life insurance.

JEFFREY WERNICK: Like the general economic shift from the "old" economy to the new high-tech economy, the Mafia is being forced to reinvent itself, too. Part of it has to do with law enforcement. RICO statutes can now bring a whole family down because of some screw-up on the lowest level. Snitches, or rats, are endemic. No longer is it "do the crime, do the time." It's more like, do the crime, make a deal. And, finally, competition from other gangsters is fierce. Colombian drug dealers or Russian credit card forgers do not play by the same rules as Uncle Luigi. I'm sure Tony Soprano looks to a young, bright, with-it guy like Christopher Moltisanti to take the family into new growth opportunities. God knows someone has to.

THE BODY COUNT

VICTIM #1: EMIL KOLAR
A young Czechoslovakian-American, nephew of Evzen Kolar, an interstate waste carting operator. Through a marginally trustworthy informant, told that Kolar was killed execution-style at Satriale's Pork Store on Kearney Avenue in Kearney. Body never found. Minor criminal record for drug-possession. If a hit, probably an unsanctioned hit, perhaps perpetrated by a young, un-made Soprano (Moltisanti?) for purposes of earning his stripes for made status. One shot, close range, back of head, followed by seven more shots to the body. Talk of cocaine use.

whoops . . .

VICTIM #2: HECTOR ANTHONY, Driver, Comley Transport
Killed during the execution of a daylight hijacking. Assailants unknown, but have reason to believe that an associate of Christopher Moltisanti, Brendan Filone, was involved (see Vic #3). Given the entry of the fatal bullet, looks like an accident more than an execution. Probably an assailant's gun slipped, went off, and killed the guy. How pathetic is that?

Clean through the eye

VICTIM #3: BRENDAN FILONE
A known associate of Soprano soldier Christopher Moltisanti, believed killed as a result of the unsanctioned, boneheaded hijacking referenced above. Comley Transport pays protection to Junior Soprano, who has no love for Christopher (thinks he's an irresponsible brat, which he is). Filone shot through the eye while taking a bath, a clear mob message. Simultaneously, at another location, Moltisanti was severely beaten — same message. Re the old adage that the mob only kills its own: it sometimes happens that way.

VICTIM #4: FRED PETERS A.K.A. FABIAN "FEBBY" PETRULLO
Peters garroted to death in rural Maine, outside of trailer headquarters of travel business, "Peter's Travels / Italian Holidays." A well-liked man in the local community, Peter's real identity is Fabian "Febby" Petrullo, convicted DiMeo / Soprano soldier who flipped in the late 1970s and helped us bury a half dozen wiseguys. His defection was apparently devastating to Tony Soprano's father, Johnny. Death by strangulation with extreme prejudice. Killing occurred while Tony Soprano was reportedly in the area escorting his daughter, Meadow, around to exclusive Ivy League-type colleges (Colby, Bowdoin, et al). Absolutely no hard evidence linking Tony — pure speculation. Could have been any one of a hundred guys that hated Febby. Let this be a lesson to all rats — they never forget.

VICTIM #5: RUSTY IRISH

A local drug dealer and reputedly a good earner, killed by being thrown off the bridge over Paterson Falls. Believed killed by Michael "Mikey" Palmice, a lieutenant of reportedly newly named boss Junior Soprano, as punishment for selling cocaine to the grandson of a civilian friend of Junior's. Some evidence that other capos in family didn't concur. Irish was an earner in several other illicit businesses, especially sports betting.

VICTIM #6: IDENTITY PENDING, Colombian National

A reputed drug dealer, killed execution-style in his apartment in Newark area. Jailhouse Latino informant believes his friend was killed by Soprano family members for invading Soprano business territory and failing to pay required tribute.
Real motive

Police reconstruction w/ dummy:
Rusty Irish homicide

probably robbery. As we all know, these guys carry suitcases full of cash for face to face transactions and there was none found at crime scene. Territorial dispute just a convenient rationale for getting in the door.

VICTIM #7: JIMMY ALTIERI

Killed execution-style, again with extreme prejudice. We're pretty sure why Mr. Altieri was killed — he was working for us and someone found out. Too bad. He was an excellent informant, fearless, willing to wear a wire into almost any situation. Young Russian prostitutes, believed to be waiting to

Jimmy the rat

rendezvous with Altieri and set-up man, were questioned but said nothing. Who can blame them?

VICTIM #8: MIKEY PALMICE

Palmice is a well-documented Soprano operative, loyal to Junior Soprano. Killed in woods near his home. Wife says he went out for morning jog and never returned. Again, we are absolutely sure why Palmice was whacked. Once Tony Soprano heard our tape of his Uncle Junior and mother plotting his murder, we feared heads would roll. Not even

The moral midget

Look what we caught

a monster like Tony can kill his blood relatives, but there's no sanction against weasels like Palmice. Too bad. We probably could've gotten Palmice to flip at some point. He was the kind of moral midget we like to prey on. Unauthorized hit - they should have gotten Junior's permission, which he would have never given.

VICTIM #9: CHARLES "CHUCKY" SIGNORE
Chucky reported to Philly Parisi (see Vic #10) in the Soprano organization, but also took orders from Mikey Palmice (see Vic #8). Vanished at the same time Palmice was assassinated. Last seen on leisure boat docked at marina. Went swimming with the proverbial fishes. Possible scenario: Chucky takes killer for boatride, gets whacked and dumped, killer drives boat back to dock. Who's a master boatman? One guess.

VICTIM #10: PHILLY PARISI
Soprano family soldier, reports to Junior. Killed execution-style in front of house in Orange, possibly by Gigi Cestone, Soprano family soldier, reports to Tony. Follow the bouncing ball. This is obviously an inter-family dispute, probably involving Philly's notoriously big mouth, e.g., spreading the rumor that Tony tried to snuff out his own mother. Of course Cestone is not around lately to answer questions and all other family members call it "a tragic loss." Check with Boston authorities. Cestone may have relocated.

VICTIM #11: FREDERICK "FREDDIE" CAPUANO, BUSINESSMAN
Owner of the Green Grove Retirement Home, residence of Livia Soprano and other aging LCN relatives. Disappeared, believed dead. Crime scene: empty car, still running, found under exit 16W on the NJ Turnpike, driver's door open and Freddie's cut-rate hairpiece nearby. Standard kidnap/murder MO. Freddie had a mouth. One source inside home says Freddie hinted at "relationship" between Livia and Junior. I'm sure Junior liked hearing that. Also gabbed about Tony "fluffing up" Livia's pillows, ie, snuffing her. Known to brag about Green Grove as "the place where the mob brings their moms." Loose lips sink bald guys.

Elvis lives? Not this one.

VICTIM #12: JIMMY BONES
Struggling Elvis impersonator and weekend wiseguy, killed in his duplex in Dover, surrounded by images of The King. Death by repeatedly pummeling to the head by hammer, probably ball peen. God knows why. He was reportedly a fatmouth - maybe someone just got tired

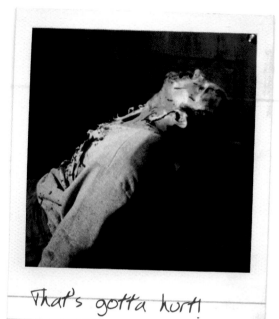

That's gotta hurt!

of his act. Skip Lipari remembers meeting him at the Party Box with Big Pussy. Made Pussy very nervous. Put this one in the never-to-be-solved file.

VICTIM #13: SEAN GISMONTE
Street punk, petty thief, wiseguy wannabe, known associate of the late Matt Bevilaqua (see Vic #14) and Christopher Moltisanti. Cousin of Louis Gismonte, incarcerated, East Jersey State Prison. Killed in street altercation in front of diner in North Arlington. Died with Glock 9 in his hand. Plenty of witnesses, none talking. Very ugly scene, bullet holes everywhere, none traceable so far. Moltisanti was hit. Maybe he was intended victim, maybe at the orders of Richie Aprile. All speculation at this point.

VICTIM #14: MATT BEVILAQUA
Same profile as Gismonte. Also known as Matt Drinkwater, nephew of wiseguy Ivo Bevilaqua. Executed point blank in an abandoned refreshment stand at Hacklebarney State Park. Beaten badly, hands tied with gaffer tape, mouth sock found next to body. Many shots to the head and body. Definitely a grudge kill, only days after Gismonte shoot-out and Moltisanti's hospitalization. Of course there is absolutely no hard evidence to connect anyone, unless that eyewitness Larry Arthur agrees to testify, which he won't.

POSSIBLE VICTIM #15: RICHIE APRILE
Major figure in Soprano family, brother of late acting boss, Jackie Aprile, close associate of Junior, probably chief rival to Tony Soprano. Disappeared off the face of the earth. Could be in the wind, but highly unlikely. Fiancée Janice "Parvati" Soprano suddenly cancels escrow on fancy new honeymoon home, hightails it back to Seattle. Anonymous reports of late night gunshots heard at Livia Soprano's home in West Orange. Is this the upshot of a lover's quarrel or a power struggle? Probably both.

Did Tony do him?

POSSIBLE VICTIM #16: SALVATORE "BIG PUSSY" BONPENSIERO, CW16
A loyal and trusted Soprano soldier for 35 years and as you know, one of "ours." Ask Skip Lipari for details. Again, a disappearance, not a confirmed hit. For a while we thought he might have split because of the pressure from both sides, but Skip doesn't buy that theory. He thinks it's an inside job. If so, it must have been the most painful thing Tony and crew ever had to do. Sure, there's a code, but it's broken all the time. Pussy was a close friend of Tony's father, a godfather to Tony's own son and like a brother to Paulie and Silvio. What a nasty business. Kind of takes the bloom off the Mafia rose, doesn't it?

"Out there, it's the 1990s. In here, it's 1954."

Tony Soprano, to his kids

The children of Tony and Carmela Soprano – Meadow, age 17, and Anthony, Jr, called AJ, age 14 – have broken no laws and are under suspicion for no crime. In many ways, they have been raised much like other suburban kids – pampered, encouraged to excel, and sheltered from unpleasant realities. And they have an increasingly rare blessing – an intact family.

Even so, it's tough enough being a kid in the age of Columbine. Being a kid with a dad who buries Kruggerands and loaded guns in the backyard is a whole other problem.

Again, thanks to Mr. Wernick's resources, we can peek into the private lives of Meadow and AJ. The same email scavengers who tapped into FBI correspondence earlier in the book also have a rich download on Meadow. She loves to go online and chat about her life. Her current handle is "Bella82."

CHATROOM: "FRIENDS – SECRET PASSAGE." TIME: 1834.

CapdogNY: STOP Favia
Favabean07:   make me, love of my life . . .
Katethevirg: you 2 are tres disgusting!
Favabean07:   oh, kate, let me be the one . . . pleeeeezzzzz . . .
Bella82:   hi, room.
Prettyinpink: hey, look whos back...La costra bella!!!!!
Katethevirg: hey, bella.
Favabean07:   still not buyin it, but hi too . . .

Bella82:	shut up, please, iii got a prob . . .
CapdogNY:	we know...
Bella82:	**Blow me.**
Favabean07:	you mean . . . blow me up!!!!
Bella82:	**alright I'm leavin, good night...**
Katethevirg:	fav you leave, d-head. what's all up, bell??
Bella82:	**ok, so a little par-ty at my gramma's old house got, you know, whacky last nite, but it's not my fault!!!**
HairyMat:	it never is.
CapdogNY:	whose that?
Favabean07:	who cares? More, more . . . take drugs, get naked, horizon bopppp????
Bella82:	**fav, you are sooooooo stupido...**
Katethevirg:	duh. So?
Bella82:	**so not much, iii didn't get punished or anything...credit card taken away for three weeks...**
HairyMat:	man, you are so lucky...
Bella82:	**it's the bigger pic, you know...they have no life but me and my lit bro and they are unhappy and stressed out...like iii'm not...and**
Favabean07:	my dad thru a JB bottle at my mom the other night and almost hit ME!!!!!!!
CapdogNY:	we know...bell, is you dad going to big house?
Bella82:	**iii don't know. can't wait to get outa here. I hate my life, crazy fam, etc, etc...**
Prettyinpink:	who doesn't. I think I'm preg!!!
HairyMat:	ii know a doc...
Favabean07:	bummer . . . hey, kate, tell me, am iii da man??? Im good, just ask pretty.
Prettyinpink:	you suck, fav.
Bella82:	**gotta go. Here comes Il duce...**
Katethevirg:	by, bell...all who agree that fav sucks, speak up now.
CapdogNY:	Eihhhhhhhhhhhhhhhh.......

JEFFREY WERNICK: Growing up a well-known mobster's kid is probably much like growing up the child of a celebrity. First of all, your father is pretty self-involved, like an actor or a politician. If he shows up at your soccer game, everyone makes a big deal out of it and rushes up to shake his hand. But, at the same time, people tend to tiptoe around you, wanting to impress you but not wanting to say the wrong thing or be too nosy. As much as they say, "We don't care who your father is," they do. And their parents do. In fact, their parents probably bug Meadow and AJ for gossip about you-know-who. How do you deal with that as a kid? A lot of celebrity kids, we know, end up in drug wards. And then there's the ethical and moral vacuum.

Hollyweird:	i swear, none of em cared, one just handed me the soap and said do me, pleez... i love college girls...
BigBeef:	u are so full of shit...
Turtle499:	Hanson stupid.
Favabean07:	freaking music critic. wheres bella???
Bella82:	**ii'm here.**
Favabean07:	is your bro mafia, too?
Bella82:	**a, there is no mafia, tweeb, and b, no he's a dorky little kid who spends 2 much time playing video.**
BigBeef:	borrring. Gots go. LOL.
Turtle499:	bye beef.
Bella82:	**and he knows nothing about nothing.**
Favabean07:	mentally challenged, huh?
Katethevirg:	u should know.
Favabean07:	mi amoure!!!!! Pleez, let me fondle yor tender . . .
Turtle499:	oh my god.
Hollyweird:	shut up, fav.
Bella82:	**so he gets into this fight with a poser at school and he thinks kid is afraid of HIM!**
Hollyweird:	I'm afraid of him.
Favabean07:	does he have guns and stuff???
Bella82:	**he has a poster of Keith Van Horn and a fishing rod or something. No glocks.**
Hollyweird:	whats that?
Favabean07:	glock go boom, kill hollyweird.
Turtle499:	where do I get one?
Katethevirg:	Do you love him?
Bella82:	**Bite me.**
Favabean07:	is he stupid?
Bella82:	**he's....14.**
Hollyweird:	I'm still afraid of him.

GERALD MCFADDIN, MATH & SCIENCE TEACHER: The boy is well liked, a kind of "everybody's friend" kind of kid, but not a good student. In fact he's an awful student. He goes out of his way to be helpful to others, but I don't think he takes himself seriously.

FATHER PHIL: In general, a father like the type we're discussing doesn't want his son to pick up what you might call the "outlaw" gene, the one he got from his own father. Of course, if it is an actual gene, and we're learning more about the genetic code everyday, then it's too late. I'm sure that's what the father thinks – the die is already cast.

PETER GALANI, MA, PHD, MSW
SCHOOL PSYCHOLOGIST

PSYCHOLOGICAL EVALUATION/REPORT TO PARENTS
VERBUM DEI MIDDLE SCHOOL. STUDENT: ANTHONY SOPRANO, JR.

Dear Mr. and Mrs. Soprano:
I have now completed an exhaustive array of medical, psychological, and behavioral tests with Anthony. Here are the highlights of my diagnosis.

A. Anthony has no observable evidence of physiological impairment or disease. He is in excellent health. He has a slight weight problem, but who doesn't?

B. Anthony has no observable evidence of learning disability or other cognitive dysfunction. His intelligence, problem-solving skills, and verbal and math comprehension are within the norm. Despite his low grades, he may even be above-norm in some areas. Which leads me to:

C. In terms of ADD (Attention Deficit Disorder), the results are inconclusive. Out of nine possible symptoms, a subject must manifest at least six to be given an ADD diagnosis and subsequent treatment. Anthony manifests five symptoms. They are:

   1. Difficulty awaiting his turn.
   2. Acts in a fast mode, as if driven by a motor.
   3. Interrupts others.
   4. Fidgets with hands and feet.
   5. Doesn't listen to elders.

In conclusion, it is best to call Anthony a borderline ADD and simply hope his behavior improves with maturity. It is my recommendation to do nothing at this time but to observe him carefully and reward good behavior. Please do not hesitate to call me if you notice other indications of inattention, impulsivity, or hyperactivity on Anthony's part. Remember, he is only one symptom away from intervention.
Thank you.

Cordially,

Dr. Peter Galani
Cc: Father Hagy
Mr. Miskimkin

CONVERSATION CONTINUES:

FIELDER: Dad, are you in the Mafia?

HER DAD: Am I in the what?

FIELDER: Whatever you want to call it, Dad - organized crime?

HER DAD: That's total crap. Who told you that?

FIELDER: Dad, I've lived in the house all my life. I've seen police come
                with warrants. I've seen you going out at three in the morning.

HER DAD: So you never seen Doc Cusamano go out at three in the morning on
                a call?

FIELDER: Did the Cusamano kids ever find fifty thousand dollars in
                Krugerrands and a .45 automatic while they were hunting for
                easter eggs?

HER DAD: I'm in the waste management business, everybody immediately
                assumes you're mobbed up. It's a stereotype, and it's offensive.
                And you're the last person I would want to perpetuate it.

FIELDER: Fine.

HER DAD: There is no Mafia.

                (BREATH) Alright, look...Fielder, you're a grown woman - almost.
                Some of my money comes from illegal gamblin' and whatnot.

                How does that make you feel?

FIELDER: At least you don't keep denying it like Mom. The kids in school
                think it's actually kind of neat.

HER DAD: As in "The Godfather", right?

FIELDER: Not really. "Casino", like, Sharon Stone...the Seventies
                clothes, pills.

HER DAD: I'm not askin' about those bums. I'm askin' about you.

FIELDER: Sometimes I wish you were like other dads. But then like, Mr
                Scangarelo, for example, an advertising executive for big
                tobacco, or lawyers, ugh. So many dads are full of shit.

HER DAD: And I'm not.

FIELDER: You finally told me the truth about this.

HER DAD: Look, Fielder, part of my income comes from legitimate business.
                You know, the stock market, I...

FIELDER: Dad, please okay. Don't start mealy-mouthing.

JEFFREY WERNICK: The last thing thing that most career Mafiosi wants is for their kids to follow them into that business. They often do, of course – Bill Bonanno, John Gotti, Jr., Sammy "the Bull's" son out in Phoenix. And the ones that do usually fall on their face. What did Jefferson say? "I fight wars so that my sons can study philosophy." That's one place that *The Godfather* got it exactly right. Vito didn't want Michael to be a mobster. He wanted him to be, "Senator Corleone, Governor Corleone..." I bet he would have settled for Dr. Corleone or even Mike Corleone, State Farm Insurance.

GERALD McFADDIN: The girl? She knows, for sure. She made the National Honor Society, for crissakes.

DISCOVERY
FINANCIAL SERVICES

Closing date: May 11, 2000   page 1 of 2

Cashback Bonus ® Award	this period	to date
qualified purchase	$1531.90	$6022.37
Cashback Bonus award earned	$4.69	$18.45
Cashback Bonus anniversary date	June 18	

Discovery Card Account Summary

account number	▇ ▇ ▇ ▇		
payment due date	June 12, 2000	previous balance	$974.03
credit limit	$9,500	payments and credits −	923.36
credit limit	$9,500	purchases +	1531.90
credit available	$6,500	cash advances +	0.00
cash credit limit	$4,750	balance transfers +	0.00
cash credit available	$4,750	FINANCE CHARGES +	29.68
		new balance =	$1612.25

You may be able to avoid Periodic Finance Charges, see the reverse side for details.

Transactions

Payments and Credits

April 28	PAYMENT – THANK YOU	$	− 800.00
May 07	BANANA REPUBLIC.COM RET		− 123.36

Merchandise/Retail

April 12	E-BAY.COM	76.24
April 12	EARTHLINK *INTERNET	19.95
April 14	ESSEX FELLS LIQUORS	54.19
April 17	MINDSPRING *INTERNET	16.95
April 19	E-BAY.COM	20.14
April 19	MCDONALD'S	1.19
April 20	M.O.B.COM SUBSCRIPT	17.95
April 20	BLOCKBUSTER VIDEO	47.95
April 21	TICKETMASTER	156.00
April 22	INDULGE.COM	49.19
April 23	GENERAL CINEMA	9.50
April 24	GENERAL CINEMA	19.00
April 25	GENERAL CINEMA	9.50
April 25	SUNOCO	26.85
April 27	TERESA'S FANCY NAILS	9.67
April 29	SEPHORA	72.05
May 01	BANANA REPUBLIC.COM	123.36
May 02	JESSICA MCCLINTOCK	168.00
May 02	US POST OFFICE	0.33
May 02	J. CREW.COM	84.60
May 06	CRATE & BARREL	54.72
May 07	VICTORIA'S SECRET.COM	106.09
May 08	SUNOCO	24.77
May 09	AMAZON *SUPERSTORE	114.33
May 10	THE WALL	30.00
May 11	E-BAY.COM	209.88
May 11	GENERAL CINEMA	9.50

BigBeef:	Tell us everything…every little thing like who he killed, etc…
Favabean07:	still not buying it . . .
HairyMat:	you are too you poser
Prettyinpink:	fav, a poser? he's mr. no-BS. Not.
BigBeef:	I WANT DETAILS!!!!
Favabean07:	yeah, like whats his crew???
Bella82:	**go away, fav.**
BigBeef:	pleez tell soemthingggg)))))
Bella82:	**don't really know, no lie, gambling and stuff, goes to tittie bar, people give him money, worries a lot.**
Turtle499:	hello in there.
Prettyinpink:	turt-man is back.
BigBeef:	where you from?
Turtle499:	Lawrence, Kansas.
BigBeef:	not you, suckface!
Turtle499:	oh…
Bella82:	**ii'll never tell…ii already said too much…anyway, I want to talk about me, not him.**
Favabean07:	Chicago! Shes from Chicago!!! I hear the accent. So am I!!!!
Bella82:	**wrong again.**
Turtle499:	N'sync real stupid.
Prettyinpink:	big f-king deal. Her dad's a crook. All dads are bullshit. Mine does feminine hygiene ads and thinks he's steven freaking spielberg. I'm sure all our dads would blow their boss for a raise.
BigBeef:	mine already has. Wears knee patches…
Favabean07:	someday hes gonna do something to make you puke and youll turn him in . . .
Bella82:	**never in a billion years. Slit my throat first.**
HairyMat:	I think your dad is a dick.
Bella82;	**he is who he is. Fuck you.**
Turtle499:	that is so cool.

CLOSE FRIEND OF MEADOW, NAME WITHHELD: I don't know anyone who doesn't think Meadow will get everything she wants in life. She won't marry the first guy that comes on to her, that's for sure. She won't be a hospital volunteer and book club organizer like her mom. I think she'll be more like, you know, her grandma, who I think is pretty cool. She's funny, you know, sarcastic. And no one tells that old lady what to do. If she had grown up now, like Meadow, she'd be bigger than Meadow's dad. In fact, I bet Meadow ends up bigger than her dad. And if something should ever happen to her mom, and there was no one left to take care of him, she'd do that, too. Gladly.

Bella82:	**my mom is so into this college thing, it's disgusting!**
UCLAORBUST:	Tell me about it!
Jackflash69:	how many schools, bell?
Bella82:	**4000.**
Jackflash69:	no way! You must be rich.
Sexaddict:	jack, that training program at Mickey D's looking pretty good, huh.
HardbellyTX:	I took so much crank for SAT I finish hours before anyone else, then puked bigtime.

UCLAORBUST:	how'd you do?
HardbellyTX:	1360. Full ride to LSU. Belle, are u dying to know?
Bella82:	**I'm dying to leave! And make my mom happy!**
Sexaddict:	is she coming with u?
Bella82:	**probably wants to. U know, I heard about a mom doing that, moving into the dorm and everything, going to class, etc, but the girl was a total crip. Even so, how awful is that?**
Jackflash69:	just wish I was blind, black, w/ single mom who escaped from Cuba.
Sexaddict:	you would.

FATHER PHIL: When the parents don't complete college, it's only natural that they want their son or daughter to get an advanced education and do well in the world. They read the papers, they understand. If you don't go to college now, you are in for a constricted life. What are you going to do – marry a nice boy from the neighborhood? Wrong century.

ADMISSIONS OFFICE WORKER, GEORGETOWN UNIVERSITY, NAME WITH-HELD: Of course we are legally barred from releasing any information about our admissions process or the candidates therein, but I can tell you, in the strictest confidence, that the candidate in question had some excellent references. Her family must be very prominent in their area. We ended up wait-listing the girl, which I, for one, thought was a poor decision. The committee decided they had met their Italian-American quota and needed more "sky's." You know, Wachinsky, Makursky, Polish people.

FROM THE DESK OF JOAN O'CONNELL SCRIVO

May 4, 2000

Mr. Quentin Penn
Office of Admissions
Georgetown University

Dearest Quentin,

I am writing yet again to recommend another fine young scholar for admission into Georgetown. Re: the Martinez boy. He was a most worthy candidate, but I was disappointed to recently learn that he was only using Georgetown as a backup to Harvard. When I discovered this fact, I immediately withdrew my recommendation. I promise his agenda, which I considered deceitful, was not revealed to me by his college counselor.

But now I have the considerable pleasure of introducing you to Meadow Soprano. She comes from a very good family who just happen to live next door to my sister, Jeanne, and her husband, Dr. Bruce Cusamano. Meadow is an excellent student, an excellent athlete, and a young woman of exceptional character. She is also a published author! Her research paper on the melting icecap ran in her high school paper, to considerable fanfare.

I promise, Quentin, this will be my last recommendation for this incoming class. This is the best candidate for Georgetown that I have found since helping to start the alumni association in this area in 1985 – are we getting that old?

Trust me, Meadow Soprano will make Georgetown proud. I recommend her without qualification.

Say hello to Beth for me!

Cordially,

Joan O'Connell Scrivo

BA '81
LLB '83

NAME OF CHAT ROOM; "COLLEGE BLUES." TIME: 2250.

UCLAORBUST:	call me CSUN-OR-BUST, ok?
HardbellyTX:	sorry, ucla. Come to Baton Rouge. We'll get f*********ed up!!!!!!!
UCLAORBUST:	send me an app.
Jackflash69:	what about Vito's little girl???
Bella82:	**Bingo! I'm sorry, I worked el butto off, deal with it... Berkeley, thank u, thank u.**
Favabean07:	go, pleezzzz . . . I'll join you there . . . I wanta be MADE!
HardbellyTX:	where'd u come from?
Bella82:	**And NYU. And BU.**
UCLAORBUST:	and Georgietown, natch.
Bella82:	**no, waitlist.**
HardbellyTX:	get outa town!!!!
Bella82:	**and waitlist Columbia, but no Penn, no Bowdoin.**
Jackflash69:	so where you gonna go?????
Bella82:	**stay tuned, sports fans............**

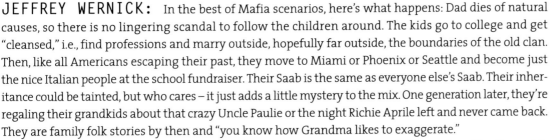

GERALD MCFADDIN: AJ? Hard to predict. Could end up teaching high school science, once he realizes that he's pretty good at it. Don't let the C's and D's fool you. Or he could go into business with his dad. Not any kind of dirty business. A real clean-cut business that his dad finances and sets up AJ to run. "AJ's House of Video & Sports Memorabilia." Something in the leisure field.

Tony and AJ take the boat out for a spin

JEFFREY WERNICK: In the best of Mafia scenarios, here's what happens: Dad dies of natural causes, so there is no lingering scandal to follow the children around. The kids go to college and get "cleansed," i.e., find professions and marry outside, hopefully far outside, the boundaries of the old clan. Then, like all Americans escaping their past, they move to Miami or Phoenix or Seattle and become just the nice Italian people at the school fundraiser. Their Saab is the same as everyone else's Saab. Their inheritance could be tainted, but who cares – it just adds a little mystery to the mix. One generation later, they're regaling their grandkids about that crazy Uncle Paulie or the night Richie Aprile left and never came back. They are family folk stories by then and "you know how Grandma likes to exaggerate."

What's lost? Only a real connection to the past, a sense of family stability and continuity, a rich neighborhood life of uncles and cousins and friends that would literally die for you. That's all. We have this manic urge in America to completely uncouple with our past. Soon we'll succeed and then where will we be?

NAME OF CHAT ROOM: "FRIENDS – UNDER 21." TIME: 0313.

Meadow gets on down

Katethevirg:	so sorry about your dad getting busted, Bella. will we read about this?
Bella82:	**oh my God I hope not.**
Turtle499:	kill all boy groups!
Favabean07:	shutup, shutup, SHUTUP!!! $&X?&!!!
Turtle499:	sor-ry.
Prettyinpink:	both shutup, bella's in trouble...are u scared?
Bella82:	**no, my dad is sexy and smart...he'll get out of it.**
Katethevirg:	but what if he doesn't???
Bella82:	**then I'll get him out of it.**
Prettyinpink:	sad?
Bella82:	**a little. Night-night.**
Favabean07:	wouldn't u like to meet her??? God . . .

"I mean, in this day and age, who wants the fucking job?"

Tony Soprano

And now, some final thoughts from the experts. If you only get your news from the mainstream media, then you probably hold the view that the Italian-American Mafia is on life support, soon to be eradicated from the face of the earth. Or if not eradicated, reduced to a few desperate crack dealers hiding in the alley. If this were a made-up story line, then the life imprisonment of the last leading man left standing, John "The Teflon Don" Gotti, would be a fitting dénouement to this 70-year-long tragedy.

But, as any Mafia fan knows, they said that when Al Capone got sent up, and again when Lucky Luciano got deported, and when Joe Valachi went public with "La Cosa Nostra," and again when the mob was run out of Vegas in the late 70s. Ask a bookie in New Rochelle or a tradesman at the Fulton Fish Market if the mob is dying and he'll probably look at you funny and say, "Yeah, right..."

FRANK CUBITOSO, FBI, NEWARK: The short answer is, they've scaled back, in some cases, way back, and they'd gone back to a life of secrecy. I mean, what could be more disconcerting than to be a part of a fairly intricate secret society and see the biggest name in the organization with his picture on the cover of *Time* magazine? It's one thing when you're famous because "you're connected" and someone in Hollywood made a movie about Bugsy Siegel. It's another when tourists are asking for your autograph. That's called blowing your cover.

From FBI surveillance: "(Unintelligible) Uncle thinks he's King of Kings.
Truth is, every (unintelligible) is run by me."

JEFFREY WERNICK: I think a lot of the historic breakdown has to do with economic parity, or the lack thereof. The original wiseguys were poor immigrants, trying to make a few bucks more than the working stiff next door. That original poverty line created a common worldview – everyone was a "brother," "family," one of "our" friends. And it worked. It was a deadly business, but money was made, big money. But as the business matured, the bosses naturally got richer, just like Bill Gates and Steve Jobs got richer, and the underbosses got a little richer, too, and the capos got their taste, and soon there were economic classes *within* the organization. That changed everything. Over time, it bred not obedience, but resentment. Not loyalty, but distrust and deceit.

DISTRICT ATTORNEY, NAME WITHHELD: It's my humble opinion, after chasing these guys for more than 20 years, that you will never get rid of them. These families, often with very orderly successions of power, have outlasted most South American governments. Only Fidel Castro has had a longer run than some of these guys. Sure, the next generation may not be as bright or as tough or as grounded as the old guys, but how grounded do you have to be to take over an extortion operation which has been running smoothly for 30 years?

JEFFREY WERNICK: RICO hurts. The rapidly growing population of rats and informants hurts. Young guys laughing at old guys wearing pinky rings hurts. The UN of criminal competition on the streets hurts.

Paulie and Chris in the old country

Okay, this is probably not the best time in history to choose a career in the Mafia. But you got to look on the bright side. Because inter-family violence has proven so costly, your chances of getting killed over a territorial dispute have lessened considerably. Your best friend might send you up the river for 20 years, but you won't get shot in the eye for dissing the boss. That's progress, of a sort.

FRANK CUBITOSO: We finally, after many failures, have Tony Soprano in a bind. We have the evidence to prosecute. We will need cooperation from others involved, but assuming we find it, we will go to trial with a very strong case. Will we bring home a conviction that will stick and get Tony out of the way for a little while? Will we get even luckier and put together a RICO that will send everyone scurrying for cover? Stay tuned.

JEFFREY WERNICK: Sure, the mob is reeling, but I bet you they're glad to be thought of as reeling, at least in *Time* and *Newsweek*. I'm sure they wish people out there in Media Land would forget that the Mafia even exists. They don't need any more press, good or bad. But I promise, in reality, their hold on the Northeast remains strong. Very strong.

DISTRICT ATTORNEY: Crime families like the Sopranos provide services that have been around for thousands of years. They service primal human appetites – the urge to make a fast buck, to get high, hell, to get laid by someone other than your wife. I mean, prostitution has been around since men got dicks. These are more than appetites, really. They are cravings. Morality aside and even with all the ugliness and brutality involved, from a strictly commercial point of view, you could do worse.

JEFFREY WERNICK: Whatever happens to Tony, the Sopranos are not going to disappear any time soon. Even if Silvio opens the new Copa, Furio goes back to the Cammorista, Tony's son becomes a video game designer, and Hesh gets kicked in the head by a horse, Paulie Walnuts is not going anywhere and Christopher has his whole career ahead of him. My guess is that Tony, in the tradition of the really smart ones like Carlo Gambino and Meyer Lanksy, will die in his sleep, surrounded by his children and grandchildren. But I could be wrong. Way wrong.

NEWS ROUND UP • • • • • • • • • • • •

Belleville Man Disappears

BY OUR LOCAL REPORTER

Matthew Bonpensiero, 20, student at Villanova University, reported yesterday that his father Salvatore Bonpensiero has been missing for more than a week.

Bonpensiero's wife, Angela, told reporters she was not concerned, that he would probably show up. Police suspect foul play.

UNITED STATES DISTRICT COURT

State of New Jersey

CRIMINAL *Division*

THE UNITED STATES OF AMERICA

vs.

ANTHONY SOPRANO, AKA Tony Soprano <u>et al.</u>

Defendants.

INDICTMENT

Wire fraud (Title 18, USC 1343); Mail fraud (Title 18, USC 1341)
Interstate transportation of stolen property (ITSP) (Title 18, USC 2314)

A true bill.

‾‾

Foreperson

Filed in open court this __5th_____ *day*
of __June_____ *A.D.* 2000_____

‾‾

Clerk

Bail, $__1 million_____

"Psychiatry and cunnilingus brought us to this."

Tony Soprano

AN INTERVIEW WITH DAVID CHASE

A few years back, TV writer-producer David Chase decided to create a dramatic series based on the lives of the Sopranos. Through a stroke of good fortune, he gained access to Jeffrey Wernick's unedited research files. From this came "The Sopranos."

The stories in "The Sopranos" are strikingly close to the real-life drama without an extensive abuse of dramatic license. But what is even more remarkable is that the actors are so similar in look and tone to their real counterparts as to be almost unsettling. As you read on, you will no doubt be struck by the many parallels.

The result of Chase's efforts is "I, Claudius" meets "The Godfather" and the blurry confusion of fact and fiction.

This interview with the creator and executive producer of *The Sopranos*, David Chase, took place in his Los Angeles office on May 5, 2000. The next day David left for New York to begin work on season three of the show.

David Chase (original family name De Cesare) was born in Mount Vernon, New York and spent his early years there, just north of the Bronx. His family moved to Clifton, New Jersey when he was six and later to North Caldwell, New Jersey, where, it just so happens, Tony Soprano lives today.

David first went to Wake Forest University in Winston-Salem, North Carolina, then transferred to New York University in his junior year, where he majored in English. Then he and his new bride, Denise, moved to Palo Alto, California as he attended the Graduate Film Program at the Stanford School of Communication.

In 1971, they moved to Los Angeles where David began writing for television, first for the series, *The Night Stalker*, then *The Rockford Files*, starring James Garner. He won his first writing Emmy for an original TV-movie about a teenage prostitute returning home from New York to Minnesota, called *Off The Minnesota Strip*. He worked as a writer/producer, or "show runner," on the series, *I'll Fly Away* and *Northern Exposure* and created and produced a short-lived series for CBS called *Almost Grown*.

The pilot for *The Sopranos*, one of the most acclaimed shows in the history of American television, was written in David's 27th year in the business.

Q: I think of *The Sopranos* as a comedy. Is that how you see it?

DC: Who knows? When we were in France we went to Pere Lachaise Cemetery. They have a list of professions of everyone buried there. They have all these different levels of writers and artists and under Simone Signoret, it says "comedienne." Simone Signoret. Other actresses it says "actrice." I know that comedienne is a common French reference for actress, but still, it's very strange. Simone Signoret. Did you ever laugh your ass off at Simone Signoret?

Q: It could be that *The Sopranos* is the funniest thing on TV because we are in a very bad period of comedies. Do you watch television? Is there a comedy that you watch?

DC: I loved *The Larry Sanders Show*.

Q: Do you like television?

DC: You mean network television?

Q: I guess...

DC: I think when we say TV, up until very recently, we mean network TV. HBO has carved out a very unusual niche and has changed the face of everything to a certain extent. But when you say network television, and there are some exceptions, but I loathe and despise almost every second of it.

Q: How old were you when you left film school to start on *The Night Stalker*?

DC: That was my first job. 23, 24, something like that.

Q: So, having spent so much time in network television, why do you loathe it?

DC: I loved TV as a kid. I fell out of love with TV probably after *The Fugitive* went off the air. And then when I had my first network meeting, that didn't help. I didn't watch any television in the 60s or the 70s except *Medical Center* and that was a completely absurd thing. Chad Everett told every patient that they were "copping out." My wife and I never missed an episode. It was very funny.

I watched *I Spy*, which in its last seasons, I thought was brilliant. That to me was great writing. What the show became in its last two seasons was a couple of jamooks wandering around the world talking and bullshitting with each other. Plot was almost entirely out the window. It was the greatest show on the air as far as I was concerned.

Q: Aside from *I Spy* and *The Fugitive*, you came to loathe TV after you got here, right? After you watched the way it was made.

DC: You've known me a long time. We both grew up in the late 60s so I hated everything that corporate America had to offer. I considered network TV to be propaganda for the corporate state – the programming, not only the commercials. I'm not a Marxist and I never was very radical, but that's what I considered it to be. To some extent, I still do.

Q: But look at the shows you've been involved with ... *Rockford Files* ... *Northern Exposure*...

DC: *Northern Exposure* was part of my career but I didn't create *Northern Exposure*.

James Gandolfini (Tony) and Oksana Babiy (Irina) hang out on The Stugots.

I really came on the last two years as part of a caretaker government. And before I got to *Northern Exposure* I didn't like it much.

Q: Too self-conscious, huh?

DC: Too self-congratulatory. And again, it was disguised but it was propaganda for the corporate state. What I mean is, it was ramming home every week the message that "life is nothing but great," "Americans are great" and "heartfelt emotion and sharing conquers everything."

Q: And *I'll Fly Away*?

DC: *I'll Fly Away*, I thought – and since I didn't create it, I feel very safe in raving about it – that was an excellent show. Josh and John were brilliant in what they created there.

Q: How would you describe your career to this point?

DC: I've been extremely lucky to work on shows which I didn't create which were really good shows, and to work with true talents.

Q: *Off The Minnesota Strip* [an ABC TV-movie starring Mare Winningham] won an Emmy, right? Was that a highlight?

DC: That was a real huge highlight.

Q: Was that an original idea?

DC: *Off The Minnesota Strip* was Meta Rosenberg's idea. She had the one liner which was, "It would be great to do a movie about a girl who goes to NY, [becomes a prostitute], and then comes back and tries to reintegrate into small town life." When we first conceived of it we thought, well, this being TV and us being middle-class white people, what will happen is she went astray for a little while but she'll come back to the fold. You know, like in a TV show. But after you've gone to one juvenile detention center and interviewed one teenage prostitute, you know they're not going back anywhere. It's just not going to happen. They're extremely damaged people, going back to childhood, and they're not going to reintegrate with society.

Q: I know you've written a lot of movie scripts. Were you always thinking, "I have got to get out of this TV thing, I'm getting stuck here."?

DC: My whole thing was...I would take these TV development deals. But, when I got out of Stanford, I wanted to be a movie director.

Q: With that little Mafia movie you made? That was your directorial debut, wasn't it?

DC: No, at Stanford, I made three films. One, my first year, was about a techie who bought an incredible high-end stereo. And he put it together and he kept adding speakers and components, until he finally blew his ears out, and blood came out of his head. Then I did one, it was sort of an existential sort of thing...about a guy who, as he was being killed, he was imagining his escape on a jetliner. He's running down the beach, and these killers are about to shoot him and he's flashing on that silver bird of escape, his plane, which is now taking off. See, they'd grabbed him at the airport. At the moment they pull the trigger, you see the jetliner in the air freeze. So you don't know which was real and which was fantasy. It was pretentious.

Q: So, tell me about your mob film at Stanford.

DC: It was called *The Rise and Fall of Bug Manousos*. It was about alienation. It was about a guy driven crazy by the cheesiness, sanctimoniousness, and fakery of American society. He was frustrated – he shotgunned his TV set. And what got to him were the commercials, the astronauts, and the fact that white bread Nixonians ruled America. That's what got to him. And he dreamed of becoming a gangster, an old-fashioned gangster in a pinstriped suit, and he got his wish. He got killed in the end, but the film was poorly thought out.

Q: Back to TV. You worked in it, yet you loathed it. Did that cause a certain amount of tension in your life before *The Sopranos* came along?

DC: A great deal, a great deal. I always wanted to be in movies, but then also, during that time, I saw television take over American cinema. I saw TV executives moving in to movies. I saw the pandering, cheerleading, family entertainment shit dominate everything. Low attention span stuff. It all came from TV. TV ruined the movies as much as the blockbuster mentality did.

Q: Hmm...

DC: I think my attitude toward TV is an informed attitude. Because I've worked in it for so long. And because I think I understand how the wires and pulleys are hooked up. And I know exactly what they are trying to do. What they are doing is that they are lying about human behavior. Humans don't behave like that. I'm only talking about fiction TV. I'm not talking about CNN or the History Channel...

Q: If a 21-year-old kid came up to you today, and said he wanted to be a television writer, just like you, Mr. Chase, what advice would you give him?

DC: I would be highly suspicious.

Q: Highly suspicious of him asking the question?

DC: I suppose. What does that mean, "just like me"?

Q: You know..."Listen, I love *The Sopranos*, I love to write, I want to make the kind of TV that my friends watch, etc."

DC: It is a terribly, terribly tiny target, and I'm there doing it so I *know*. I mean, I think anybody in this business who has had any kind of success, and doesn't attribute so much of it to luck, I don't know what's wrong with them. There is so much luck involved. But in my case it also meant that I didn't take just everything, that I refused to work on some shows. Even though they would say, "We'll pay you this or that," I'd say no. So, it does take that. But a big success is an extremely small target to hit.

Q: It's been your life story.

DC: Yes, but to have a hit show of any kind – even a bad hit show – but especially to have

David Proval (Richie), Steven Van Zandt (Silvio), Tony Sirico (Paulie) and James Gandolfini (Tony) in front of Satriale's Pork Store.

a hit that you love, and which actually turns its back on conventional TV, which is what you've just cited. That's an infinitesimally small target to hit. What *luck*.

Q: So you tell them to consider a career in medicine?

DC: What do I tell them? I'd tell them you are up against tremendous odds. You know, one of the things about me, this [the *Sopranos* success] happened to me really late in life. Really late. Until then, I was like, at best, a captain in the Genovese family. [Laughs] I wasn't even a street boss.

James Gandolfini
(Tony) and
Tony Ray Rossi (Febby
Petrullo) grapple on
the set of "College."

THE Sopranos

Q: I guess the question stated badly is, what took you so long? Especially in a medium which cherishes people doing things between the ages of 24 and 28, and then disposes of them?

DC: It wasn't that way when I started.

Q: You were a young man in a much older business.

DC: I think, actually, looking back on it, I was like the first counterculture – horrible term – person in hour drama. I was one of the early ones. So my humor, in *The Night Stalker*, was filled with strange, deadpan, kind of cruel ... pop culture-oriented humor. New at that time – later came SNL, but not much later. And that wasn't drama.

Q: You kept holding on to that image of yourself as that guy, outside of things...

DC: I think so.

Q: You obviously didn't give it up, because you came up with this idea.

DC: And I wrote many pilots in the meantime. And I had one other show that got on the air. *Almost Grown*. I'm proud of that show. That was when I was 38 or 39.

Q: And who starred in that show?

DC: Timothy Daly and Eve Gordon. That was a show about a couple from New Jersey, who met in high school, traveled to California in the late 60s ... and at the time we meet them, it's late 80s, and they have two kids of their own. The show went back and forth in time, using rock and roll and pop music as a memory device. I always wanted to be a rock and roll musician much more than I wanted to be anything else.

Q: And what instrument did you play?

DC: I started out playing drums, then bass for a while. When I was like 17 or 18 back in Jersey, my friend Donny and I, we used to get high in his basement and we'd put a single on the stereo, like "Peppermint Twist," and play that single against *whatever* was playing on the TV, and turn the TV sound off. You would notice strange synchronicities like the rhythm of the cutting of the TV show would miraculously fall in with the rhythm of the song. And the chance juxtaposition of, say, Joey Dee and wheat harvesters rolling across the plains was very funny. It blew out the idea of "score."

Q: You use music a lot for juxtaposition. In one of the episodes, they are singing "tra-la-la..."

DC: Oh yeah, "The Happy Wanderer."

Q: Is that the one where they go to college?

DC: No, it's the episode with the poker game. Where Tony talks about his anger at people who are happy wanderers. And he doesn't know *why* he gets angry at people who are happy and well-adjusted. "Happy fucking wanderers," he says. "Why should I be angry at guys like this? I should say ah, salut ... good for you ... go with God." But he says, " I don't. I want to rip their fucking heads..." Frank Renzulli wrote that. But it was something that I immediately understood. Unfortunately.

Q: But TV didn't knock the instinct out of you to do something well. You didn't turn into a hack. And at 50-whatever years old, to come up with a show as fully, in your mind, as *The Sopranos*. How do you explain that?

DC: Naiveté. Continuing and unending naiveté is the reason why. Honestly. [laughing]

Q: What, you figured if you did something well, someone would buy it.

DC: That's right. I thought quality counted. Schmuck! And, um...constantly being shocked with each project. That they *didn't* like it! Not that I wanted their approval, but I thought I'd finally get them to say yes, to get into production. We have to jump back a second, because I did this only to finance my move into movies, which never happened.

Q: Well, your life isn't over yet.

DC: No, but it hasn't happened, and it didn't happen in all those years. First of all, everything I was doing – I was living very well, which was maybe my problem – was that I made a compromise, *I took the money.* Not always, but enough. I really thought that the job definition of being a writer or entertainer or filmmaker, or whatever, was to be innovative. Do stuff people *hadn't* seen before! It turns out that's not what the system is ever looking for. They only want things people saw yesterday. But it's not like I was some noble, valiant knight following a cause. I was naively going along thinking the wrong thing. That quality and innovation mattered.

Q: But now that's all changed. I can imagine that people would trip over themselves to get you to do anything you wanted to do.

DC: That's what they say, that's not what they do. To begin with, there's been a strange course of events. One is, that I've reached a particular age. I had this show happen, and have been paid an amount of money such that I am never going to do television again. Don't have to, don't want to, and won't. Okay. But even if I was going to, they would, in fact, yes, you are right, trip all over themselves to make a deal. And then they would be unhappy, disillusioned, and finally angry, that it didn't work out. "You know what we paid that David Chase...?"

Q: And do you know what he gave us? He gave us some kind of dark twisted thing...

DC: That's exactly what they would say... "some dark fucking thing." Even after *The Sopranos*! And that's why I was lucky that I found myself with Brillstein-Grey [Productions]. Because, those guys, Brad Grey and company, for whatever reason, I think, have a lot of balls. And they weren't afraid.

Q: Explain.

DC: [Lloyd Braun, then an executive at Brillstein-Grey] said to me, "We believe you have a great TV show inside of you. Would you be interested in doing, like, a TV version of *The Godfather*? I said, "The mob has been a lifelong love of mine, but no, I don't want to do a TV version of *The Godfather*. So, I went home and on my way home I really took this guy's words to heart. He had talked to me and he had inspired me. Very hard to

Cast and crew
take time out
from filming

do in those days. And then I remembered this movie idea that I had. About a guy, a mob guy...originally it was going to be DeNiro and Ann Bancroft as his mother. And I don't have to go through what it was because you saw it, it was the first season of *The Sopranos*. I thought, "I wonder if that could be a TV show?" And that's what we did.

Q: And you were lucky, huh?

DC: Very lucky.

Q: Did you read a lot when you were a kid?

DC: I was an English major in college. At NYU. Unfortunately, I read little of what was assigned and now I regret it. I mean, I'll be honest with you. I went through college in 1965–1969, or something like that, and what I was really studying, this is no joke, was the Rolling Stones. I did read a lot of Shakespeare. What really got me when I was in high school was *Death of a Salesman*, O'Neill, *View From the Bridge*, those plays. I never

went to see any of them. In fact, I've only ever seen about four plays in my life, I read them. I did see... maybe on a CBS Midnight Movie, or whatever, they had the movie version of *Death of a Salesman* with Frederick March. And that's probably, now that I think about it, one of the most influential things I ever saw.

Q: Do you have any brothers or sisters?

DC: No.

Q: You're an only child. You moved to New Jersey. Didn't you grow up in New York?

DC: No, I was born in Mount Vernon, NY. In Westchester, which is right above the Bronx. Where the Bronx becomes Westchester. I have to say that to make sure I get my street creds in there – Bronx. Then we moved to Jersey. We moved there because my mom couldn't stand to be away from her sisters, and she made my father forego this opportunity he had in California to build printing presses with some guys. He was a designer, a draftsman for a printing press designer. She said, "No way." She threw a fit and said, "All my sisters are here and my family is here." So he had to move back to Jersey with her. And there's an episode of *The Sopranos* where Johnny can't go to Reno because Livia pitches a fit.

Q: So you grew up where in New Jersey?

DC: Basically in Clifton. I was in Clifton, New Jersey I guess, from K through 7. And then we moved to this leafier suburb. My parents struggled to have the WASP's dream house in North Caldwell, New Jersey, which at that time there were actually even horses there. At any rate, we moved to that suburb. My father built that house himself, he was the general contractor on it, he worked every Sunday on it. I helped him.

Q: How would you describe your mob education?

DC: Mostly from books, newspapers, and certain movies.

Q: Those newspaper stories were probably more prominent in Newark than they ever were if you lived somewhere else.

DC: *The Newark Evening News* was a paper that was in business then. I used to read all those mob stories, and my parents...I have a cousin, she married a guy who, I guess,

was "a guy." I don't know if he was made or not, but he was connected. I didn't know that then, but he had a certain style...he was different from the rest of the family. At weddings he would always give us the money to go make a phone call or whatever. He was always the guy giving you a buck to do whatever you wanted.

Q: Tony Sirico had an uncle like that.

DC: Then my other cousin, who lived in Westchester, he lived with his mother and father, and two uncles, Uncle ▮▮▮▮ and Uncle ▮▮▮▮. Who were these very slender, very small guys with the glasses. They always wore like, jackets...their ties undone and their feet in those thin socks, and their feet up on a hassock and reading the paper. These guys were mob guys, they were killers. I didn't know that, but there was something going on. My parents told me later. And the two of them were middle-aged men, living with their sister. The Corleone brothers, it wasn't.

James Gandolfini (Tony) and Aida Turturro (Janice) get ready for a scene.

Q: Were your parents ashamed of being Italian?

DC: My mother was very sort of proud/defensive about being Italian. If I had friends over, she would serve them some kind of food...it could be broiled chicken, but it would have garlic on it...garlic and a little oregano, and she'd put it under the broiler. And she would say "Well, this is *our* way of doing it." Like a challenge. And at the same time, she so much wanted to be in North Caldwell with, you know, the Martin Mulls of the world. She and my father both. And um...that's what she wanted more than anything else. She wanted me to be a lawyer, a minister, you know. See, I was Protestant, that's another weird thing.

Q: Yeah, where did you get that?

DC: My grandfather was a socialist. My mother's father was a socialist.

Q: And this is an act of protest to leave the Catholic...

DC: No, no. Socialists/anarchists renounce all religion. So he was an intellectual and he had left the Catholic Church. He had no religion. But, as it turns out, my mother was looking around for places to hang out as a kid, she found her way to this largely Italian Protestant church in Newark and she became a Protestant. So her parents are powerless. An Italian Protestant.

Q: Would this be a Congregationalist church, a Christian...

DC: A Baptist.

Q: A northern Baptist...

DC: Northern Baptist, right. And my father was another, they were these Italian Baptists. They met in that church. Most of my aunts and uncles, most of my mother's sisters are Catholic. Many of my cousins are Catholic. My mother hated Catholics, because of sibling rivalry.

Q: When did you decide to pursue a career in film?

DC: I only knew I wanted to be in show business in a vague, dumb way. I wanted to play in a rock and roll band. When I went to Wake Forest, oddly enough, where they had a Friday night film festival, in a Southern Baptist college in North Carolina in 1965, I saw *8½*.

Steven Van Zandt (Silvio) and James Gandolfini (Tony) on the set of "Funhouse."

Q: A movie you probably didn't understand.

DC: I didn't totally understand it but I liked it. I saw my family in there. I saw those Italians, I saw those faces looking into the lens. I saw those gestures, I saw those "operatic" men and women and I thought, "I'm home, this is where we came from." And then when I transferred to NYU, I continued to be interested in foreign films.

Q: Like?

DC: The one that really did it was Polanski's *Cul-de-Sac*. Not only, "Who was this guy Polanski?" but "Hum, there's a guy named Polanski who did this movie and that other *Repulsion* movie?" These movies do not come out of a factory...like a Ford. They're personal. That would be interesting to do.

Q: It comes up over and over again that your mother Norma gave you a lot of ideas about Livia. Is that true?

DC: My mother is not Livia. By any stretch of the imagination. In the first season, in the first few shows, in the pilot, some of Livia's dialogue is actual dialogue from my mother. My mother had a very Livia-like attitude. She was very unintentionally funny. Because she was so downbeat.

Q: Like Livia, as in ... "My son. The mental patient."

DC: Yeah, right. My mother was like that. [Laughs]

Q: Are you mining your family here?

DC: Well, in terms of all of it, my mom is not Livia. She never plotted to have her son killed. My mother did say to me, during Vietnam, "I would rather see you dead than avoid the draft." And I found that odd. Kind of hurtful. Maybe Nixon could say that, but your mom? And I know she was serious.

Q: You did avoid the draft.

DC: It turns out I had a back problem, which I still have. I was classified I–Y. And I was very lucky. Again, see? Luck. I know that.

Q: Are there any other characters who are kind of close to someone?

DC: Uh...there's a dollop of my daughter in Meadow. They are not the same person by any means, but there's a dollop there.

Q: The great thing about *The Sopranos* is that it's a mob story where the women are more powerful, more conniving than the men, more, you know... stronger. More of a presence.

DC: More conniving? No. More of a presence, that's fair enough. I have to go back to Livia, though. I mean, being based on my mother. You see Livia, if you ever look at the first season, Livia never says, "Let's kill my son." And Livia has total "plausible deniability," as we said during Watergate. Not only with the outside world, but with herself. She doesn't think she ever did that. "Did I say that? I never said that!" This is what my mother could do. My mother could stand in two emotional places at the same time constantly. But she was an ethical, law-abiding woman, unlike Livia.

Q: But the women are really strong.

DC: My mother was very strong...but my mother came off like Livia does, as the number one victim in American society. And that's how she worked her show, coming off as the victim. My mother was powerful by pretending to be powerless. She was always the focus of attention.

Q: Has *The Sopranos* changed you in any way? Changed your outlook?

DC: I guess I feel a certain relief that I've proved my point and that's about it. If you're asking if my life is better, absolutely. But, no, it has not changed my basic attitude.

Q: You mean you worry just as much as you used to?

DC: I rage and I worry just as much as I used to.

Q: You probably worry a lot about this show, right?

DC: Yeah. Anxiety and anger, I guess, are the two themes. And I have plenty of both. Neither one of them are like they were when I was 25. But it wasn't *The Sopranos* or success that has brightened my attitude. That had already happened to a certain extent.

Q: I guess the other thing is that you're worried there's going to be a downside to this, a backlash, though it hasn't happened yet.

DC: No, it hasn't happened yet. But I already see people carping. I see critical carping. It will continue. It's inevitable.

Q: But they can't make it go away.

DC: No, but here's the advice I would give. I mean, to get back to your 21-year-old. If you accept their compliments – critics, studio heads, agents – if you internalize their praise, if you accept their awards, that also means you have to accept their lack of praise, their negativity, and their criticism. So, you shouldn't do either one. You should try to just do it for yourself. That would be my advice.

David Chase
considers the action

**Selected film
credits include:**
A Civil Action
Night Falls on Manhattan
Crimson Tide
Angie
True Romance

THE Sopranos

Anthony Soprano: *James Gandolfini*

James Gandolfini was born in New Jersey in 1961. His father still lives there. He has relatives in Italy that live on the same mountain they grew up on. A self-described lower middle-class kid, he went to Rutgers, managed nightclubs for a while, then decided to try acting at around 25. He was 31 before he got his first paid acting job. He finds talking about his own life boring. "I wasn't raised by wolves or anything."

Gandolfini received a 1999 Emmy nomination and the TV Critics Association Golden Globe and SAG Award for his portrayal of Tony Soprano.

"I think that without the humor the show would be in the worst kind of trouble. I think it's a comedy. It's a comedy that says a lot about life, but it's got to be funny or no one will watch it. Who wants to watch people being miserable every week?

"We don't have any true outlaws any more. The outlaws are now the people in power – the actual politicians, the actual cops ... I think [Tony's] an outlaw, he's outside the law, he's the cowboy in the black suit. I think people are still fascinated by them, they always have been.

"People would probably never say this but I think the character of Tony, David Chase, and myself all have a sense of self-loathing that we share in common. Which is the only way that character works. I think he can write it, I can play it, and Tony has it. It all kind of works out in the end. It's a good thing.

"I think the immigrants still carry a lot of the old world values with them that the kids growing up today don't have. They have American values, whatever that nonsense is. I don't think any of us really knows what it is. You know, American dream, entrepreneurs ... step all over everybody. Tony has a lot of the old history ... and Italian-American values like honor, loyalty to family. There's also a lot of craziness in Italian families. We're told not to trust the government too much, not to trust other people too much, be careful. My mother instilled that in me."

Selected film credits include:
Judy Berlin
Bullets Over Broadway
Laws of Gravity
Oz (TV)
Side Man (Broadway)

Carmela De Angelis Soprano: *Edie Falco*

Edie Falco was raised on Long Island among many strong Italian women. She hates it when *The Sopranos* is referred to as a "mob show." "Everything in my system seizes up," she says. To Edie, Carmela is a wife and a mother and "her husband does what he does." She won the 1999 Emmy, the 2000 Golden Globe, and the 2000 Screen Actors Guild Award for her role.

On why Carmela stays with Tony: "I understand this less intellectually than I do kinesthetically, but it's a combination of history... she was probably a different person when they made their original connection ... it was probably a less rational time of her life ... he got under her skin quite some time ago before she was aware of the fact that it wasn't the smartest life-career move.

"There is something about his personality type, the brutishness of him, that she's really turned on by. I think there is something quite agreeable about the arrangement with her. She is not a stupid woman, and if it was really an unacceptable situation, there's no question to me that she would have been out a long time ago.

"There is something, I think, about his running around, his evasiveness about what he does, that provides something that she needs. If he were to suddenly become the husband she pretends to want, I don't know that it would be as fulfilling or satisfactory to her as it is right now. The complaining, the confusion, and the anger and the disappointment, I think that's a very integral part of their connection. I don't understand it completely, but I think it's real. And I think she would deny this fact, if asked about it."

THE **Sopranos**

Meadow Soprano: *Jamie-Lynn Sigler*

Eighteen-year-old Jamie-Lynn Sigler grew up on Long Island and before *The Sopranos*, did mostly community theater and briefly toured in a stage production of *It's A Wonderful Life*. A week before she got the role of Meadow, she announced that she didn't want to act any more. Now she can never imagine doing anything else.

"I don't think Meadow really knows what she wants to do when she grows up. I think she might go into psychology...she's very smart, very bright...psychology is a very broad major, but it's something where she can help her Dad out. One of those mob wives is the last thing she wants to be.

"My friends love this show. Teenagers love this show...it's the Mafia, there's cursing and there's killing...anything that's supposed to be bad, they love...last year, my friends came over to watch every Sunday. It was a lot of fun."

Anthony Soprano, Jr., aka "'AJ'": *Robert Iler*

Robert Iler is 15 and goes to public school in New York City. Most of his schoolfriends don't watch *The Sopranos*. Many don't get HBO and the others are too busy with their own lives. He began acting in commercials at the age of 6.

"[AJ] is just a regular kid, just a little dumber than most of them...I don't think he has talent, I don't think he has patience. I think by the time he grows up if they're not going to have a job playing video games or something, he's probably going to be a mobster like his dad...as his path is going, if his dad wasn't who he was, he'd probably be one of those dumb guys that drive other guys around... I've been doing acting since I was younger and I always thought it would, like, give me money to go to college or if I don't go to college, maybe get me on my feet while I look for a job. But in doing this, and meeting people who I idolize, I think I do want to be an actor. I just think it's so great how my life has changed and I love what I'm going through. Before *The Sopranos*, I never wanted to be an actor when I grew up."

Selected film credits include:

Bruno

Lessons in the Tic Code

Saturday Night Live with Rosie O'Donnell (TV)

LIVIA SOPRANO: *Nancy Marchand*

Nancy Marchand was born in 1928 in Buffalo, New York and her distinguished list of acting credits goes on for pages. She was in the original, live *Philco Television Playhouse* presentation of *Marty* on NBC in 1953. She starred in TV mini-series like *The Adams Chronicles* and *North And South*, and walked away with four Emmys for her role as autocratic newspaper publisher Margaret Pynchon in the classic series, *Lou Grant*. She has won multiple awards for her theater work and her movie credits range from *Jefferson In Paris* and *The Bostonians* to *Naked Gun*.

Nancy Marchand passed away on June 18 2000, from complications due to lung cancer and emphysema. She was 71. This interview, believed to be her last, was conducted via telephone on April 20 2000.

Q: What do think of playing Livia Soprano after your distinguished career of playing everyone from pre-revolutionary women to Lou Grant's boss?

NANCY: This has been a big boon for me. I love doing it. When I came there and saw the script, I just loved it. This is not a tasteful lady. I was thrilled.

Q: Are you tired of playing tasteful ladies?

NANCY: Well, you know...

Q: Have you ever met anyone like Livia Soprano?

NANCY: Yes, and I have met many young men who, having seen a couple of episodes of the show, have said to me, "My God, that guy knows how to write about my mother!" And I get remarks from other guys who say, "She's just like my mother-in-law."

Q. Does this reflect badly on American mothers?

NANCY: I don't know. I think there's a lot for the future of American women, but now, when they get older, I think they experience some disappointments in life.

Q: Why is Livia so bitter about the world?

NANCY: I don't think she feels her lot has been fair. A lot of women feel that way.

Q: What do you find most admirable about Livia?

NANCY: I have to stop and think about that. [Pause] She's a tough old bird.

Q: Ever met a woman this tough?

NANCY: No, but it comes in handy. I just moved into a retirement home. I'm enjoying it. And I'm treated with kid gloves.

Q: And you think that's because of Livia?

NANCY: I don't know. Nobody in my close association watches the show. Or they claim they don't watch it.

Q: Did David Chase know you from *Lou Grant* or something else?

NANCY: My agent got a call from Georgianne Walken. Now, how she knew me, I don't know. She gets around.

Q: Do you have children?

NANCY: Yes, I do. I just received a Mother of The Year award. I have three children and seven grandchildren.

Q: Do you think of David as another one of your children?

NANCY: No, not at all. He's my boss.

Q: Not a bad boss to have.

NANCY: No, he's not. He's, to a fault, a kind man. And he's bright, very insightful, I think he loves his work. Whose idea was it to write this book?

Q: David's. Okay, thank you so much for your time.

NANCY: I wish I could be a little more, I don't know, with-it.

Q: You were plenty with-it. Thank you again.

Christopher Moltisanti: *Michael Imperioli*

Michael Imperioli is a New York-based actor and writer – he wrote, among other things, *The Sopranos* episode, "From Where To Eternity," in the second season. He grew up in Mount Vernon, New York and spent his early career doing theater in New York City, producing, directing, and acting. His movie break came in *Goodfellas*, where he played Spider, the kid who was maliciously shot in the foot by Tommy De Vito, the Joe Pesci character. Before *The Sopranos*, he was not looking to do another mob role, feeling "there was not many more places to go in that genre." He was also a producer and writer on Spike Lee's *Summer of Sam*, in which he also had an acting role.

"[*The Sopranos*] is a certain kind of representation of the American dream. Their business is about ruthlessness for the sake of acquiring wealth ...

"If you're not the boss, like Tony, if you're like Pussy or Paulie Walnuts, you got to work week to week to make money. It's not like cash rolling in over time and you got the life of Riley ... it's not like sitting back and drinking coffee all day ... it's work and it's not necessarily very lucrative if you're not the boss, because the money flows up in that world ... they've got little houses in New Jersey, you know ...

"These are the people that [Christopher] loves, this is his world; if he doesn't have that, he really doesn't have anybody. I mean, who does he have, these idiots in Hollywood who don't give a shit about him? This is the meaning in his life, this is really his family. It's not just the money or the glamor, it's not climbing the economic ladder that's going to make him happy...

"I like his guts, his balls, he speaks his mind and if he needs to do something, he goes out and does it. If he's upset with somebody, he's upset with them, he lets people know it ... there's an honesty about him that I like."

THE **Sopranos**

Dr. Jennifer Melfi: *Lorraine Bracco*

Lorraine Bracco grew up in Brooklyn and Long Island. Her father, she explains, was "a bit of a character" and worked in the Fulton Fish Market, where there were (and are) plenty of wiseguys and stories about wiseguys floating around. She became a fashion model after moving to France in 1974. Her most prominent film role to date, for which she won an Academy Award nomination, is the role of Karen Hill, wife to notorious wiseguy-turned-rat, Henry Hill (Ray Liotta), in Martin Scorsese's *Goodfellas*.

"I've always thought that Dr. Melfi is the moral through-line of *The Sopranos*. He [Tony] comes to her and he talks about how he's feeling and what his life is, and since she isn't part of that life, she is always that point in his moral never-never land. I've made Melfi very lonely and I want her to stay there until something happens for her or to her ... I think today, in film and television, you don't really see that, a fairly good-looking woman who is lonely, and I can tell you, there are millions of women like that out there.

"[Because of this show], I'm much more aware of being an Italian-American, for the good and the bad of it. I'm surprised at a lot of people's reaction to it, the whole defamation of character thing. I went into a delicatessen the other day and the guy turned around to me and said, 'I hate that show. I liked it until the last show where they killed Pussy,' but now he thinks it's terrible and will never watch it again. I want to go, 'Guys, it's only a @?*&!#* TV show!'

"I think [with Tony] it's that whole I'm-not-available thing. I believe it's one of the great reasons it works...one, I am his equal, I'm as powerful as he is, and two, besides the sexuality, he's so attracted to her because she's so much smarter than him, and knowledge is seductive ..."

THE Sopranos

Corrado "Junior" Soprano: *Dominic Chianese*

Dominic Chianese grew up in an Italian-American neighborhood in the Bronx. Like Junior, his relatives were working people – stone masons, painters, laborers. Unlike Junior, Dominic has spent almost 50 years acting on stage, on TV, and in movies.

"When I was a kid in the neighborhood, I'd be walking to school, and these guys were shooting dice in the street. These were not criminals, but ordinary guys, but they were older, in their 20s and 30s. Every time a police car would come by, an unmarked police car, the guys would run like hell ... and I'm sure that one out of those ten guys running probably ended up in a life of crime ... probably felt, what's the word, beleaguered, probably felt put down, probably felt something about the cops, said 'I'll get even with you.'

"There were no Italian cops in those days, I'm talking in the 30s, when I was 5 or 6 ... the cops would come in unmarked cars ... 'We'll catch you, you crazy wops,' that kind of thing, and some of the guys probably hated that, to be called a wop when they were born in this country, you know ... and Junior was probably one of those guys ... and Johnny Boy [Junior's brother] was probably running the game and he was pissed off because he was making good money."

Silvio Dante: *Steven Van Zandt*

Steven Van Zandt, a legendary musician and member of Bruce Springsteen's E Street Band, was inducting The Young Rascals into the Rock & Roll Hall of Fame on TV one night when David Chase was watching. Chase immediately knew that he needed him for *The Sopranos*. Even though Van Zandt had never acted before, he knew this guy. Like Silvio, he's a student of mob lore, mob movies, and the cultural era of the 40s and 50s that Silvio so embodies. It's almost like he's a conscious actor playing an unconscious actor playing a wiseguy.

"You certainly ran into guys all through the music business, especially in the early days, who were mob guys or wannabe mob guys, all the time...guys who were either union-related, sometimes, or club-related ... they would tolerate you, you know. Almost across the board, they hated rock and roll, but they recognized that that was what was in and they had to put up with it. They never stopped listening to Sinatra, Tony Bennet, Jerry Vale, Dean Martin, Connie Francis...and a lot of guys listened to Doo-Wop, 50s rock, Dion, Four Seasons...they're basically pop oriented in their musical tastes. Today they'd be listening to Celine Dion, Whitney Houston, New Kids On The Block...

"[Mob guys] tend to try to keep control of the script themselves, you know, and the actors, and create their own world. That's why Silvio got so upset when he had to kill Pussy. That just wasn't part of the script, man. That didn't fit into his movie."

Peter "Paulie Walnuts" Gualtieri: *Tony Sirico*

Tony Sirico grew up on the streets of Brooklyn where wiseguys were as respected and admired as a kid's own father. He did five years in prison, off and on, before he took stock and chose another direction. Inspired by boyhood idol, Jimmy Cagney, an Irishman, he became an actor. His mob-related credits are extensive: *The Godfather Part II*, *Goodfellas*, *Mickey Blue Eyes*, *Miller's Crossing*. He's also a fixture in Woody Allen movies such as *Mighty Aphrodite* and *Bullets Over Broadway*.

"He's got a great sense of humor. Paulie's still a good-hearted guy, even though he kills people. He's been doing this all his life, but he never lost his sense of humor, he cracks jokes about himself, he makes himself the clown ... that's how he gets by in the rough world that he lives in.

"Some of the funniest guys you want to meet are wiseguys. That's how they survive, you know, their life is hard, they're always on the go, always looking behind them, the tension is fucking unbelievable. Some guys are lucky, they got a sense of humor, it keeps them from drowning ... it's that float when you're in the water, the thing that keeps your head above the water.

"I mean, I wouldn't laugh at Paulie Walnuts, unless I explained to him why I was laughing at him, but Paulie would laugh along with a joke on himself just like the next guy. In fact, it would probably be a breath of fresh air for him."

Salvatore "Big Pussy" Bonpensiero: *Vincent Pastore*

Vinnie Pastore grew up in New Rochelle, New York over an Italian-American social club. He ran his own New Rochelle nightclub, "The Crazy Horse Café," until, at age 40, he was nudged by friends into making a stab at acting.

"The wiseguy, I sometimes think, is a very creative person. He doesn't want to work nine to five. He gambles with his life. He wakes up and in the same way that an actor wonders if he's going to get an acting job or a writer wonders if he's going to get a writing job, they wonder if they're going to get a score. They have to plan and think through it. It's not an easy life. The more I investigate it, working on these characters, I realize, it's not an easy life. It's a life that's very similar to an artist's.

"When Tony Soprano comes home and he walks into the house and tells them to shut the music off, he says, 'I was working all night,' and the audience says, 'Working? He was running a card game.' Yeah, but he was working, he was making money. And that's how he knows how to make money, running a card game for three straight days.

"I didn't think about it too much a few years ago, but I think about it now. The more I meet these guys and try to play them, I compare it to my life. You know what, I'm not working on *The Sopranos* now, I'm looking for a job, fortunately I got something coming up, but I'm no different from a guy sitting at home saying, 'I gotta go make some money, I gotta pay the bills, I gotta make a score.'"

Adriana La Cerva: *Drea de Matteo*

Drea de Matteo grew up in Whitestone, Queens, a very Italian neighborhood, then traveled across the bridge to go to high school in Manhattan. It was a torturous transition. "Everyone teased me non-stop, the way I spoke, that I was trash, that I was Italian, had the long nails and big hair..." She made it through and is now playing a woman from her old neighborhood.

"At 17, my great-grandmother decided she didn't want to be with her husband any more – and in those days, no one would get up and leave their husband. She took her kid into Manhattan and put herself through school to become a midwife. She supported herself her whole life, she had two other husbands, and if she didn't like them, she threw them out. She was the boss.

"What makes *The Sopranos* so great is that the women are ruling over the men, and are not these quiet women who are getting the shit kicked out of them. The men fear the women more than their male enemies. I swear to God, they do. They can't get rid of us. What are they going to do...kill us?"

Selected film credits include:
R'Xmas
Deuces Wild
Sleepwalk
Shadowboxers (Theater)
The Heart Transplant (Theater)

Arthur "Artie" Bucco: *John Ventimiglia*

John Ventimiglia, AKA Artie "Prince Rogaine" Bucco, grew up in the Ridgewood section of Queens and the suburbs of Teaneck, New Jersey. He didn't live in an Italian neighborhood, but he lived in a thoroughly Italian family. Both of his great-grandfathers came over from Sicily at the turn of the century, then both got homesick and went back. They did, in John's words, "the reverse trip." His parents came over in the 1950s and stayed.

"I've spent a lot of time in Sicily, and the whole root, where all of these attitudes and ideas about respect and things like that, I've really seen the other half ... Artie's idea of what is right and when you have done wrong comes from the same place that Tony's does...the beliefs are the same...the idea of having to revenge or correct a great injustice, it's something that's inbred...

"I think Artie is kind of a conscience or sounding board for Tony. Aside from the shrink, Artie is also somebody who can call Tony on certain things. He is Tony's one true non-mob friend."

Selected film credits include:
Manhattan Murder Mystery
The Public Eye
Law & Order (TV)
Mad About You (TV)
Northern Exposure (TV)

Herman "Hesh" Rabkin: *Jerry Adler*

Jerry Adler, who plays the only non-Italian character in the main cast of *The Sopranos*, played a rabbi on *Northern Exposure* for producer David Chase. He has no experience of playing mob types, but thinks the character of Hesh is important to the show in expanding its references. He's also well-known as the next-door neighbor that Larry Lipton (Woody Allen) thinks killed his wife in the Allen movie, *Manhattan Murder Mystery*.

"I have admiration for the gentleness of them [the Sopranos] toward their families and friends, and then the extraordinary ruthlessness in their attitudes toward their enemies. In their gentleness toward the family, there is a kind of Jewish *gemütlichkeit* about them – a German word for sympathy, warmness, and tenderness – that really appeals to Hesh.

"I think Hesh doesn't feel that Tony is quite as put-together and sharp as John [his father] was, and he feels he needs help, and that's why Hesh hangs around, so he can be of help...Tony has a kind of insecurity in certain areas where Hesh can help.

"Hesh has a kind of warmth, gentleness, and humor that's in contrast with almost everyone else on the show...People think there's not much steel in the guy, but I think there is, he's just not ever shown it."

Selected film credits include:
The Shawshank Redemption
Nunzio
Mean Streets
Picket Fences (TV)
Requiem For a Heavyweight (Broadway)

Richie Aprile: *David Proval*

David Proval grew up in the East New York neighborhood of Brooklyn, the setting for the movie, *Goodfellas*. He thoroughly understands the provincial, "four block world" of wiseguys. Because of this, he was able to take bad guy Richie Aprile, a man who felt maligned and disrespected by Tony Soprano, and make him almost admirable.

"Usually what these guys become are the living dead, you know, you can't live a life like that without paying the price of a piece of your soul. You can justify it that you're a soldier, this is a war, we do what we have to do. But the action itself after a while gets to you. I've heard guys talk about the last time they saw a guy's face when they were hanging him out a window, what his face looked like, the terror on his face. Having to live with that, that's not an easy thing to keep going on in your life.

"They go into a strange, automatic pilot thing, and you know food becomes part of that, they kind of put it all away with food, so, if you notice, everyone's pretty big on the show, and that's one of the most accurate things, because most of the guys I knew became fat guys, because they just replaced it with food. After they did something, they'd go eat, all the time."

Janice "Parvati" Soprano: *Aida Turturro*

Aida Turturro has acting in her blood. Noted actors John and Nicolas Turturro are her cousins. She grew up on the Lower East side of Manhattan and went to school in the Village. Her father was an artist and surrounded the family with a highly diverse group of people. She has never done anything before where "everybody knows you."

"Janice is very selfish at times. If she has what she needs, then it's OK, she has room, she's not selfish, but if she doesn't have what she needs, she's selfish. She does have a heart. At times she really does love her mother, even though she wants to kill her at times. She doesn't see straight. She sees one way and it's like, 'This is what I need. I have to have this.' Even though she was the oldest, she feels like she got gypped, everybody loved Tony. It all stems from 'I'm not wanted, I'm not acknowledged, my mother was mean.' She was really resentful at what he got, being a boy, that power that men have.

"The mom being a crazed psycho dysfunctional really hurt her. People are quick to blame the world and not themselves...and that's what Janice does."

Selected film credits include:

Illuminata

Celebrity

Angie

True Love

A Streetcar Named Desire (Broadway)

Season One

The Pilot

Written and directed by David Chase.

Tony visits Dr. Melfi for the first time and talks about his life, his panic attacks and the ducks. Uncle Junior wants to whack a guy at Artie's restaurant, but Tony foils the effort by blowing the place up.

Tony Soprano makes his first visit to psychiatrist Dr. Jennifer Melfi, complaining of a mysterious blackout and shortness of breath. He tells her he's a "waste management consultant" and fears that "I came in at the end. The best is over." He then launches into a story about a family of ducks who settled into his swimming pool. We see in flashback how much these ducks mean to him.

As Tony talks, we see his life unfold. His daughter wants to go skiing in Aspen. His wife is preparing for his son's birthday party that evening. Tony drives around in his "hothead" in-law Christopher's $60,000 Lexus. They spot a deadbeat and Tony runs him down with the car.

Tony meets with his crew and complains about "the Kolar Brothers" moving into his territory. He's worried about his Uncle Junior's plan to kill a weasel named Little Pussy at his old friend Artie Bucco's restaurant. He visits his mother to try to soften her up about moving into a home and also dissuade Junior of his plan. That night, standing over the backyard barbecue, he sees the ducks fly away and collapses.

While getting an MRI, Tony argues with Carmela about their life. Meanwhile, Christopher whacks Emil Kolar without permission. While Big Pussy helps Christopher dispose of Emil, Tony and family show Livia the Green Grove retirement community. Suddenly, Tony passes out again.

Worried that Uncle Junior is going to ruin his business, Tony tries to get Artie out of town with two free tickets to the Caribbean. Artie's wife, Charmaine, says that "someone donated their kneecaps for those tickets" and won't take them. Tony, out with his mistress, runs into Melfi. A few nights later, in the same restaurant, he tells Carmela that he's seeing a shrink and taking Prozac. Carmela is thrilled. Tony is worried about being seen as weak.

While Tony spends some quality time with Meadow, Silvio blows up Artie's restaurant, thus preventing the hit. Tony tells Melfi that he's feeling good. When the subject of the ducks comes up, he cries, fearful he will lose his family just like he lost the ducks. Later, Junior tells Livia he's fed up with Tony. Livia says nothing.

46 Long

Written by David Chase. Directed by Daniel Attias.

Christopher and Brendan hijack a truck protected by Uncle Junior, then Brendan accidentally kills a driver. Pussy and Paulie replace a Saturn that was stolen from AJ's teacher and Tony puts Livia in a retirement home.

Ex–Genovese soldier and best–selling author, Vincent Rizzo, and US Attorney Brown are on the *Harvey Levin* TV show talking about the demise of the mob in America. Tony and the boys watch while counting money in the Bada Bing. Rizzo says that as long as people want gambling, porno, and drugs, the mob will be around. Silvio breaks into his famous *Godfather* routine – "Just when I thought I was out, dey pull me back in."

Christopher and his friend, Brendan Filone, hijack a Comley Trucking semi in the middle of the night. The driver asks that they beat him up so it looks like he put up a struggle. The boys drive away with a truckload of DVD players.

Around the breakfast table, AJ announces that his science teacher, Mr. Miller, had his Saturn stolen. Carmela asks Tony to look into this, being that Pussy has a body shop and AJ is making a D+ in science. Back at the Bing, Christopher and Brendan pass around DVDs but Tony, waiting on a call from "Serge," is more interested in the meathead bartender, Georgie, who can't work the phone system.

Livia is cooking when Tony calls. As she puts the phone down, she gets distracted by an African-American mail carrier, and sets the kitchen on fire. Carmela rushes over to Livia's and tries to convince her that she needs help. Livia just wants to talk about how her husband Johnny was a saint.

At the Great Seattle & Tacoma Roastery Company coffee boutique, Pussy and Paulie look for the punks who stole Mr. Miller's Saturn as Paulie complains about how these people are ripping off the Italians. "They ate pootsie until we gave them the gift of our cuisine." Meanwhile, Melfi tells Tony that maybe his mom was "not an ideal candidate for parenthood."

Livia hates Perrilynn, the new Afro-Caribbean housekeeper, and accuses her of stealing "the beautiful plate Aunt Settimia took from that restaurant in Rome." At the Pork Store, Junior tells Tony and acting boss Jackie Aprile that Comley Trucking is his client. Jackie rules that Christopher and Brendan pay Junior retribution.

Perrilynn quits, and Pussy and Paulie tell the guys who stole and chopped up the Saturn to go steal another one. Livia hits forward instead of reverse and runs over her friend, Fanny, prompting Tony and Carmela to move her to the Green Grove Retirement Home. Meanwhile, Brendan decides to rip off another Comley truck with two friends, Special K and Antjuan. A gun goes off and the driver is killed. Tony is interrupted in a moment of intimacy to hear all of this from Christopher.

A new Saturn with different keys and a new paint job miraculously appears in Mr. Miller's parking space. AJ hails his father and "my Uncle Pussy" as heroes. As

Tony cleans out his mother's place, he almost collapses from another "episode." Melfi tells him he has to admit hatred and rage toward his mother. Tony walks out and ends up back at the Bada Bing where he repeatedly whacks Georgie the bartender on the head with a phone receiver for being such a dunce. The dancers stop, look, then go back to undulating.

*Written by
Mark Saraceni.
Directed by
Nick Gomez.*

Denial, Anger, Acceptance

Tony helps out a Jewish motel owner and ends up a partner in the business. Meadow gets "cranked up" for her SATs. Brendan gets killed and Christopher gets beaten up for their hijacking shenanigans.

Christopher and Brendan return the Comley truck, but Junior is pissed because Tony gets all the credit. Tony is troubled that his friend Jackie Aprile, the acting boss of the family, is dying of intestinal cancer. While visiting Jackie in the hospital, Silvio tells Tony about a Jewish friend, Shlomo Teittleman, whose daughter can't get a divorce unless he gives her husband, Ariel, 50% of his motel business. Tony decides there could be a business opportunity here.

Meanwhile, Meadow blows it in choir practice because of the stress of studying for the SATs. She has to get accepted at Berkeley and can't "wait until the whole North American land mass is between me and Tony and Carmela." Tony, guilty about torch-

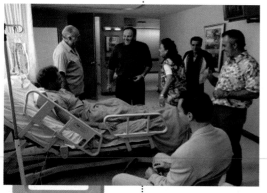

ing Artie's restaurant, offers to help him get back on his feet. Then he joins Paulie and Silvio in a sitdown with Shlomo and his son, Hillel. Despite Hillel's warnings, Shlomo gives Tony the go-ahead to deal with his son–in–law. Paulie and Silvio drop by the motel and beat the crap out of Ariel.

Carmela hires Charmaine and Artie to cater a hospital benefit while Meadow and friend Hunter visit Christopher in search of "crank." Tony shows up at Jackie's bedside to surprise him with a comely "nurse", i.e. a stripper, to "check his vitals." In a visit to Melfi, he gets so angry she gets scared. She tries to link all of his repressed feelings – about Jackie, his own mortality, the ducks – and he storms out, yelling and cursing.

After Christopher slips Meadow the crank, Carmela treats Charmaine like a common servant at the benefit. Tony and Artie argue in the kitchen and get into a spaghetti fight that dissolves into laughter. The next day, Charmaine, out of spite, tells Carmela that she and Tony slept together in high school. Meanwhile, after a rendezvous with his Russian goomar, Irina, Tony joins Paulie and Silvio at the Pork Store for another round with Ariel. He won't give in, so Tony calls Hesh whose advice is to threaten Ariel with "finishing his bris."

Tony meets with Shlomo, or in his words, "ZZ Top." Shlomo wants to renege on the deal, having worked out his own deal with Ariel. No go – Tony wants his 25% interest in the motel, and gets it. Back at the hospital with Jackie, he sees that his old friend is fading.

Junior visits Livia at Green Grove and tells her he needs to get some respect back by dealing with Christopher and Brendan. Livia tells him that Christopher is off-limits but that she doesn't know Brendan. Junior gets the message.

Tony expresses his sadness about Jackie to Melfi, then joins Carmela at Meadow's concert. Meanwhile, Christopher is dragged to the Meadowlands by two Russian thugs and given a mock execution. He is terrified, thinking that Tony arranged this because he gave Meadow the meth. In another part of town, Mikey Palmice finds Brendan taking a bath and puts a bullet through his eye, "Moe Green style," while Junior lingers in the shadows. Tony, listening to the beautiful music, cries freely.

Meadowlands

*Written by
Jason Cahill.
Directed by
John Patterson.*

Tony has second thoughts about therapy and orders Det. Makazian to tag Dr. Melfi. AJ picks a fight at school and learns the meaning of "Soprano." Boss Jackie Aprile dies.

Sitting in Melfi's office, Tony sees Hesh pass by the window. He peers into the waiting room to find Silvio having sex with a lap dancer and Paulie and Pussy reading the paper. He sees Jackie on a couch, hooked to tubes, as Anthony, Jr. walks by. Melfi turns in her chair and it's not Melfi – it's Livia. Tony awakens from this horrible dream.

Adriana picks up a banged-up Christopher from the hospital and asks him if it's true that he "made number two" in his pants when they held a gun to his head. They arrive at Brendan's and find him dead in the bathtub.

At school, Anthony, Jr. picks a fight with an old friend and comes home with a torn shirt. Tony tells Melfi he's having second thoughts about this therapy thing. She explains that it'll be fine as long as he says nothing incriminating. Tony explains, "Just my being here incriminates *me*." Meadow assures Christopher and Adriana that she said nothing to Tony about the crank. Christopher offers to buy her a Happy Meal.

Carmela discovers AJ's torn shirt and says he has to earn the $40 to pay for it. Tony brings some macaroons to Livia at Green Grove and she complains about "mothers throwing their babies out of skyscraper windows." Tony meets with Detective Vin Makazian outside and makes a deal – he checks Melfi out and Tony will lay off the vig on his heavy gambling debts.

Christopher tells Tony that he wants revenge against Mikey Palmice. No way, says Tony. Tony then bumps into Mikey and staples his parking ticket to his chest. At the Sit–Tite Loungenette, Junior and Tony have it out. "The next time you come in," says Junior, "you come in heavy."

Vin and partner stop Melfi and her date, attorney Randall Curtin, and rough Randall up in search of the goods on Melfi. Vin then fills in Tony: Melfi works ten hours a day, eats tuna subs, and shops at Pathmark, i.e., a dull life. Tony meets up with three other capos – Raymond Curto, Larry Boy Barese, and Jimmy Altieri. The subject is who becomes boss when Jackie dies. It's a problem.

AJ confronts Jeremy at school and tells him to cough up $40. A fight is scheduled after school, but Jeremy shows up with $40 in hand. Tony has another panic attack and uses the occasion to tell Carmela that he wants to stop therapy. Carmela refuses to hear it and walks out. Melfi writes Tony a prescription for Xanax and tells him that the way to deal with Junior and Livia is "to let them have the illusion of being in control."

Tony is reading *Eldercare: Coping with Late Life Crisis* when he hears the TV report that Jackie has died. The whole crew is broken up. Tony returns to the Sit-Tite, tells Junior he's the rightful heir, and gets Bloomfield and the Paving Union in return. AJ asks Meadow why Jeremy backed out of the fight. Meadow fills AJ in on his dad's occupation.

Melfi tells Tony about her friend Randall's run–in with the cop. Tony almost tells her the truth, then announces he's going to stick with the therapy. At Jackie's funeral, the black suits are out in full force. The other capos acknowledge that Tony is the real boss and Junior will take the hits.

Written by James Manos, Jr. and David Chase. Directed by Allen Coulter.

College

While visiting colleges in Maine, Tony tells Meadow the truth, then bumps into a rat in hiding. Carmela and Father Phil have an all-night rendezvous.

Tony and Meadow head off for Maine for a college tour. After a stop at Bates College, a place Meadow calls "the world's most expensive form of contraception," she asks Tony if he's in the Mafia. After a little bullshitting, he admits some of his income is derived from illegal activities. She tells him her friends think it's cool.

While being berated long-distance by Irina that he's not her "knight in white satin armor," Tony spots someone he knows and gives chase. He thinks it's Fabian "Febby" Petrullo, a notorious rat, and calls Christopher to check. Meanwhile, Father Phil drops by the house to minister to a sick Carmela.

Tony continues his heart-to-heart with Meadow and tells her if he hadn't taken this path, he'd be selling patio furniture on Route 22. Father Phil and Carmela continue their schmooze fest when Melfi calls Tony about changing an appointment. Carmela, assuming Tony is screwing her, won't take down her number because she "lost my pencil up his ass."

While Carmela and the good Father settle in to watch *Remains Of The Day* on DVD (stolen in *46 Long*), "Peters", AKA Febby Petrullo, tracks down Tony at the Odenoki Motel where he's putting a tipsy Meadow to bed. Carmela and Father Phil are about to kiss when he becomes ill, wobbles to the bathroom, and throws up.

The next morning, Peters watches Tony and Meadow leave the motel and breathes a

sigh of relief. Tony drops Meadow at Colby College, then backtracks and gets the jump on Peters. Peters begs for his life, brings up his daughter. Tony tells him, "One thing about us wiseguys, the hustle never ends," and garrottes him to death.

Meanwhile, Carmela and Father Phil say their awkward goodbyes, agreeing to remain "good friends." Tony and Meadow arrive home and Carmela tells him Father Phil spent an innocent night there. Tony thinks it's weird – is Father Phil gay? Then Carmela casually says, "...your therapist called. Jennifer?" Tony gets the message.

Pax Soprana

Junior takes over as boss and exacts a hefty tribute from Hesh. Tony has both cannoli and Carmela problems, and Paulie steals Dr. Melfi's car to fix it.

Written by Frank Renzulli. Directed by Alan Taylor.

Junior takes over. His goon, Mikey Palmice, announces that all poker games are to pay a tax to the new boss. Tony brings Melfi a gift of coffee and she explains it is inappropriate for her to accept gifts. Junior, trying on a new suit, learns that one Rusty Irish sold his tailor's grandson drugs. Tony shows up at Irina's and in her words, "Tony's cannoli doesn't want to stand up?" Tony says he just wants to talk. Irina throws things, he walks out.

Hesh tells Tony that Junior wants to stick him with an exorbitant tax. That night, Tony dreams of getting a blow-job from Melfi. Later, at Il Granaio, he confers with Johnny "Sack" Sacramoni, a New York capo, about the Hesh situation. He returns to his table to a livid Carmela – it's their 18th anniversary and he's jawing with Johnny Sack.

While Melfi complains about car problems, Tony complains about the "side effects" of the Prozac. Meanwhile, Carmela's buying furniture. Back at Melfi's, Tony kisses Melfi on the lips. She's unnerved.

Melfi hears a noise that night – it's Paulie stealing her car in order to fix it. Mikey Palmice throws Rusty

Irish off a bridge, which irritates Tony and the other capos. Junior's overdoing it. Tony sits with Junior and using Augustus Caesar as an example, convinces him to be generous with his "subjects." Melfi is furious with Tony for fixing her car. He tells her he loves her. She tells him he's confusing love and therapeutic progress.

Junior distributes Hesh's tribute to all the capos and Tony gives his share back to Hesh. Tony and Carmela kiss and make up – she now understands Melfi's role in Tony's life. At Junior's coronation, Tony and the other capos toast Junior as an undercover waiter snaps their pictures. On the FBI wall, Jackie Aprile's photo is replaced by Junior's in the slot marked "Boss."

Down Neck

Written by Mitchell Burgess & Robin Green. Directed by Lorraine Senna.

AJ gets tested for ADD and Tony flashes back to his childhood in Down Neck where he sees his father in his element.

AJ and friends drink some sacramental wine and show up drunk at gym class. Tony has to leave a shakedown at a construction site to join Carmela for a school meeting with Vice-Principal Father Hagy and school psychologist Dr. Galani. Dr. Galani thinks AJ may have ADD – Attention Deficit Disorder. At dinner that night, Livia points out that Tony stole a car before he could see over the dash.

The next morning, while staring in a mirror, Tony flashes back to Down Neck, 1967. He sees his father and Uncle Junior beat the crap out of a man from the neighborhood. He tells Melfi about this incident and his worries that he's responsible for AJ's bad behavior. Meanwhile, Dr. Galani shows AJ some pictures. He relates them to an episode of *South Park*.

AJ tells Livia that Tony is seeing a shrink, which Livia dubs "a racket for the Jews." Tony realizes AJ is clueless about his criminal life. In another flashback to the 60s, young Tony hides in his dad's Caddie while Johnny takes Tony's sister Janice for a trip to "Rideland." On a later trip, he watches the cops arrest Johnny Boy and Junior – they're using the amusement park as a front for fencing goods.

Tony tells Melfi that AJ is doomed because of the Soprano legacy. Tony flashes back to an incident in 1964 where his dad wanted to go to Reno and start over, but Livia refused. He asks Livia about it and, of course, she remembers nothing. Dr. Galani says that AJ's ADD diagnosis is inconclusive. Tony gets angry – maybe AJ is just being a boy. That night, a distraught AJ joins Tony in the kitchen for a giant ice cream sundae. Father and son connect.

THE Sopranos

Season 1

The Legend of Tennessee Moltisanti

*Written by
Frank Renzulli and
David Chase.
Directed by
Tim Van Patten.*

While Tony frets about federal indictments, Christopher frets about the "character arc" of his life and Melfi's ex-husband harangues her about treating Tony.

Christopher has a terrible nightmare about Emil Kolar, the guy he killed in the pilot episode. At a wedding reception for Larry Boy Barese's daughter, rumors of indictments spread among the capos. At home, Tony tells Carmela to round up all the valuables stashed around the house. The Feds are coming.

Christopher is trying to write a screenplay on a new stolen computer when he flips on the TV to see a conversation about the Sopranos that mentions his dead friend Brendan as "a loyal soldier." Chris is furious that Brendan gets press and he doesn't.

Melfi, at dinner with her family, catches grief from ex-husband Richard for treating a sub–human like Tony. Tony calls Christopher to pick up some baked goods for the boys. Christopher gets dissed at the bakery and, in the style of *Goodfellas*, shoots the counter boy in the foot. Meanwhile, while Carmela distracts Livia, Tony hides money and guns in her closet at the retirement home.

Christopher complains to Paulie that his life is going nowhere – where's his "character arc?" Tony takes Chris on a drive to discuss his reckless behavior. Chris talks about his feelings of despair and emptiness, feelings Tony knows all about. The FBI shows up at the Soprano home and confiscates AJ's and Meadow's computers. Tony misses a session with Melfi and over Chinese take-out, tells the kids that he's being harrassed because he's Italian.

Melfi charges Tony for his missed session and he calls her "a fuckin' call girl." Chris's mom calls in tears to tell him he's mentioned in the paper with other lowlife wiseguys. Chris is jubilant. In a family therapy session, Richard continues to whine about Melfi's mob patient. The therapist, Dr. Reis, proudly proclaims that his uncle was a driver for Louis "Murder, Inc." Buchulter Lepke. Meanwhile, Chris pulls a paper from a vending machine and reads about himself, ecstatic in his 15 minutes of fame.

Boca

*Written by
Jason Cahill and
Mitchell Burgess &
Robin Green.
Directed by
Andy Wolk.*

Meadow's soccer coach is revealed as a child molester. Junior takes his girlfriend to Boca and returns to find the whole town talking about his special skills.

The Verbum Dei girls soccer team, led by Meadow, Heather Dante, and Chiara Bucco, is enjoying a winning season, thanks to Coach Don Hauser. Hauser is offered female companionship at the Bada Bing, but no, he's a married man. Detective Makazian drops by to tell Tony that Mikey Palmice is having him followed. Meanwhile, at a local park,

Meadow and friends discover that soccer star Ally Vandermeed has slit her wrists.

Junior's lawyer, Melvoin, tells Junior to take a trip to Boca Raton while he deals with the indictments. Junior shows up at the Jointfitters Union office and announces to his girlfriend of 16 years, Bobbi San Fillipo, that they're off to Boca. Tony meets Larry Boy Barese and Jimmy Altieri at Green Grove where they all have their mothers parked and learns from the newspaper that Coach Hauser is leaving.

Down in Boca, Bobbi tells Junior how good he is at oral sex and Junior asks her to keep that under her hat. Back in New Jersey, Bobbi tells her pedicurist that she doesn't want to yak about their sex lives. However, Carmela already knows. Meanwhile, the boys try to convince Hauser to stay by bringing him a big-screen TV, a gesture he takes the wrong way. Christopher kidnaps, then returns his dog.

Meadow tells Tony that Ally has been sleeping with that swine Hauser. Tony and Silvio are ready to kill him but Artie holds them back. Playing golf, Tony teases Junior about his proficency at cunnilingus and the insults fly. Later, Junior hints to Mikey that Tony may have to be silenced.

Junior is furious at Bobbi for revealing his secret and smashes her in the face with a pie. With intervention from Melfi and Artie, Tony doesn't give the signal to pop Coach Hauser. He's arrested by the police. Tony, blitzed on Vicodin and alcohol, tells his wife, "Carm, I didn't hurt anybody."

Written by Joe Bosso and Frank Renzulli. Directed by Matthew Penn.

A Hit is a Hit

Tony rubs elbows with the "mayonnaisers" while Hesh gets shaken down by Massive Genius, and Christopher and Adriana try their hands at the music business.

Paulie, Pussy, and Chris whack a Colombian drug dealer and make off with a big score. Tony gives his neighbor, Dr. Cusamano, a box of Cuban cigars for recommending Melfi, then joins some of the goomars and crew in a classy hotel room to celebrate the score.

Chris and Adriana run into a rapper named Massive Genius and visit his mansion in Englewood. Massive asks Chris to arrange a sit-down with Hesh who allegedly stole royalties from 50s black singer, Little Jimmy Willis. Later, Chris complains he's the real gangster, not Massive. "Fuckin' drum machine and ignorant poetry and any fuckin' fourth-grade ditsoon is Chairman of the Board."

The next morning, Carmela tells Tony they've been invited to a barbecue by the Wagners, a couple they met at a hospital fundraiser. Tony is nervous about hanging out with "mayonnaisers," i.e., whitebread Italians. Adriana has a brainstorm – that Chris get into the music business by managing a group she knows called Visiting Day. Massive can help.

At a dinner party at the Cusamanos, mayonnaisers talk about fuckin' and whackin' and living next door to Tony. Massive shows more interest in Adriana than Visiting Day, but plays along in order to meet with Hesh and shame him into paying the stolen royalties. Tony worries that he's selling out by mingling with the "meddigan," i.e., white guys.

Tony plays golf with Cusamano and friends and they press him for mob gossip. Suddenly, Tony feels stupid, like a dancing bear trotted out for their amusement. Chris, at a recording session for Visiting Day, loses it after the 300th take and smashes Richie Santini, Adriana's friend, with a guitar. Later, they play the demo to Massive and then Hesh. Hesh doesn't bullshit them: "There's one constant in the music business – a hit is a hit. And this, my friend, is not a hit."

Tony tells Melfi a story about Jimmy Smash, a kid from the old neighborhood with a cleft palate who was a constant source of derision among the other kids. That's how Tony felt around the Cusamano crowd – like a freak.

Hesh blows off Massive by phone and Massive responds by saying he'll sue. Adriana is crushed when Chris tells her that Massive is only interested in getting in her pants. Tony ends his experiment with respectability with a little joke on Cusamano. He hands him a mysterious box (filled with sand) to keep for him. The Cusamanos stare at the box. Is it a gun? Drugs? What?

Nobody Knows Anything

Written by
Frank Renzulli.
Directed by
Henry J. Bronchtein.

Tony gets the word that Pussy wears a wire, Det. Makazian commits suicide, and Junior decides it's time to take Tony out.

The Feds raid Jimmy Altieri's social club and Pussy gets caught making a run for it. Junior meets Livia at Green Grove and gets an earful – Tony meets with other capos there and talks about Junior. Junior says, "I'm the boss...blood or no...I have to act." Livia says nothing.

Down at Madam Debby's bordello, Tony and the boys are relaxing when Pussy's back goes out and they have to help him down the stairs. They bump into Makazian who breaks the very disturbing news to Tony that Pussy is wearing a wire. He had to cut a deal because the cops had him for trafficking heroin to send his kid to college.

At the annual Soprano open house party, Tony watches Pussy's every move. He's doubly upset when he finds out there is no medical explanation for Pussy's back problem. He confers with Melfi who tells him that stress – i.e., keeping secrets – can throw your back out. Tony wants hard proof from Makazian and not just rumors from "a degenerate gambler with a badge."

At the Bing Tony tells Paulie about Pussy. Paulie volunteers to exact justice. Tony tells him to be 100% sure. "I want you to see the wire." Tony visits Pussy and gives him an opening to come clean, but Pussy misses the point. Paulie takes Pussy to the Russian baths and tries to get him to strip down, but Pussy refuses, saying that heat is bad for his blood pressure. Paulie is not buying this.

Tony finds out that Makazian owes Pussy $30,000 in gambling debts, perhaps a basis for the smear campaign. Makazian gets busted in a raid on Madam Debby's, is subsequently suspended, and ends up doing a swan dive off a local bridge.

Meanwhile, Mikey Palmice and Chucky Signore, with Junior's backing, plan a hit on Tony. At the Soprano house, capo Jimmy Altieri shows up and asks Tony a lot of questions. Tony gets suspicious – how did Jimmy get out of jail so quickly?

Tony races to the Bing to save Pussy's life, now that he's sure that Jimmy is the flipper. Silvio hasn't seen Pussy or Paulie since Paulie took him to the "schvitz." Paulie walks in. Tony: "Did you fuckin' do it?" Paulie says no and they all raise a glass. "To Pussy. Wherever you are, fat boy."

Written by Robin Green & Mitchell Burgess. Directed by Allen Coulter.

Isabella

A severely depressed Tony has an encounter with a fantasy beauty named Isabella and narrowly escapes the two hitmen sent by Uncle Junior to kill him.

Tony, severely depressed in the wake of Pussy's disappearance, looks out the bedroom window and sees a vision of loveliness: Isabella, a young Italian girl of heartbreaking beauty, hanging sheets on a clothesline next door. He is thoroughly enchanted.

Junior meets with Mikey and Chucky to finalize the hit on Tony. Mikey has hired two African-American guys to nail Tony the next day at his favorite newsstand. While Carmela takes AJ shopping for a suit for his first formal dance, Christopher visits Tony at home and is shocked by his disheveled appearance. When he leaves, Tony wanders outside and strikes up a conversation with Isabella. She's a dentistry student from Italy housesitting for the Cusamanos while on vacation. Tony is ga–ga.

Chris follows Tony to the newsstand, where the hitmen, Rasheen and Clayborn, hide in wait. An unsuspecting Chris blocks their way and foils the assassination. Tony tells Melfi about Isabella and about his suicidal depression. She ups his Prozac. Back in town, Tony sees Isabella and takes her to lunch. As she tells him about her small Italian hometown, Tony fantasizes seeing her in a peasant kitchen in 1907, singing to a little baby – Tony!

Junior is pissed that the hit didn't go off. Carmela catches Tony staring out the window at Isabella and explodes. "If I had an ounce of self–respect, I'd cut your dick off." She then takes AJ out to buy an Armani suit and reminisces about her first date with Tony. AJ is worried that his dad is going to jail.

The next day, the hitmen strike. One goes down with a stray bullet and Tony gets away, wounded, only to crash his Suburban into a tree. At the hospital Tony rejects an offer of protection from the Feds. Although Livia feigns ignorance about the events that have taken place, she and Junior act fast to offer sympathy.

Tony meets Melfi in a deserted parking lot to announce that he's feeling better. In a later chat with Carmela, he realizes that Isabella is a delusion and calls Melfi to tell her. Melfi tells him to stop taking his Lithium, then suggests that Isabella is a Madonna fantasy, a substitute for his unloving mother. She also thinks Livia, with her constant droning about infanticide, may have been behind the hit. Tony's feeling good and will feel even better when he finds out who tried to kill him.

I Dream of Jeannie Cusamano

Written by David Chase. Directed by John Patterson.

Jimmy Altieri, Chucky Signore, and Mikey Palmice go down. Artie goes ballistic, Melfi takes a hike, Junior is indicted, and Tony tries to settle the score with Livia.

Tony gets Junior's blessing to whack Jimmy Altieri. Chris takes Jimmy to a motel to meet up with some sexy Russian woman. Silvio jumps out of the closet and blows Jimmy away.

Meadow is making out with boyfriend Jeremy Herrera when she sees Livia wandering around in a fog outside. Tony tells Melfi that Livia may have Alzheimer's, but Melfi thinks she has a borderline personality disorder and is probably the one who wanted him killed. Tony goes ballistic and calls Melfi "a twisted bitch...that's my mother you're talking about."

Jimmy is found dead in an alley, a rat shoved in his mouth. FBI agent Cubitoso plays Tony the tape where Livia and Junior discuss cracking "his coglioni for putting

you in here." Tony is crushed. Meanwhile, Livia tells Artie Bucco that Tony burnt down his restaurant (in the pilot episode). Tony meets the boys at the Bing and tells them to take care of Mikey Palmice and Chucky Signore.

Tony kills Chucky himself, with a gun pulled from the mouth of a dead fish. Tony apologizes to Melfi, then tells her to get out of town. Back at the Pork Store, a crazed, gun-toting Artie is ready to waste Tony for burning down his place. Tony badmouths his senile mother and talks his way out of it.

Livia continues her addled and confused act at dinner, then Tony confesses to the boys about his therapy. They seem okay with it. Paulie saw one, too. "I had some issues. Enough said. I learned some coping skills."

Carmela goes to church, sees Father Phil making nice to her friend Rosalie Aprile, dumps the ziti in the trash. Mikey Palmice is jogging in the woods when he's chased down and killed by Chris and Paulie. Paulie is pissed – he's covered with poison ivy.

Tony is delighted to see Junior arrested by the Feds. He has only one task left – kill Livia. He gets to Green Grove to find that she's had a stroke, which he doesn't buy. Pulled back by security guards, he screams, "I'm here to tell you that I don't die that

fuckin' easy, Ma. I'm gonna have a nice, long, *happy* life! Which is more than I can say for you."

Carmela tells Father Phil that he manipulates "spiritually thirsty women." Melfi has taken Tony's advice and gone on vacation. Tony drives the family to Artie's new restaurant, "Nuovo Vesuvio," in a rainstorm. The electricity's out but Artie manages to feed them anyway. Silvio, Paulie (covered with calamine lotion), Christopher, and Adriana are there, too. They're all feeling pretty good about things. Tony toasts his family. "You two'll have your own families someday. And if you're lucky you'll remember the little moments. Like this. [Beat] That were good."

Season Two
Guy Walks into a Psychiatrist's Office...

*Written by
Jason Cahill.
Directed by
Allen Coulter.*

Pussy returns and wins Tony's forgiveness. Sister Janice arrives from Seattle to help with Livia. Tony has another panic attack but Melfi refuses to see him.

As the second season opens, Christopher has hired an Asian guy to take the stockbroker's test. In a montage to "A Very Good Year," we see: Livia hooked up to life support, Junior in jail, Melfi seeing patients at the Anthony Wayne motel, Paulie screwing a girl on a pool table, Christopher doing coke, Carmela cooking ziti, Tony teaching Meadow to drive, Tony screwing Irina, and finally, Tony sneaking into bed next to Carm.

The next morning Pussy reappears, saying that he knew his friends had turned "their hearts to stone against me" so he split for Puerto Rico. He came back to take care of his wife and kids. Tony: "Don't you ever pull shit like this again."

Junior has been indicted for 12 RICO predicates and his "piss boy," Philly Parisi, runs into Gigi Cestone (working for Tony) at the airport and gets summarily whacked. Tony tells Melfi to come home, but she's nervous. Down at Pitzer and Koolhoven Brokerage, Christopher naps while Matt Bevilaqua and Sean Gismonte harass brokers to sell a stock called Webistics. Carmela calls Tony to announce that his aging-hippie sister, Janice (who calls herself Parvati), has just returned from Seattle.

As the boys celebrate the return of Pussy at the Bing, Silvio tells Tony that the brokerage called and "Chip and Dale sent one of the brokers to the emergency room." The next morning, Tony comes downstairs to greet his sister and, after she explains her current disability scam, they chat about Livia. Tony says he's selling her house and never to mention her name around his house again.

Tony busts Christopher's balls about Chip and Dale. Then, while driving the Suburban and listening to Deep Purple, Tony has another panic attack and crashes into a post. Melfi won't see him, so he visits another shrink, Dr. D'Alessio, who doesn't believe he's in the commercial and non-putrescable waste business.

Sister Barbara, husband, and kids come to Tony's and the big family reunion begins. Tony knows the only reason Janice came back was "for the house and a $400 car...that's the level she works at." Pussy's joking out by the barbecue eases the tension.

Tony finds Melfi and asks again for her help. Her reply: "How many people have to die for your personal growth?" She tells him to get out of her life. He returns to Carmela and some homemade pasta.

*Written by
Robin Green &
Mitchell Burgess and
Frank Renzulli.
Directed by
Martin Bruestle.*

Do Not Resuscitate

Junior gets out of jail, Tony runs a scam on a construction site, Parvati makes nice to Livia, and Freddy Capuano disappears without his hairpiece.

Tony visits Junior in prison and the tension is thick. Junior wants Tony to make peace with Livia, who, he insists, had nothing to do with the hit on Tony. Meanwhile, at a

Massarone Bros. construction site, African-American jointfitters, led by Rev. Herman James, Jr., picket for jobs. At Livia's house in West Orange, Tony and Parvati argue about selling the place as Parvati leaves to visit Livia in the hospital.

As always, Livia and Parvati immediately go at each other. Parvati talks about a self-help video she's trying to peddle – *Lady Kerouac, or Packing for the Highway to a Woman's Self-Esteem*. Livia whines. "Open the window and just push me out. I can't take this anymore."

Tony meets up with Jack Massorone who asks him to help him out with the jointfitters, even though they are Junior's territory. Later, at the Pork Store, Tony tells Junior's boy Bobby Bacala that Tony is taking over, reducing Junior's take but still calling him boss. Pussy meets with Federal Agent Skip Lipari and we learn that he has been working with the feds since 1998. Skip wants him to pass along more info on Tony, but Pussy resists, citing his 30-year friendship.

Through the good efforts of his attorney, Harold "Mel" Melvoin, Junior gets out of jail for health reasons and is placed under house arrest and required to wear an electronic bracelet. Tony meets Junior at Junior's cardiologist's office – off limits for bugs – to talk about the jointfitters' problem. Tony tells Junior that Livia "played you like a fuckin' child." Junior tells Tony that Freddie Capuano, who owns Green Grove, is spreading rumors about the family. A few days later, Freddie's car is found empty and still running, the door open and his hairpiece on the ground.

AJ works on his DNA assignment for school while Meadow practices driving with Parvati, taking her aunt to score some pot and share complaints about Tony. Parvati visits Livia and senses Livia is making "tremendous strides." As Tony later points out, "How can she make tremendous strides when there's nothing wrong with her in the first place?"

Tony and Pussy watch as a gang of Tony's boys take baseball bats to the African-American protesters at the construction site. Parvati visits Livia again. Livia announces she wants to return to Green Grove. A nurse raises the possibility of a Do Not Resuscitate agreement with Parvati.

AJ overhears Tony and Parvati arguing over the

DNR – which he confuses with DNA – and asks Livia what it means. She flips, refuses to go back to her old home with Parvati, and threatens to give all of her money to her physical therapist. Junior takes a mean fall in the shower. Meanwhile, Tony shows up at the house of Rev. Herman James, Jr. to settle up their "business arrangement."

The good Reverend is in cohoots with Tony, i.e., "I'm lining my pockets with their blood." Massarone's payoff for services rendered is to put five no shows on his payroll – Tony gets three, Rev. James gets two.

Livia calls Carmela to tell her to watch for Janice – "she's a real snake in the grass." Carmela hangs up.

Toodle-Fucking-oo

Written by Frank Renzulli. Directed by Lee Tamahori.

Meadow throws a party at Livia's home. Richie Aprile comes home from prison, hooks up with Parvati, and runs over Beansie. Melfi frets to her shrink about abandoning Tony. Tony drops by Livia's old house to discover that Meadow's had a designer drug-and-drinking party there and the place is trashed. Meanwhile, Richie Aprile is back in town. While Tony and Carmela worry about Meadow, Richie confronts Peter "Beansie" Gaeta at his pizzeria and wonders where the payments have been for the ten years he was in jail. Beansie protests, so Richie beats him up with a coffee pot and chair.

"The bride of Frankenstein," as Tony refers to Meadow, comes down the next morning and manipulates her parents into a punishment of taking away her Discover card. Tony meets Richie and Christopher at the Pork Store. Richie busts Chris's

chops for manhandling his niece, Adriana. When Richie starts to talk business with Tony, Tony walks out. Silvio explains. "No more talkin' business with the skipper directly."

Melfi bumps into Tony at a restaurant and in a moment of girlish abandon, signs off with "Toodle-oo." The boys think she's an old fling. Melfi, talking to her own shrink, feels stupid for saying "toodle-oo" and guilty for abandoning Tony. Parvati spots her old flame, Richie after a yoga class. They reunite.

Tony and Richie talk business in the mall. Tony tells him "what was yours before you went away, will be yours again." Richie doesn't take well to Tony giving him orders. "What's mine is not yours to give me." Tony tells him to lay off Beansie.

Tony and Parvati have it out over the mess she finds at Livia's house left by Meadow and friends. Tony gets enraged, then tells his sister that she only came to "pick the friggin' bones" of their mother. Richie meets up with Junior at Dr. Schreck's, where Junior utters the immortal line, "The federal marshals are so far up my ass I can taste Brylcreem." The boys throw Richie a party at the Bada Bing but Beansie doesn't show.

Carmela and Parvati make up. Parvati talks about her son, Harpo, AKA Hal, now in Montreal with his father, Eugene. Richie finds Beansie and runs over him with his

car. The next day, Richie and Parvati meet at Livia's hospital and Tony and Carmela argue about throwing Parvati out. Carmela won't do it. "It's not Christian."

Melfi has a nightmare where Tony suffers a panic attack and crashes his car because she abandoned him. Tony visits a mangled Beansie in the hospital, finds out that he'll probably never walk again, then goes after Richie for assaulting the guy. He reminds Richie that he's the boss and if Richie doesn't show him respect, they have a major problem. Tony shows up at Livia's to change the locks. When he looks through the window, he sees Meadow hard at work, scrubbing the floor.

Written by David Chase. Directed by Tim Van Patten.

Commendatori

Tony, Paulie, and Christopher travel to Naples, meet a tough lady boss, and recruit Furio. Pussy whacks Jimmy Bones for being in the wrong place.

Paulie destroys a defective stolen DVD because it won't play *The Godfather*. A Mercedes ML430 is carjacked at gunpoint from a family and their dog, "Churchill." Tony looks at pictures of such stolen cars as he meets with Junior to discuss his business trip to Italy. He's off to meet boss Zi Vittorio "on the other side."

Pussy is filling Skip Lipari in on the stolen car operation at the Party Box when they run into Jimmy Bones, an Elvis impersonator and old friend of Pussy's. Pussy is freaked

that Jimmy saw him. Carmela lunches with friends Rosalie Aprile and Angie Bonpensiaro where Angie threatens to divorce her unfeeling husband, Pussy.

The music of Andrea Bocelli takes us to Tony, Paulie, and Christopher arriving in Naples. They meet Furio Giunta and a guy named Tanno at the hotel. Paulie loves it when they're called "Commendatori." Tony meets the number two guy, Nino, and they talk cars, with Furio translating. Tony offers

the popular Mercedes ML series for $90,000 a car. The beautiful Annalisa wheels in her father, the aging Zi Vittorio, and everybody rises. Meanwhile, Chris and his newfound junkie friend, Tanno, do drugs back at the hotel.

Furio tells Tony that Annalisa is the link to the acting boss, Mauro Zucca, in jail for life. Tony and Annalisa make small talk as shots suddenly ring out. It's a kid with firecrackers. Furio summarily pounds the poor kid. As one of the Italians proclaims, "This is Naples University."

Carmela and Tony have a strained long-distance chat, then Tony dreams of screwing Annalisa from behind – she's dressed in a toga, he's dressed in a centurion's breastplate. Meanwhile, back home, Pussy has a nightmare about Jimmy Bones. Tony heads off to visit Annalisa while Parvati drops by Carmela's to complain about Italian men. "... Swaggering mama's boy, fuckin' hypocrites ... emotional cripples ... and they expect their wives to live like the fuckin' nuns of Mount Carmel College." Carmela thinks she's putting down her own marriage and takes offense. She trashes Richie and Parvati tries to explain Richie's newfound sensitivity toward women.

Tony is impressed that Annalisa is the *de facto* boss. All the men, she explains, either kill each other or go to jail. While Paulie drinks espresso with the locals, Tony tells Annalisa that he wants to take Furio back to the states. She refuses. Tony asks to speak to her husband, which doesn't sit well with her. "My husband. Fuck you. He is never coming back, so you have to fucking deal with me." Tony walks.

Pussy drops by Jimmy Bones's place and kills him with a ballpeen hammer. Furio talks Tony into staying. Carmela, in response to her own shaky marriage, tries to talk Angie into not leaving Pussy. Back in Naples, Paulie screws a prostitute and is elated that they're from the same village.

Tony and Annalisa walk around the Cumae – Cave of the Sybil – and get down to business. They finally agree on a price for the cars – $75,000, plus Furio. Pussy picks the boys up at the airport where they wait while Chris buys Adriana a present in the airport gift shop. Carmela is putting the laundry away when she hears Tony shout that he's home.

Big Girls Don't Cry

*Written by
Terence Winter.
Directed by
Tim Van Patten.*

Furio comes to town, Chris goes to acting class, and after a couple of tantrums, Tony reunites with Melfi.

Christopher is at the Bahama Skies Tanning Salon (e.g., whorehouse) to collect from Dominic, a heavy coke addict. Dom's Filipino girlfriend throws a fit, says they can't pay. Chris sticks a paintbrush up Dom's nose, then leaves.

Much to Charmaine's chagrin, Tony and crew are lunching at Artie's Nuovo Vesuvio again. Tony asks Artie to hire Furio as a buffalo mozzarella cheese maker. Artie tries to say no, but since Tony will pay Furio's salary, he can't.

Christopher is late for the "Acting for Writers" class that Adriana has steered him to.

He introduces himself as Chris MacEveety, a stockbroker who tried to write a script with the book, *How to Write a Movie in 21 Days*, but failed. Meanwhile, Tony is at home watching a TV news report on the Soprano family. He hates that "every piss I take is a fuckin' news story."

Tony meets Paulie and tells him, a) Furio is coming over to join the crew, and b) Paulie gets a bump up. Paulie is thrilled. At Elliot Kupferberg's office, Melfi describes her *Wizard of Oz* dream about Tony and Elliot ponders, "I'm concerned that treating a mobster provides you some vicarious thrill." Melfi curses at him and walks.

At breakfast, Tony gets a call from the bank about Parvati trying to borrow against Livia's house and destroys the phone. Tony drives over to confront Parvati but finds Richie in his underwear. Tony wonders what Richie is up to. "There are men in the can better looking than my sister." At acting class, Christopher gets an acting assignment of the gentleman caller from "The Glass Menagerie" but later demands another.

At Furio's welcoming party, Pussy and Chris wonder what's going on. Chris: "Guess I didn't get the memo." Tony goes to Hesh for commiseration on his temper tantrums, tells Hesh he's seeing a shrink, and learns that Johnny Boy also had anxiety attacks. Chris gets a new scene, from *Rebel Without A Cause*.

Tony is entertaining Irina on the boat when some Russians give them a hard time and Tony whips up on one of them, i.e., another tantrum. Chris does James Dean in acting class and is a big hit. Melfi returns to Elliot and announces she is thinking about taking Tony back.

Outside the Tanning Salon, Tony preps Furio on what to do. Furio walks in, destroys the place with a baseball bat, shoots Dominic in the knees, and attacks his girlfriend, too. Tony picks up his cell phone and it's Melfi, wine glass in hand, inviting him back. Tony's reaction: "Ah, fuck it. No cure for life."

At acting class, fellow classmate Mitch improvs the wrong attitude to Christopher and Chris beats him up. Later, Adriana tells him that he was reacting to Mitch as the father figure in *Rebel Without A Cause*. Chris mocks her, so she leaves, upset.

Melfi comes in to find Tony in her waiting room. In their session Tony tells her about his father. Her reaction pisses Tony off. "I want to stop passing out. I want to direct my power and my fuckin' anger against the people in my life who deserve it." She tells him she can't make him a better gang leader. He says he wished it was him who went into the tanning salon. Melfi: "Giving the beating or taking it?" That night, Chris throws all of his scripts and discs in the trash.

The Happy Wanderer

Tony learns about an uncle he never knew and stages a high-stakes executive card game where old friend Davey Scatino loses a fortune.

It's college night at school and Tony runs into old buddies Davey Scatino (with son, Eric) and Artie Bucco. Davey, a problem gambler, asks Tony if he can get into Tony's high stakes executive card game. Tony defers. "I don't want to see you get hurt. These guys, they play deep."

Melfi asks Tony how he's feeling. Honestly, he says, "I'd like to take a brick and smash your fuckin' face into fuckin' hamburger." He can't understand why he's angry and why he resents clear-headed people "always fuckin' whistlin' like the happy fuckin' wanderer." Melfi tells him his parents kept him from experiencing joy. That makes Tony angry, too.

Season 2

THE SOPRANOS

Written by
Frank Renzulli.
Directed by
John Patterson.

At a card game at Richie's Social Club, Davey wants to keep playing even though he's into Richie for "seven large" [$7000]. Meanwhile, Meadow and Davey's son, Eric, rehearse "Sun and Moon" from *Miss Saigon* for chorus class. Meadow complains that she wasn't offered a solo for Cabaret Night, but Mrs. Gaetano gave it to Gudren, Meadow's classmate.

Tony and Junior meet again and Junior tells him how he and Johnny Boy started the executive card game 30 years ago. Then Junior drops a bomb: that he and Johnny had another brother – Eckley, short for Ercoli, or Hercules – who was "slow" and put in an institution for life. This is shocking news to Tony. Over at Davey's sporting goods store, Richie is pissed when Davey hands him a light envelope.

The card game is on at the Flyaway motel, with the boys joined by: Frank Sinatra, Jr.; Dr. Fried, a penal implant specialist; and a professional dealer named Sunshine. Davey shows up unannounced and weasels his way into the game by borrowing "five boxes of ziti" [$5000] from Tony.

Chris awakens Tony at 9 am and tells him that Davey's now down 45 boxes of ziti. Richie walks in, sees deadbeat Davey, and causes a ruckus. Frank, Jr. and the other guests split and Tony and Richie argue in the parking lot. Tony tells Davey he wants his 45 large

the next day or 5% interest will be exacted weekly. Davey doesn't know the hell he's about to visit. The take on the game, after expenses, is 80K, including the two boxes of ziti that Silvio himself donated.

Tony goes home to have Meadow tell him that the father of his brother-in-law, Tom, has died. Meadow has no details. Tony tells Melfi that Tom, Sr., fell off the roof while putting up a satellite dish. At the funeral, Parvati and Richie bring in Livia, or in Tony's words, "Fuckin' Bette Davis." Tony tells Richie he gets Davey's money first. On the way home, Parvati baits Richie about Tony's alleged mistreatment of him. Tony is forced to slap Davey around for non-payment. Davey goes to Artie for help and when Artie hears the problem is Tony, he backs way off. Davey, desperate, gives his son's Jeep to Tony for payment and Tony gives it to Meadow. Both Meadow and Carmela flip out, but Tony shuts them up with a speech about the facts of life. "So take that high moral ground and go sleep in the fuckin' bus station if you want."

Backstage at Cabaret Night, Eric is livid about the car and refers to Meadow's dad as a "real lowlife fuckin' asshole." Meadow reminds him that his dad gave Tony the car and Eric walks out on their duet. The PA announcer broadcasts a change in the program. Meadow will now be singing a solo, "My Heart Will Go On," from *Titanic*. Davey and wife leave as Gudren opens with "The Happy Wanderer."

Written by
Todd A. Kessler.
Directed by
Allen Coulter.

D-Girl

AJ questions the meaning of life, Christopher gets the Hollywood runaround, and Pussy wears a wire to a confirmation party.

AJ takes Carmela's Mercedes for a joy ride and busts the sideview mirror. Down in SoHo, Christopher and Adriana meet his cousin Gregory and Gregory's fiancée, film development girl (D-girl) Amy Safir. Amy works for actor Jon Favreau and invites them to the set of a movie Favreau is shooting in NY. Chris whispers something to a guy that's bothering Amy and the guy splits. Amy is impressed.

Luckily, Adriana has saved a copy of Chris's script to "slip" to Amy and Jon. She's excited: "Would it be so fuckin' horrible to attend a premiere?" Back at the Sopranos, Carmela and Tony confront AJ about the damaged car. AJ goes into a dark existential rant. When Carmela asks for God to forgive him, he announces, "There is no God." Tony and Carmela are horrified and blame the new English teacher from Oberlin.

On Pussy's back balcony, Skip presses him about a bomb blast in Philly killing one Waldmar Wyzchuk. Pussy gives a mealy-mouth response, prompting Skip to say, "Sometimes, Sal, you don't act like a guy facing 30 to life for selling H." Tony tells Melfi about AJ's blasphemy. She explains that it may be Tony's fault – "...in your family, even motherhood is up for debate."

Chris visits the set of *Female Suspects*, which stars Janeane Garofalo and Sandra Bernhardt, carrying his script, *I Bark, You Bite*. He meets Jon Favreau, who's very deferential to "the guy from Jersey." Janeane (playing "Zephyr") has a problem with the word "bitch" in the script – it's not interesting enough. Chris steps up and suggests "pucchiacha" (meaning cunt). Sandra (playing "Gina Schecter") uses the word and Chris is the star of the moment.

Chris takes Jon and Amy to a Newark pizzeria and regales them with mob stories. Jon wants to do the Crazy Joe Gallo story. Chris tells him about a wiseguy named Joey Cippolina who got fooled by a guy in drag and proceeded to cover his body in acid.

Tony asks Pussy, AJ's confirmation sponsor, to talk to the boy about God and bad grades. Pussy takes AJ and his own son Matt to the batting cages. Christopher goes to

the Soho Grand Hotel to hang with Jon the movie star, but ends up at Amy's. She starts to critique his script, i.e., its lack of "the seven-part hierarchy of human needs that explains and clarifies what drives us," then ends up having sex with him.

While AJ turns to Livia for wisdom, Chris hangs out with Jon, who exposes himself as a complete mob-struck fan. After showing off his gun, Chris play-fights with Jon and scares the living shit out of him. Jon is vague about his reaction to Chris's script. At lunch, after an embarrassing scene with Chris, Adriana mentions his script to Tony, which is news to him. Skip and Agent Grasso tell Pussy he has to wear a wire to AJ's confirmation. Pussy loathes the idea.

Chris waits for Amy at the hotel and they have sex in the elevator. The next morning they chat and when he asks her if she's ever shagged another skinny guinea, she hides in the bathroom. He finds Jon's script, *Crazy Joe*, and sees that he stole the Joey Cippolina story. Jon, of course, has headed back to the coast.

Pussy attaches the wire in his bathroom and when his wife Angie tries to interrupt him, he attacks her physically. Meanwhile, Chris tracks Amy down at a talent agency and she tells him, coldly, that regarding his script, "...we're going to have to pass..." She also passes on their relationship, prompting Chris to utter the final line... "Fucking D-Girl!"

At AJ's confirmation party, AJ gets caught smoking weed, Pussy gives AJ more heart-

felt wisdom while the Feds listen in, and Chris shows up late. Tony lays it on the line. He tells Chris that if he's still here in ten minutes, "then I'm going to assume you got no other desire but to be with me. And your actions will show me that every fucking second of every fucking day."

Pussy is in the bathroom, sobbing. Chris joins the family inside. He has made his choice.

Full Leather Jacket

Written by Robin Green & Mitchell Burgess. Directed by Allen Coulter.

Carmela wrangles a college recommendation for Meadow, Adriana gets an engagement ring, Tony insults Richie over a silk-lined leather jacket, and Chris gets shot.

At dinner, the conversation is about college. Meadow has many options – Bowdoin, Holy Cross, Georgetown – but has her eye on Berkeley. No fucking way, says Tony. At a hosiery company, Chris and his friend Matt bust a safe while Sean relieves himself in the corner. Chris tells them this is how Pussy started, until he stepped up for Johnny during "the unrest of '83."

Late at night, Carmela wonders why Meadow wants to go as far as Berkeley. Tony tells her to take a Xanax. Silvio and Paulie drop by Richie's social club and order him to modify Beansie's house. Richie exudes pride that he made Beansie into "a shopping cart ..."

Carmela approaches her next door neighbor, Jeannie Cusamano, about getting her twin sister, Joan

O'Connell, to write a recommendation letter for Meadow. Jeannie is hesitant.

Christopher goes to Adriana's house to make up after all the D-girl business. Her mother, Liz, tries to keep him out and when he hands Adriana a wedding ring, Liz cracks, "I bet it was in Zale's window this morning." Adriana leaves with her true love. While Junior and Tony discuss black-market videos, Richie shows up to give Tony a silk-lined, Corinthian leather jacket that he took off Rocco DiMeo. Carmela finds a letter from Berkeley in the mail and bins it.

As Sean, Matt, and Chris crack another safe, Chris announces he spent all of his cut on the diamond for Adriana. "She loves me and these are her childbearing years." A guilt-ridden Carmela fishes the Berkeley letter out of the trash. The next morning, the Spatafores show up at Beansie's house to do the handicap house modification remodelling and aren't deterred by Beansie's wife, Gia, slamming the door in their face.

Sean and Matt meet with Richie and get snubbed. Richie badmouths Christopher and leaves them with, "If there's ever anything you can do for me, let me know." Jeannie asks Joan to write the Meadow letter. Joan says no, she already wrote one for a young Dominican from the projects. At a family dinner, Richie calls Livia "Ma" and asks Tony about the jacket. Tony says it's terrific. Jeannie calls Carmela with the rejection from Joan.

Carmela goes to see Joan herself and more or less orders her to write the letter. Her offering is ricotta pie with pineapple. She even gives her a good excuse for the Dominican boy. While Tony snubs Matt and Sean in the men's room of the Bada Bing, Paulie and Silvio bust Richie's balls about doing a bad job at Beansie's. Jeannie brings Carmela the good news – Joan wrote a terrific letter to Georgetown, and loved the pie.

Richie drops by Carmela's with some tripe and tomatoes when he notices the maid's husband wearing the jacket he gave Tony. Matt and Sean are pissed that Furio took their money to give to Tony. Meanwhile, Tony tries to explain to Melfi why he's not responsible for Davey the degenerate gambler.

Christopher is ambushed by Matt and Sean. A wounded Chris kills Sean and Matt runs for his life. He shows up at Richie's social club and explains they shot Chris as a favor to Richie. Richie chases him down the street with a baseball bat.

Christopher is on life support, Adriana and Tony at his side. Tony asks, "How could this happen?"

From Where To Eternity

Christopher has a vision of hell, sending Paulie to both a psychic and a priest. Carmela and Tony argue about a vasectomy and Matt Bevilaqua pays a heavy price for ambushing Chris.

Christopher lies in the ICU as Silvio and wife, Gabby, drop by and Christopher's mother, Joanne, implores Silvio to make the shooter suffer. Detectives talk to Tony and others about Sean and Matt, but they are mute. Richie shows up with Janice, making

THE Sopranos

Written by
Michael Imperioli.
Directed by
Henry J. Bronchtein.

everyone nervous. "He's full of negative energies," says Pussy. Richie tells them that the word is out on the street about Matt.

After Gabby tells Carmela that a Brazilian goomar just made Ralph Rotaldo a daddy, Carmela lays into Tony about getting a vasectomy to avoid the prospect of a bastard child. Back in the

waiting room, Adriana wakes up to a Code Blue. Everyone gathers as Christopher's spleen is removed. Carmela prays to give Chris "vision." The next morning, the doctor announces that Chris suffered cardiac arrest and "the worst is over, but he was clinically dead for about a minute."

Chris tells Tony and Paulie about his visit to the other side. There was a tunnel, a white light, and his father in hell, dressed in an old-style, pinstripe gangster suit. Hell is an Irish bar where it's St. Patrick's Day forever and the Irish win every roll of the dice.

Tony indulges in more rationalization with Melfi. Who deserves hell? "Only the worst people, the real twisted and demented psychos who kill for pleasure...the fuckin' Hitlers and the Pol Pots..." People in the life are a different story. We're the children of exploited immigrants who "wanted a piece of the action." "We're soldiers. Soldiers don't go to hell. It's war..."

A freaked-out Paulie wakes up Christopher to hear more. Chris says his dad loses the same hand of cards and gets whacked at midnight, every night. Since there are no horns in sight, Paulie decides it's Purgatory. Paulie's theory is that you multiple your mortal sins by 50 and your venal sins by 25 and that's your time in Purgatory. He's looking at 6,000 years.

While Melfi waxes about "living in a moral never-never land with this patient," Carmela visits Chris to learn that Tony lied to her about Chris's vision. Back home, Tony tells her she's a hypocrite, that "the Pope doesn't even believe in Trojans and you want me to get snipped?" Then he turns on AJ. "I'm supposed to get a vasectomy when this is my male heir?"

A drug dealer named Quickie G tells Pussy where Matt Bevilaqua is hiding for $20 dollars. Paulie goes to a psychic and runs into the spirits of people he's whacked, like Sonny Pagano, his first murder. He tells Tony that he's "draggin' a bunch of fuckin' ghouls around with me..." That night, after Tony makes up with AJ over pizza, he meets Pussy to hunt down Matt. They find him and drag him to an abandoned refreshment stand at Hacklebarney State Park. Matt blames Sean, of course, and after he downs a diet drink, Tony and Pussy shoot him full of holes.

Father Felix at the church tells Paulie that psychics are heretics and thieves. Paulie's not so sure. "You've been slackin' off on me," he tells the priest, "and you left me unprotected. I'm cuttin' you off for good." After sharing a steak with Pussy, Tony crawls in with Carmela and agrees to get snipped. No, says Carm, she might want another baby, then admits, "Tony, all I want is you." They begin to make love as the camera pans to her angel collection.

*Written by
Frank Renzulli and
Robin Green &
Mitchell Burgess.
Directed by
John Patterson.*

Bust Out

Tony and crew bankrupt Davey's business for debts unpaid. Tony barely escapes a murder rap when a witness changes his mind, and Carmela has a brief encounter with a wallpaper artist.

Larry Arthur, a witness to the Matt Bevilaqua murder, tells the police that he saw Tony getting into a car with another "heavyset" man. As Tony waits for Richie at a mall, he sees a lost little boy and flashes on shooting Bevilaqua. Richie is pissed because he's being overcharged by Barone Sanitation, half-owned by Tony. That night Carmela reads *Memoirs of A Geisha* while Tony announces he wants to spend more time with AJ. He

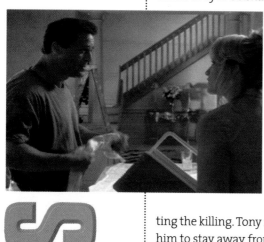

wants to toughen him up so that he doesn't end up like that "poor prick they found dead, kid was 23 or something."

At Ramsey Sport and Outdoors, Davey Scatino's store, Tony, Richie, and Paulie conduct a bust out, ordering everything in sight. Tony asks Davey about blank airline tickets he ordered. Davey smells a disaster. Tony explains it's a promotion gimmick and Davey can put it on different lines of credit. Later, as Tony and AJ hang out by the pool, Agent Harris and Detective Harold Giardina arrive to invite Tony down to the station to talk about the Bevilaqua case.

Skip Lipari knows that Pussy was the "husky accomplice" in the murder, but Pussy denies it. Skip wants Tony on tape admitting the killing. Tony meets with lawyer Neil Mink to plot their legal strategy. Mink tells him to stay away from the police while he figures out what to do. Meanwhile, Carmela holds a Senior Grad Night confab, then meets Victor Musto, an "artist with wallpaper," through his sister, Christine Scatino, Davey's wife. Carmela is smitten by Vic but Christine tells Vic to steer clear.

Davey contemplates suicide while Janice and Richie make love with a gun to Janice's head. Janice tells Richie he should be boss and Richie gets steamed every time he thinks of the jacket incident [in *Full Leather Jacket*]. Carmela has a sex dream and Tony, down at Ramsey's, wonders why the police want to talk to him and not Pussy. Paulie walks in to announce that the witness is not a rat, but an eyewitness, "a flag salutin' motherfucker."

Christine has lunch with Carmela and tells her Davey's gambling is a disease and since the store is in her name, he can't piss it away. Carmela wants to know about Vic. Tony brings a gift home to AJ, a high-priced rod and reel. AJ begs to go to the mall instead of fishing. Tony pines to Melfi about AJ, but Melfi sets him straight – kids grow

up. Tony then says he may be going away "for a long time for something I didn't do." He's clearly scared.

Wandering around Ramsey's, Tony sees Davey asleep in an Arctic tent. They talk about the old days, but Tony cuts him short. "Don't reminisce on me." When Davey asks how this whole thing is going to end, Tony tells him it's a planned bankruptcy. "This is how a guy like me gets along, it's my bread and butter." Davey can't respond through his tears.

Tony misses AJ's swim meet, but arrives in Neil Mink's office with $400,000 for the family if he has to split. Carmela busts Tony's chops for missing the meet and notices that he's acting strange. The next morning, as Vic begins a wallpaper job at her house, Carmela finds herself in his arms. They back away and agree it shouldn't happen again. Meanwhile, Richie and Janice show up at Junior's to give him some jogging suits and salami and eggs. Richie says that Tony's got to go and Junior reacts with outrage.

Meadow shares her college victories with Livia – acceptance at Berkeley and NYU, waitlist at Columbia and Georgetown. Livia gives her $20.

Vic calls Carmela and they plan a lunchtime rendezvous. Larry Arthur, the witness, and his wife are sitting at home when she comes across an article about the Bevilaqua murder and "a high ranking mafia member." Larry runs for the phone. Vic meets his brother-in-law Davey at a bar and Davey tells him he's lost everything. Vic tells him that he's out of his sister's life as soon as their son goes off to college, which Vic will now have to pay for.

While Tony watches "Patton" on the History Channel, Paulie calls to say that the witness has changed his mind. Tony can breathe again. Meeting with Melfi, he realizes that he's dodged a very big bullet and checks out of therapy for the day. He finds Beansie in a wheelchair and hands him $50,000. Beansie is reluctant to take it, but Tony insists and thanks him three times. He walks away happy.

As Carmela finishes preparing a picnic lunch, the doorbell rings and it's not Vic. He's at another job. As liquidators finish up, a county official hangs a "For Lease" sign on Ramsey's. Tony and AJ ride *The Stugots* and Tony lets AJ take the helm. As father and son plow through the water, they're oblivious to the fact that they capsize a small boat in their path.

House Arrest

Written by Terence Winter. Directed by Tim Van Patten.

Confined to his house, Junior reunites with an old friend. Confined to Barone Sanitation, Tony goes stir-crazy as Melfi confronts her drinking.

The show opens with a Zanone Bros. carting truck dumping garbage in the parking lot of the Towne Deli. A phone call to Richie sets Siraj, the owner, straight – pay double and they'll try to make a pickup every day. Meanwhile, Tony gets the word from his lawyer, Neil Mink, that he needs to spend more time at his legit businesses like Garden State Rendering or Barone Sanitation.

Junior is in serious pain and refuses to use a bedpan – "I'm not a cat. I don't shit in a box." Marshall Michael McLuhan shows up with his electronic bracelet to monitor his house arrest. Tony wanders around the house, and later tells Melfi (who gulps Vodka before their appointment) that he's bored with life.

As Bacala wheels him out of the hospital, Junior bumps into old friend Catherine Romano. They talk about old times, including her late husband, Lou, a detective and "a real straight shooter," according to Junior. Tony shows up at Barone's to play at working and meets the new secretary, Connie DeSapio, a born-again Christian. Dick Barone tells Tony that Richie has guys selling blow on his routes. Melfi admits to Elliot that she drinks on the days she sees Tony and feels compelled to keep seeing him.

As Junior tries on his new breathing mask, Tony and Carmela attend the Garden State Carting Association's golf tournament. Tony chides Richie about selling drugs on asso-

ciation routes. Richie complains that his earnings are being clipped. When he walks away, Tony collapses.

The ER doctor tells him the rash he's developed has no physical cause. As Junior's trying to get something out of the disposal, Bacala leaves to take his kid to karate. Junior gets his hand stuck in the drain.

At Carmela's book club, the group compares Frank McCourt's new book, *'Tis* to *Angela's Ashes*. Silvio calls to announce that a shipment of WWII artifacts just arrived and that Tony should come down and see. A tipsy Melfi has lunch with Jason and tells off a smoker. Later, Elliot suggests that she consider a 12-step program and prescribes Luvox.

Tony and Junior meet at Dr. Schreck's and argue about selling coke with garbage. Junior pines for the old days when they all worked together. Tony: "Yeah, I remember that picture of Albert Anastasia lying all amicable on the barbershop floor." Tony has his rash checked out again and bored to tears, goes back to Barone and screws Connie the Born Again from behind. Catherine and Junior finally hook up and reminisce about Perry Como and Sons of Italy Hall.

Tony and Carmela visit an $850,000 house that Richie and Janice want to buy. Barone tells Tony about a Richie-instigated coke deal the Feds have on video. Junior gets off the phone with Livia and rejoins Catherine, utter-ing the classic line about Livia – "She could fall in a sewer pipe and she'd come up holding a gold watch in each hand."

Melfi tells Tony about a psychological con-dition known as "alexithymia," that affects antisocial types who "if they stop moving, they think about feelings of emptiness and self-loathing haunting them since childhood. And they crash."

Tony returns to the boys at the Pork Store, tired of the legit act. They hear a car crash outside. "It's that dipshit Carmine again." Paulie pulls out his sun reflector as Agent Harris shows up to introduce his new partner, Joe Marquez. Life goes on.

The Knight in White Satin Armor

*Written by
Robin Green &
Mitchell Burgess.
Directed by
Allen Coulter.*

Richie tries to move against Tony and ends up getting killed by Janice. Irina tries to kill herself, Carmela is furious, and Pussy tries to be a superior informant.

Richard "Rick" Aprile, Jr., Richie's son, and his dancing partner waltz around Richie and Janice's new house. Jackie Aprile, Jr. drops by and Tony comments on his deadbeat lifestyle. Janice says Richie wants to take AJ to a dirt bike championships. Tony says no. They argue and Tony leaves.

After sex, Tony tells Irina he wants her to find a husband and settle down. She threatens suicide. Later, Tony meets with Dick Barone, Richie, Albert "Ally Boy" Barese (Larry

Boy's brother) and Jackie, Jr. to discuss garbage routes. A big route is up for grabs but Tony won't let Richie have it, because of his coke dealing.

Richie meets with Junior and Bacala to complain about Tony. He wants to take him out. Junior makes no commitments, tells him to talk to Ally Boy. Pussy greets Skip Lipari and hands him a blank airline ticket from the Scatino bust out. Skip wants to wire Pussy for Janice's engagement party. No problem. At the party, Richie makes a toast to everyone for "celebrating with us this historic-making union of the Apriles and the Sopranos." Carmela, having sniffed out more CK One on one of Tony's shirts, cries in the kitchen.

Tony has to split in the middle of the night because Irina took 20 halcyon and a quart of vodka to end it all. The next day, Carmela tells Janice to expect a goomar in Richie's life. Janice replies, "I'd like to see a goomar that's gonna let him hold a gun to her head when they fuck." Carmela is shocked. Janice explains it's a fetish and "usually he takes the clip out."

Richie talks with Ally Boy about Larry Boy. Ally Boy is against making a move on Tony. Carmela stages an encounter with Victor Musto, her passing love interest from "Bust Out," and he apologizes for cancelling their lunch date.

Tony asks Melfi for the name of a shrink for Irina. Richie and Jackie, Jr. show up at Junior's to announce that Ally Boy is out. Richie wants to do it anyway, and take out Larry Boy at the same time. When they leave, Junior turns to Bacala and tells him that he's siding with Tony. Richie, it's clear, is not respected.

Pussy drops in on Christopher at the brokerage and learns about a heist on a truckload of Pokémon cards. He can't wait to tell Lipari, who tells him to cool it. Tony encounters an enraged Irina who tells him how Svetlana's prosthetic leg fell off at a Gap store and her boyfriend picked her up and carried her out "like a knight in white satin armor." Where is her knight? Pussy tracks Chris and Tommy Mac on the big Pokémon caper. Not looking, he hits a worker on a bike and runs away.

Carmela confronts Tony about Irina and he says it's all over, but she's depressed and tried to commit suicide. Carmela is outraged:

"You're putting me in a position where I'm feeling sorry for a whore who fucks you?" Carmela tells her friend Gabby that Vic is the one male she can respect. Gabby tells her Vic ditched her because of Tony. "He pissed his pants."

Junior tells Tony that Richie is moving against him. Tony gives Silvio the okay to move against Richie. Meanwhile Janice, having given Livia two Nebutols, looks forward to a fun evening with Richie. He tells her to shut up and make dinner. When she tells him it's okay that his son is gay, he whacks her in the mouth, she gets out his gun and shoots him in the chest. Panicked, she calls Tony, who arrives and tells her what to do.

While Lipari explains to Pussy that he put a 7-Eleven clerk in a coma, Furio and Christopher show up at Janice's to clean up the mess. As Furio and Chris move Richie through a vertical saw, Chris comments, "It's gonna be a while before I eat anything from Satriale's." The next morning Livia comes face to face with Tony for the first time in a while. Insults fly.

Tony puts Janice on a bus for Seattle. "All in all," he says, "I'd say it was a pretty good visit." She wonders aloud why their family is so screwed up. Tony tells her not to miss the bus. Back home he finds Carmela still reading *Memoirs of a Geisha*. She announces she and Rosalie are planning a three-week trip to Rome. She tells him he'll have to chauffeur AJ and find a tennis clinic for Meadow, because if she has to do it, she "just might commit suicide."

Funhouse

Written by David Chase and Todd A. Kessler. Directed by John Patterson.

Tony gets violently sick and suffers a prolonged nightmare that ends with Pussy as a talking fish confessing his betrayal. Tony, Paulie, and Silvio take Pussy on a fateful boatride. The Feds arrest Tony for stolen airline tickets. Despite it all, everyone gathers for Meadow's graduation party.

Tony and sister Barbara meet with Livia to work out her living situation. Barbara's husband, Tom, won't allow Livia to live with them. Green Grove is out. "She was abusive to the staff." When Livia insults Carmela, Tony gets two airline tickets to Tucson for Livia and her sister Quinn.

Tony and Pussy meet with Sundeep Abadir at an Indian restaurant to collect money for a calling card scam. Later, at Nuovo Vesuvio, Tony is served zucchini flowers and mussels by Artie as he explains the scam to Furio. Tony is feeling good as Pasquale "Patsy" Parisi (brother of the late Philly Parisi) walks in with a garment bag for him.

Back home, Tony gives Carmela a sable coat from the bag. She makes love to him wearing only the coat. Suddenly Tony is on a deserted boardwalk in Asbury Park in winter. Hesh, Paulie, Pussy, Patsy, Christopher, and Silvio are all there. Tony announces he has only until September 5th to live and Chris says Tony will torch himself. Tony turns to Patsy, but it's Philly with a bullet wound in his head. As Tony lights himself, he

awakes, jumps out of bed, runs to the bathroom, and throws up. "Fuckin' vindaloo," he shouts.

Pussy gives Lipari the tape of the meeting with Sundeep and hands over most of his cut. Tony, back on the boardwalk, catches a glimpse of Junior, then Silvio, *à la* Michael Corleone, says, "Our true enemy has yet to reveal himself." Tony peers through some binoculars and sees himself and Paulie playing cards. Tony then pulls out a gun and shoots Paulie.

The dream shifts to Melfi's office where Tony talks about Pussy. Answering back is Melfi's voice coming from Annalisa (see "Commendatori"). He wakes up and vomits again. Artie shows up to finalize the menu for Meadow's grad party. As Tony vomits some more, Artie calls Pussy to see if he's sick, too. No, Pussy says, just a touch of diarrhea.

Livia and Quinn are at the airport when security comes up to them. Tony's back in dreamland at Melfi's with an erection – he wants to fuck her, and does. He awakens to Dr. Cusamano telling him he has a small case of *E. Coli*, nothing life-threatening. Back in dreamland, Tony talks to Pussy the talking fish, who confesses that he works for the government. Tony gets dressed and heads out.

Angie Bonpensiero answers the door and it's Tony and Silvio, gathering Pussy to go look at a new Sea Ray 62 boat. Tony fakes another upchuck and finds Pussy's wiretap hardware in a cigar box. Paulie meets them at the boat, ready for a test drive. Moments later, they confront Pussy below deck. "Why you makin' me do this? You fuckin'miserable fat fuckin' piece of shit?"

Pussy explains how he told the Feds very little. They share a shot of tequila and Pussy asks, "Not in the face, okay?" Paulie tells him he was like a brother. Tony: "To all of us." Pussy sits and they all shoot. Paulie removes his jewelry and they flip him overboard in a body bag. Tony stares at the water as they drive away.

Back home, Livia calls from the airport to say she's being held for the tickets. The doorbell rings and it's Agents Cubitoso and Harris with an arrest warrant for Tony. Meadow walks in and runs upstairs crying. When Carmela tries to console her, Meadow replies, "My friends don't judge me. And fuck them if they do. I'll cut them off." Spoken like a true daughter of Tony Soprano.

Neil Mink tells Tony that this ticket case is no big deal. Tony berates himself. "I fucked up. I blew an easy one." Melfi wonders why he is more upset about this than the fact that his mother tried to kill him. He tells her about the sex dream, then walks out, singing.

At Meadow's graduation party, Tony tells Christopher that he's going to propose that he get his button. Excited, Chris says, "I fuckin' deserve it. I got no spleen, Gene." Davey Scatino announces that his son is going to Georgetown and that he's moving to work on a ranch out West. Tony lovingly hugs Meadow. As the Sopranos pose for a family portrait, we see: a Barone sanitation truck at work; a man in a sandwich board selling calling cards; the crew posing for a picture; a hooker in a tanning salon; Hillel cleaning around a junkie at the Flyaway Motel; a gutted brokerage office; Scatino leaving town; Tony lighting a cigar; and finally, waves rolling in, the ocean stretching out to infinity.

LIVIA SOPRANO, ALLEGED MOB SPOUSE, DIES

Livia Pollio Soprano, wife of the late Giovanni "Johnny Boy" Soprano, an alleged leader in the New Jersey–based Domenico Ercoli "Dom" DiMeo crime family and mother of that family's alleged acting boss, Tony Soprano, died yesterday in West Orange of complications due to a stroke. She was 71.

Though never convicted of any crime herself, Mrs. Soprano was an eyewitness, if not unindicted coconspirator, to over fifty years of organized crime in Essex County. According to FBI sources, her husband, along with his brother Corrado "Junior" Soprano, still living, have long been considered major figures in the notorious DiMeo organization, specializing in sports gambling, extortion, racketeering, and "enforcement." Johnny Boy's longest prison stretch was five years in Rahway State Penitentiary in the 1970's for a string of convictions, including attempted murder. Mr. Soprano was also a "silent partner" in Satriale's Pork Store on Kearney Avenue in West Orange.

As one police source put it, "Johnny Boy was a bad man and Livia was no stay-at-home Italian mom. She was a tough old bird. And a lot smarter than her bone breaker of a hubby."

At the time of her death,

Mrs. Soprano was under active investigation for possession of allegedly stolen airline tickets.

Born Livia Pollio, the sixth child of Italian immigrants Faustino and Teresa Pollio, she grew up in the Neapolitan community in Providence, Rhode Island, and moved to the Down Neck area of Newark as a teenager. Her father, nicknamed "Augie," was a well-known

Married to Johnny Boy, Mother of Tony

left-wing activist, union organizer, and rabble-rouser. The family was apparently impoverished. When Livia met her future husband, so the story goes, he was already a neighborhood celebrity and, by local standards, well-to-do.

Mrs. Soprano is the mother of Anthony "Tony" Soprano of North Caldwell, believed to be the current

"street boss" of the DiMeo family. Again according to unnamed FBI sources, mother and son had a tempestuous relationship. At one point, it was widely alleged that she in fact plotted his murder for forcing her into a retirement home. Charges were never brought in the matter.

The home in question was the Green Grove Retirement Home on Pleasant Valley Way in West Orange. A facility spokesman refused to comment except to acknowledge that Mrs. Soprano was in fact a past resident and that "she was a handful." Mr. Soprano himself was not available for comment.

To the best of anyone's knowledge, Mrs. Soprano was never involved in any charities, church activities, or civic organizations of any kind. She was known to lecture beggars on the street to "stop whining and haul your own freight,"

Mrs. Soprano is also survived by two daughters, Janice, of Seattle, Washington, and West Orange, a video artist; and Barbara, of Brewster, New York, a homemaker; six grandchildren; and two sisters, Quintina, of the Newark area, and Gemma, of Tucson, Arizona.

The family asks that any donations in Mrs. Soprano's memory be made to the Italian-American Anti-Defamation Society of Greater New York.

Mr. Ruggerio's Neighborhood

Written by David Chase.
Directed by
Allen Coulter.

Life goes on at the Sopranos as the FBI stages a major effort to plant a bug in the basement of "the Sausage Factory." Tony deals with a distraught Patsy Parisi, Meadow deals with a new roommate at college, AJ deals with freshman football, and Carmela deals with it all.

Tony, in his bathrobe, descends his long driveway to pick up his *Star Ledger* and reads the headline: "Mob Competition For Garbage Contracts Heats Up." At the local FBI head-quarters, a large gathering of agents agree that "CW16" (a.k.a. Big Pussy) is "compost," that it would be great if they could get Livia to testify against her own son, and that it's time to bug Tony's house. Judge Lapper issues a "sneak and peak" warrant, but warns against "a *Better Homes & Gardens* tour."

Tony disses the Fed detail as he leaves home. The office agents work out a game plan around the family maid, Lilliana. Lookout teams tail the whole family: AJ, or "Baby Bing," from home to Verbum Dei; Tony, "Der Bingle," to work; "Mrs. Bing" to play; and

Meadow, "Princess Bing," on campus at Columbia University. When Lilliana takes off for her English class with husband, Stasiu, the SET ("Surveil-lance Entry Team") moves in on "the Sausage Factory."

At the Bada Bing, Furio and Tony run into Patsy Parisi with a newly tailored sable coat for Carmela. As the SET team works, Paulie Walnuts lectures the boys on the dangers of germ-infested shoelaces and Patsy bemoans the loss of his twin brother, Philly, or "Spoons." Agents Tancredi and Jongsma watch Carmela and a skimpily clad Adriana take to the tennis courts, where they learn that Ed, the pro, is off to San Diego and the very fetching Birgit is taking over. AJ and friends skip school and smoke cigs in front of a Korean deli. Egon Kosma joins them, wearing a freshman football jersey. "Excellent jersey," opines AJ.

An agent stands outside of Meadow's dorm room as her roommate, Caitlin Rucker from Bartlesville, Oklahoma, bursts in, high from an all-night drinking binge. Lunching in a park, Lilliana tries to study up on Francis Scott Key for her immigration exam, while Stasiu harks back to their days in Lodz when he was "an engineer with twenty employees and grant from state..." At the FBI HQ, agents Harris and Cubitoso notice on a sur-veillance video that the Soprano water tank is about to blow. A base-ment lamp is spotted and before you can say "make me one with a microphone/transmitter," the tech wizards in Quantico, Virginia, have done just that.

Back at the Bing, Gigi Cestone reports that Patsy has been boozing and launching into "a single-malt diatribe" about his brother's death. Agents staking out the Soprano house hear a scream emanating from inside. As Birgit flirts with Adriana, Carmela gets a call and rushes off. Tony takes off, too, and Harris yells, "Abort!" Minutes later, Tony and Carmela wade through a flooded basement, grabbing pictures and cursing a blue streak.

Agents weasel their way past Jeannie Cusamano next door to spy on Tony. They see Patsy in the Sopranos' backyard, waving a gun. He can't bring himself to shoot Tony, but he can urinate in his pool. Soon the SET team is back in motion, dropping wires and putting the new lamp in place. AJ goes out for the freshman football squad, Meadow's friend, Hunter, gets a glimpse of screwy Caitlin, and Tony convinces Patsy to put his grief behind him. An agent detains Lilliana at the park to buy time. Finally, Agent Harris announces, "Touchdown." The tap is in.

Of course, what comes across this hi-tech intrusion is not the stuff of crime but the stuff of life. Tony works out on the exercycle and talks about his bowel movements. Carmela to Tony: "What you need is more roughage overall in your diet." The Sopranos are back.

Proshai, Livushka

Written by David Chase. Directed by Tim Van Patten.

Meadow brings home a new boyfriend, Tony has a panic attack, Livia dies suddenly, and family and friends gather for an awkward wake. Throughout it all, Tony watches* The Public Enemy *to ease the pain.

A Sani-Cruiser garbage truck explodes and Carmela walks in to find Tony passed out on the floor of his kitchen. The day rewinds. Meadow introduces Tony to her new beau, half-black, half-Jewish Noah Tannenbaum. Tony introduces Noah to reality, i.e., stay away, "ditsoon." He unwraps some gabagool, sees an Uncle Ben's box, and passes out. Carmela tends to his head wound as he mumbles about "fuckin' butterheads." Then Tony drops in on Ma. She whines – "I wish the Lord would take me now" – as he rants about clamming up re the stolen airline tickets. As he walks out, his last words are: "Fuck it – do what you want."

Tony watches *The Public Enemy* on video. Meadow comes in, livid about what Tony may have said to Noah. Tony doesn't bend: "Maybe I should have said it in Swahili!" He wanders outside, then returns to the house to hear the news: "Your mother died." He sits, shaken. Tony and Carmela arrive at Livia's house as the body is removed. Svetlana, Livia's one-legged aide, gives her farewell: *"Proshai, Livushka,"* or "Good-bye, little Livia." Back home, Meadow helps AJ decipher Robert Frost. Snow symbolizes death, she says. "I thought black was death!" Alone, AJ thinks he hears his grandma's voice.

"What are you gonna do?" Tony responds to the sympathies of his crew. He chats with

his sister Barbara, then browbeats Janice into coming back for the funeral, at his expense, of course. He returns to Tom Powers's loving Ma in *The Public Enemy*. More chums drop by; he takes Ralph Cifaretto and Albert Barese out back to order "no more fires, " refer-ring to the rash of garbage truck arsons.

Viewing caskets at Cozzarelli's Funeral Home, Janice, Tony, and Barbara argue about what Ma wanted. Tony caves, agrees to whatever, but he won't agree to Janice's "California bullshit" of voicing good thoughts. With Melfi, Tony first says he's glad Livia's dead, then berates himself for being a bad son, then sums up his Ma as "a fucking selfish miserable cunt." Melfi says it's common for adult children to wish their joyless parents dead. Later, Tony finds Janice in Livia's basement looking for buried treasure and whining that Ma saved none of her childhood relics, but all of Tony's.

Furio, Adriana, and Chris get loaded for the wake. Junior, Bacala, Assemblyman Zellman, and Rev. James, Jr. pay their respects. Backstage, Junior and Tony argue about Ralph as Ralph and his crew beat up a client. At the burial, Janice bullies Svetlana about Livia's prized record collection, which the Russian aide claims Livia gave to her. Janice is pissed.

As the afterparty begins, Artie Bucco flashes back to Livia telling him that Tony torched the Vesuvio. Tony watches Meadow press the flesh and fears that she's already "a fuckin' robot like the rest of us." We (but not Tony) see a fleeting visage of Pussy in a mirror. Janice drags everyone into the great room for Livia's favorite song, "If I Loved You," and fond memories. It's a painfully awkward situation. Carmela knocks back shots of alcohol as Janice waxes poetic re how Ma believed that "wild-flowers blossom best among rocks, with little water." Chris then launches into an endless dope-induced rap about no two people being alike. "But do they know that for sure?"

Artie is about to tell his Livia story when Carmela loses it. "This is such a crock of shit...passing out cheese puffs over a woman we all know was terribly dysfunctional." Her dad chimes in and Carm ends it on a sad note: Livia didn't want a wake because she didn't think anyone would come.

Late in the evening, Tony watches the end of *The Public Enemy*. Tom Powers's Ma gets excited that "they're bringing Tom home." As she changes his pillowcase, the door opens and a dead, hog-tied Tom drops to the floor. Tony watches, tears streaming down his face. "I'm Forever Blowing Bubbles" plays on.

Fortunate Son

Written by Todd A. Kessler. Directed by Henry J. Bronchtein.

Christopher gets made, AJ is a football hero, and Tony has a horrendous flashback that reveals a deep connection between violence, anxiety, and meat.

"This could be it," Christopher tells Adriana after a surprise call from Paulie. Meeting in a mall parking lot, Paulie tells Chris to "shoot your cuffs" and leads him to his made-man

ceremony in a basement full of Tony and crew. As Tony lays out the oath, Chris is unnerved by a black bird in the window. At the afterparty, Paulie gives Chris his sports book, with a kickback of six g's a week – "...and on it goes, this thing of ours..." Carmine, the boss from New York, tells Tony to get his mental act together.

Janice decides to move into Livia's house. Down at the Ooh-Fa Pizzeria, Chris parades his bones and Jackie, Jr. starts a fight. "Hey," Chris shouts, "don't disrespect the pizza parlor." Tony complains to Melfi about his lack of progress and Melfi says, "Dig deeper." As Tony details his latest panic attack, Melfi makes the link between meat and anxiety.

In the sports-book boiler room, Chris loses big on USC-Oregon. Later, Tony tells Chris to keep Jackie, Jr. clean, as Jackie, Jr. skips Sunday dinner and disses his mom. Chris shorts Paulie 2 g's and Paulie ups it to 4 g's. Jackie, Jr. struts into Nuovo Vesuvio with sunglasses and an attitude, and Tony tells him that his Uncle Richie was a rat and he should stay in pre-med.

At a Verbum Dei freshman football game, AJ recovers a fumble and Tony cheers wildly. Even though it's his "busy season," Tony is home for family dinner and AJ asks if they can eat with the TV on. Meadow calls, snubs Tony. Janice plays nice to Svetlana about Livia's old records, then steals her prosthetic leg. Chris freaks out about the new

pressures of "the job" – "It was that bird in the window," he tells Adriana.

Svetlana and Irina bitch to Tony about the stolen leg with the special "flex foot." Tony, snacking on gabagool, has a horrendous flashback of himself at 11 years old when his dad cuts off Mr. Satriale's pinky with a meat cleaver. Tony tells Melfi the experience was a rush, then flashes back again to a family dinner where Johnny coos at Livia over a standing rib roast and little Anthony has his first panic attack. Melfi sees the whole picture – in Tony's mind, food is always associated with violence. She mentions Proust's madeleines, which Tony thinks "sounds very gay."

Carmela heads off with AJ to visit Meadow at Columbia and dissuades Tony from coming. In front of a self-righteous Noah, Meadow tells her mom she knows the whole story and compares Tony's "racist retrograde fucking asshole personality" to Noah, "a sensitive and brilliant person." Carmela walks out. Janice stonewalls Svetlana as Chris, desperate for cash, decides to pull a college heist with Jackie, Jr. Jackie is the wheelman as Chris and Benny Fazio jack a campus benefit concert starring Jewel.

AJ announces he's not going to college. Chris hands Paulie his back money, then whines that "this being made isn't workin' out the way I thought it would." Paulie reports on the campus heist to Tony. At football practice, Coach Goodwin lauds AJ and makes him defensive captain. AJ promptly faints.

Written by Robin Green & Mitchell Burgess. Directed by John Patterson.

Employee of the Month

Melfi is brutally raped, then doubly injured when her rapist goes free. Johnny Sack moves to New Jersey and Janice is forced by some nasty Russians to return Svetlana's leg.

Tony gets a call at home from ex-flame Irina, drunk on vanilla Stoli, whining about cousin Svetlana's missing leg. Richard helps Melfi fix dinner and again complains about "stereotypical goombahs." Melfi tells Tony in session that he's not trying enough and should bring in Carmela. Melfi then tells her own shrink Elliot that Richard is right – she is being conned by a sociopath. Elliot suggests pawning Tony off on a behaviorist.

Tony tells Janice not to mess with the Russians. She claims the old LPs Svetlana stole are "a window into Ma's soul." Ralph takes Jackie, Jr. with him to visit a "sand monkey," and they bond by beating the guy up. Tony visits Johnny Sack's new Jersey digs, bothered that Johnny didn't tell him about the move. Tony then tells Ralph that he's making Gigi a captain. Melfi tells Tony that it's time for him to "move on" to behavioral mod; he senses abandonment.

Melfi steps into her empty office garage and is brutally accosted and raped on the staircase. At the hospital, she is told the rapist, Jesus Rossi, has been caught, still with her Palm Pilot. Richard notes the Italian name and son Jason comes in, huffing and puffing like the mean ass he isn't. Melfi calls Carmela to cancel her appointment with Tony because of a "car accident." Tony asks Carm to join him in therapy. She says sure.

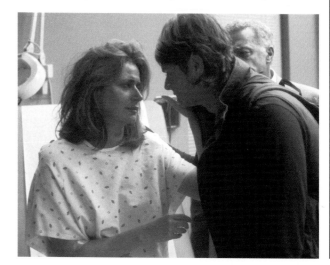

Season 3

THE Sopranos

Back home, Richard tells Melfi that the cops let Jesus go; they "mishandled the chain of custody." Melfi is crushed and turns on Richard. At the Bing, the boys tell Ginny Sack jokes – "She's so fat her blood type is Ragu..." – before Johnny walks in and directs their attention to the TV, where in-their-pocket pol Assemblyman Zellman is announcing $25 million for the new Esplanade/Museum of Science and Trucking. As Paulie puts it, "This fucking busted valise, he's worth every cent of his cut."

Melfi and Richard make up and Tony meets with Chris to tell him, as the Feds listen, to leave Jackie, Jr., a.k.a. "Little Lord Fuckpants," out of the business. Tony sees a beaten-up Melfi, then browbeats Jackie, Jr. about walking the line. Melfi orders a chicken wrap at a take-out place and there's his picture – Jesus Rossi, Employee of the Month.

Janice is at home practicing "Satisfaction" on the guitar when two Russians bust in, slap her around, and retrieve Svetlana's leg from a bowling alley locker. Melfi has a dream where a vicious Rottweiler attacks Jesus while her hand is stuck in a cola machine. She later realizes that the dog is Tony. She won't tell Tony, as she assures Elliot, but admits to enjoying the prospect "that I could have this asshole squashed like a bug."

Meanwhile, Tony picks up Janice in the ER and bitches about payback time for the Russians. Janice's thoughts turn to God. At a party at Johnny Sack's new estate, Ralph does his *Gladiator* imitation, then huddles with Johnny as Tony looks on. At Melfi's, Tony says he's ready for behavioral therapy and Melfi breaks down crying. He sweetly tries to comfort her. Tony: "What? You want to say something?" Melfi: "No."

Another Toothpick

*Written by
Terence Winter.
Directed by Jack Bender.*

Tony humiliates a traffic cop, Bacala's dad returns to terminate a local sociopath, Artie and Charmaine call it quits, and Junior announces that he has the Big Casino.

Dr. Melfi, digging at "root causes" with Tony and Carmela, provokes Carmela into pointing out Tony's need to "stick your dick into anything with a pulse." Tony huffs. Melfi senses anger. Tony: "You must've been at the top of your fuckin' class." Postsession, Tony's reckless driving brings on Officer Leon Wilmore. Tony flashes his "Police Benevolent Association" card, but Wilmore doesn't buy it. The "smoke" cop dresses him down and writes him up.

A local sociopath, Mustang Sally Intile, takes a putter to the head of Bryan Spatafore for fun. Later, brother Vito Spatafore demands vengeance as the boys stand over a comatose Bryan. While Ralph cracks wise – "he wasn't that smart to begin with..." – Gigi agrees to handle Sally the wacko.

Meanwhile, Father Phil pays homage to the late Fabrizio "Febby" Viola in a half-filled church. Afterward, Carmela disses Phil, and Tony and Junior run into old friend Bobby Bacala, Sr. Tony tells the sickly old man that his godson, Sally, stepped over the line. Junior snaps when Janice refers to Bacala, Sr. as "another toothpick."

Adriana announces to Artie that Chris wants her to quit her job as the Nuovo Vesuvio's hostess. Artie is crushed. Bacala, Jr., acting like a "gloomy Gus," cries in front of Junior because his dying dad must clip Sally. Junior confronts Tony, who convinces him it's the only way.

At Nuovo Vesuvio, a drunken Artie harasses Chris about Adriana and almost gets a fork in the eye. Privately, Artie tells Tony he's in love with Ade. Tony tells Assemblyman Zellman to deal with the unbending Officer Wilmore. To save face, Junior tells Bacala, Jr. that his dad must kill Sally as "a matter of duty." Bacala, Sr. walks in spitting blood and says he's up for the job.

Artie and his wife, Charmaine, argue about going into the packaged foods business with Tony. Eating with Johnny Sack, et al., Tony sticks to his guns re Bacala, Sr. Later, at the lawn ornament store Fountains of Wayne, Tony bumps into a moonlighting Wilmore, who announces his demotion. Feeling guilty, Tony calls Zellman.

Bacala, Sr. struggles up some stairs before sloppily whacking Mustang Sally and his friend Carlos. Driving away, he has a massive stroke and smashes into a pole, DOA. Junior asks Bacala, Jr. about the exact cause of death, then throws a fit. Artie and Charmaine go one last round before Charmaine declares: "This marriage is over."

Junior tells Tony he has stomach cancer, "the Big Casino," which is why he wanted to know how Bacala, Sr. died. "These things come in threes." Tony promises not to tell anyone, then promptly calls Janice. Drinking wine, a somber brother and sis remember their Uncle Mickey, dead at 36 from liver cancer. Janice announces that "I've really been coming to know Christ."

Meadow walks off with the FBI-bugged lamp for her college dorm room. Artie embarrasses himself at a mushy dinner with Adriana. Zellman asks Tony what to do about Officer Wilmore. Tony's final assessment: "Fuck him." Junior tells Bacala that he's not going to his dad's funeral because he's got cancer. Down at Fountains of Wayne, Tony tries to slip Wilmore some guilt money, but Wilmore, being the man he is, walks away.

University

Meadow deals with her roommate from hell, then gets dumped by Noah. Ralph goes berserk and pummels to death his pregnant goomar, Tracee.

At the Bada Bing, Tracee, a beautiful 20-year-old stripper, tries to befriend Tony with some date-nut bread. At Sunday dinner, Ralph and AJ wax about *Gladiator*, Jackie, Jr. (a.k.a. "The Fresh Prince of New Jersey") picks up some keys, and Ralph talks about how he had to drop out of high school to help his sick mom. Back at Columbia, Caitlin, in a typical hair-pulling, freaked-out mood, interrupts Noah and Meadow. The lovebirds retire to Noah's room to consummate their relationship.

Back home, Tony spews about Meadow's cold shoulder. A crazed Ralph comes into the Bing spouting more *Gladiator* lines, punches Georgie with a pool cue, then whacks him with a chain. Tony orders him to take Georgie to the ER. Meadow returns to the dorm to another Caitlin psycho show; she quickly retires to Noah's boudoir. Tracee shows Tony her new braces, trying to make a human connection. Caitlin, out on a birthday romp with Meadow and Noah, sees a homeless woman with a newspaper hanging out her backside and totally loses it. Meadow confides in her mom that Noah can go hot and cold and that at this point, she "better be" in love with him.

Teleplay by
Terence Winter and
Salvatore J. Stabile.
Story by
David Chase & Terence
Winter & Todd A. Kessler
and Robin Green &
Mitchell Burgess.
Directed by
Allen Coulter.

Tracee tells Tony that she is pregnant with Ralph's kid. Tony advises her to get rid of it. While Meadow is at home, Caitlin bugs Noah all night, and although Caitlin is all smiles when Meadow returns, Noah is apoplectic about getting a C-. Silvio tracks a missing Tracee to a *Spartacus* screening at Ralph's place and slaps her around while Ralph giggles. Meadow has dinner with Noah's dad, Len Tannenbaum, Hollywood lawyer to Tim Daly and Dick Wolf, and she feels outclassed. Later Noah announces that his dad is getting a restraining order against Caitlin.

Tracee enters the VIP lounge at the Bing and in front of his cronies, busts Ralph's balls for ignoring her. He follows her outside, insults her, then sadistically beats her to death. He tells his friends that "she fell." When Tony sees the body, he punches Ralph out for disrespecting the Bing. Back at the campus library, Noah dumps Meadow because she's too "negative." At a session with Melfi and Carmela, Tony can't get Tracee out of his head. He is beyond sadness as he talks around this "work-related death."

Meadow stomps into the family kitchen, then stomps out. Meanwhile, at the Bing, life goes on without Tracee. Girls undulate on stage as the Kinks sing "Living on a Thin Line."

Season 3

THE Sopranos

Written by Lawrence Konner. Directed by Tim Van Patten.

Second Opinion

Junior struggles with stomach cancer, Tony pays a visit to an uppity oncologist, and Carmela meets with her own therapist, who tells her the truth about her life.

Under the knife, Junior hallucinates that he rats on Tony, escapes the Big C, and marries Angie Dickinson. Dr. John Kennedy tells Tony that he took a fist-sized tumor from Junior's stomach and got all the cancer. Later, at Sunday dinner, Carmela and her mother argue about the man Carmela didn't marry, Angelo Stamfa, the drugstore mogul.

Down at the Bing, Paulie humiliates Christopher by making him strip naked in front of the boys to check for a wire and the size of his equipment. In a one-on-one with Melfi, Carmela bemoans life with Tony, whereupon Melfi suggests a therapist for Carm, one Dr. Sig Krakower in Livingston. Meanwhile, Silvio shows Tony a Big Mouth Billy Bass; Tony has a Pussy flashback, then beats Georgie over the head with the fish. Junior and Bacala visit Dr. Kennedy, who announces that Junior still has malignant cells and needs "amended surgery." When prompted to ask questions, Bacala only asks about the food Junior is allowed to eat.

Carmela bumps into Angie Bonpensiero, who complains about the doctor bills for her sick dog, Coco. Christopher brings Adriana a truckload of size-ten designer shoes and she instantly repays him. Carmela tells Tony that she's visiting Meadow's freshman dean and that Angie's dog has osteoporosis. Paulie busts in on Chris and Adriana, confiscates the shoes, and sniffs some panties while Chris silently fumes.

While Carmela argues with Meadow about "the Noah thing," Tony drops by Junior's and talks him into getting a second opinion about more surgery, even though Junior thinks Kennedy has "the hands of an angel." Carmela lunches with the oh-so-smooth Dean Ross, who tries to weasel 50 large out of her for the school's "Wall of Commitment." Meanwhile, Tony smashes in Angie's Cadillac to remind her to shut up around Carmela.

Tony refuses to hand over 50 g's to Columbia, then takes Junior to see Dr. Mehta, who suggests chemo or, better yet, convening a tumor board. Carmela sneaks

a call to Dr. Krakower, then throws her arms around AJ, back from playing video games in DC. Chris complains to Tony about Paulie to no avail.

At the tumor board, Kennedy blows up when he hears that "Sloan-Kettering Mehta" was asked for a second opinion. Junior gets his first chemo treatment and pages Dr. Kennedy. Later, Junior throws up and complains to Tony about Kennedy dissing him. Paulie catches Chris outside the Happy Days motel, tells him to stop whining to the Big Man, then pulls out another Big Mouth Billy Bass.

Tony and Furio pay a visit to Dr. Kennedy on the golf course, where Furio explains that "there's-a worse things that can happen to a person than cancer." Carmela meets with Krakower, who doesn't mince words. "Go home and pack. Leave the state...take only the children and go." Carmela hesitates. Krakower: "...you can never say that you haven't been told."

Kennedy drops in on Junior, cheers him up, and gives him his home number. Tony finds Carmela curled up in the dark on the couch. Carmela tells him they are in for the whole $50,000 at Columbia. "Tony, you gotta do something nice for me today and this is what I want." Tony quietly concurs.

Written by
Robin Green & Mitchell
Burgess and
Todd A. Kessler.
Directed by
Allen Coulter.

He Is Risen

Meadow hooks up with Jackie, Jr., Tony hooks up with Gloria Trillo, Janice hooks up with a born-again narcoleptic, and Gigi Cestone dies an ignominious death.

A zoned-out Caitlin points out Jackie, Jr. to Meadow at a frat party. "Got any more X?" Meadow asks. At a Mancuso & Sons craps game, Tony walks in and Ralphie disses him by not sharing a drink. Jackie, Jr. is about to bang a passed-out Meadow, but leaves her untouched. Silvio suggests that Tony either apologize to Ralph or bump him up to captain, but Tony says, "Over my dead body...he disrespected the Bing." Ralph fumes with friends about Tony. "What, you think I'm afraid of that fat fuck?"

In back of the Bing, the boys hand over stolen turkeys to Rev. Herman James when Tony realizes that Ralph's coming to his house for Thanksgiving dinner. Right after

Carmela and Rosalie gossip about their lovebird kids, Tony tells Carm to disinvite Ro. Carmela concocts a story about her sick father. Tony bumps into one Gloria Trillo, Mercedes saleswoman, in Melfi's waiting room. Gloria says she's "a serial killer – I've killed seven relationships." Later Tony asks Melfi about Gloria and praises *The Art of War.*

Janice's narcoleptic born-again boyfriend, Aaron Arkaway, makes an

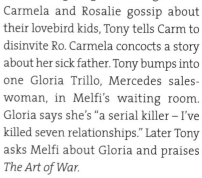

appearance at Thanksgiving dinner. Meanwhile, over at Ro's, Jackie, Jr. slips away to see Meadow. "Have you heard the good news?" Aaron asks Jackie as he walks in. "He is risen."Jackie and Meadow kiss in the car as Jackie announces that he's stopped going to classes and wants to be the next Hugo Boss. Tony tells Carmela he wants to buy a new Mercedes.

Gigi tells Tony about all the stress in his life. Ralphie tells Johnny Sack that he wants to switch families, then asks him to intercede with Tony. Johnny meets with Tony, who doesn't give an inch, then tells Ralph that Tony is "delighted" that Ralph wants to talk. While Melfi complains to Elliot about a whiny patient, Tony hears Ralph's apology, then dismisses him. Gigi complains about "spackle" in his bowels at a poker game. Ralph whines to Johnny about the sit-down with Tony. Gigi goes to the bathroom, then dies on the toilet, a victim of a bowel-induced heart attack, "the silent killer," as Paulie puts it.

Tony ponders the vacancy in the hierarchy. Junior tells Tony to "steer the ship the best you know." At Nuovo Vesuvio, Tony tells Ralph he's making him captain. Ralph is elated; Tony just walks out. At a pool hall, Meadow steals Jackie's keys and drives his car off the road, bringing on a moment of romantic fusion. Tony drops by Globe Motors for a test drive with Gloria. Melfi gets a call – Gloria can't make her session. Melfi thinks she might have heard another voice. She does – Gloria is bopping Tony on *The Stugots*.

The Telltale Moozadell'

Written by Michael Imperioli. Directed by Daniel Attias.

AJ and friends vandalize their school as Adriana opens her own nightclub, Jackie, Jr. tries to act like a big shot, and Tony and Gloria take a trip to the zoo.

Happy Birthday, Carmela. Tony gives her a sapphire rock, AJ gives her a used DVD of *The Matrix*, and Meadow chimes in with a trip to the Belladonna Day Spa. That sly Jackie, Jr. butters up Mrs. S. with a warm bottle of Gallo French Colombard, then butters up AJ with football pointers. Meadow eats it up.

Club owner/gambler Rocco De Trollio must turn over the Lollipop nightclub to

Christopher and Furio, who in turn hand it over to Adriana to book the bands. Carmela worries about the Meadow/Jackie, Jr. affair. Tony says he's better than "Jamal Ginsberg, the Hasidic homeboy." Meadow downloads an Edgar Allan Poe paper for Jackie, Jr. AJ and friends sneak into the school swimming pool and trash the place, hysterical with adrenaline.

The next morning, Meadow tries to pawn a car

out of her folks while a janitor at school shows Principal Cincotta the damage. Tony drops by Globe Motors; Gloria suggests a trip to the zoo. Carmela and Rosalie question the food at Nuovo Vesuvio. Tony lectures Jackie, Jr. about doing well in school; Jackie proudly points out the A he got on his Edgar Allan Poe paper. The cops track down the pizza evidence from the pool incident and AJ faces the wrath of Mom and Dad. Tony gets to the gist: "Your whole football career, down the drain!"

Adriana opens the renamed "Crazy Horse" and Furio must roust an X dealer named Matush from the club's men's room. Tony and Gloria drop by the gorilla cage at the zoo,

and after a little Buddhist exchange about suffering, they fornicate in the reptile house. Matush takes his problem to Jackie, Jr., who says he'll deal with it. At AJ's sentence hearing in the principal's office, Carmela and Tony are shocked when Father Nicholai, the athletic director, doesn't throw AJ off the football team, because "it would be against his best interests – and the team's..."

Melfi discusses Gloria's suicidal tendencies with her. Jackie, Jr. approaches Christopher about helping out his friend Matush, and Chris summarily blows him off. Jackie tells Matush it's all cool. AJ gets grounded for six weeks and is forced to do actual labor, like cleaning the gutters. Matush shows up at the Crazy Horse to sell more X – Furio catches wind and the boy ends up in the hospital with a wired jaw and a broken arm. Ralph gives Jackie a .38; it'll never jam, he says. Gloria gets off on massaging Tony's ankle-holstered pistol.

Melfi knows that Tony is lying to her about his

life and it drives her nuts. Tony catches Jackie at the Mancuso & Sons card game and kicks him out. The next morning, ironically, Carmela announces she now thinks Jackie is "a perfect gentleman." Tony ponders this contradiction as he watches leaves from the gutter fall by the window.

To Save Us All from Satan's Power . . .

Tony and crew are haunted by Pussy at Christmastime, Bacala has to fill in as Santa, a Russian gets paid back, and Meadow gives her dad a surprise present.
Tony stands on the boardwalk at Asbury Park, staring at the ocean, and flashes back to 1995 with Jackie, Sr. and Big Pussy. Pussy complains about "Terry's bills from Villanova and Matt and Kevin right behind her." Tony: "Don't be movin' that H anymore, Puss." Back in the present, Paulie growls, "Don't waste another second on that rat fuck," then bitches about Ralphie.

Written by Robin Green & Mitchell Burgess. Directed by Jack Bender.

Tony wakes up, "to do" list in hand, and gets hit with another panic attack. Carmela comes in and says Janice wants to fix Christmas dinner. Tony tells Melfi that he's "back to square one...back in the rat hole" and Melfi makes a crack about "Stress-mas." Tony starts to talk about Pussy but can't. Janice and Aaron are working on a Christian Contemporary Music lyric, "His blood cleans every stain," when Carm and Tony arrive to find the house a mess. Janice complains about her bum wrist. Tony writes "Janice's Russian" on his list.

Down at the Pork Store, the boys prep for the big annual Christmas giveaway started by Johnny Boy and wonder who'll play Santa with Pussy gone. Tony says no. At a Russian

nightclub, Tony passes $250 K to his friend Slava for laundering and asks him to help find "Janice's Russian," a livery cab driver. Silvio has a nightmare of Pussy in a giant rat trap, then talks about 1995 with Tony. Pussy didn't come to the big sit-down with Junior. That's the day he flipped, they realize. Later at Nuovo Vesuvio, a dolled-up Charmaine struts by looking like

"the miracle of Christmas," then busts both Tony's and Artie's balls. Tony gets a call about Igor the driver. Soon he and Furio, wearing Santa hats, pop into Igor's cab.

Tony sneers at *It's a Wonderful Life* on TV, then meets with the boys about their Santa problem. In walks Bacala. He doesn't want to do it – "I'm shy" – but has no choice. Janice watches a TV report about Igor laid out in a store window and sheds a grateful tear for Tony. Admiring the family tree, Meadow tells Carmela that Jackie, Jr. had to "visit a friend in the hospital." Tony has a fight with Charmaine at Nuovo Vesuvio, drops in on a new strip club, and there's Jackie, Jr., his head buried in bare breasts. A disgusted Tony hauls him into the john, takes away his gun, and knees him in the groin.

Carmela accuses Tony of playing around with Charmaine. He claims, "I'm the monogamy poster boy, I swear to God," but she's not buying it. Melfi wants to talk about Pussy, but Tony stomps out. As kids and moms line up for the Christmas party, Tony figures out that back in '95, an edgy Pussy was wearing a wire as Santa. Back in the present, Bacala plays a nasty Santa – "Shyness is a curse" – and Silvio later admits that despite everything, Pussy made a great Santa. "Fuck Santa Claus," says Paulie.

Christmas morning at the Sopranos, Jackie, Jr. gives a necklace to Meadow, then admits to Tony that he flunked out of college. Tony is pissed: "You bullshit me and you betray my daughter." As Jackie kisses Meadow good-bye, Carmela opens the beautiful sapphire bracelet from Tony. Meadow has a surprise present for her dad: a Big Mouth Billy Bass, singing "Take Me to the River." Tony is visibly flustered. And the ocean rolls on.

Pine Barrens

Teleplay by
Terence Winter.
Story by
Tim Van Patten &
Terence Winter.
Directed by
Steve Buscemi.

The real, wacko Gloria starts to emerge, Meadow catches Jackie, Jr. in a compromising position, and Paulie and Christopher chase a wounded Russian into the Pine Barrens wilderness.

To the strains of "Gloria," Gloria pulls up to *The Stugots*. The phone rings and she answers it. It's Irina, looking for Tony. Tony first lies, then tells Gloria who it is. She gets steamed

and throws his Christmas present in the drink. Tony sends Paulie to pick up some cash for Silvio. With Melfi, Tony and Carmela worry out loud about Meadow's love life and agree that they're "communicating" better.

Jackie, Jr. and Meadow play Scrabble; her word is "oblique," his is "ass." He leaves her with a cold while Chris and Paulie drop in on Valery, a big, drunk Russian, to collect Silvio's money. Wisecracks are exchanged, fists fly, and Paulie chokes Valery with a lamp. They throw the body in the trunk, then call Tony at Gloria's. The boys take off for Pine Barrens in south Jersey. Tony tells Melfi that Gloria makes him happier than all the therapy and Prozac in the world.

In the stark, snowy woods of Pine Barrens, Paulie opens the trunk to find Valery still breathing. In digging his own grave, Valery crows about the cold, then whaps Chris with a shovel and takes off into the woods. They give chase, shoot at him, and may or may not have hit him. Paulie informs Tony via cell phone that "the package hit Chrissy with an implement and ran off." Tony is furious, doubly so because of the bad cell connection.

As the boys wander aimlessly in the frozen tundra, Tony meets with his Russian friend Slava to clean $200,000. Slava tells him that Valery saved his life in Chechnya and is "like brother to me." Tony tells Paulie that Valery was a tough nut, a Russian Green Beret. Paulie takes a spill and Chris mistakenly shoots a deer. The cold wind blows. Paulie: "I lost my shoe."

Jackie, Jr. tells Meadow he has to get his mother's car inspected that night. As the sun goes down and the temperature drops, Paulie and Chris find an abandoned van for shelter. They suck on little packets of ketchup and relish as Tony and family back home eat and discuss the weather. Paulie calls again, begging for help. Gloria arranges a table, expecting Tony for London broil and lovemaking. Meadow can't find Jackie, decides to ask her friend Ambujam to drive her to Jersey. Tony is halfway through lovemaking with Gloria when Paulie, out of ideas, calls again with directions. Gloria loses it again and hits Tony in the back of the head with the steak. Bad idea.

Meadow catches Jackie with a slut, confirmation that he's a two-timing prick. Tony drops by Junior's, picks up Bacala in full hunter regalia, and they take off for the Pine Barrens. By 4:30 AM, the boys are fighting over Tic Tacs when Bacala and Tony arrive at the gate where Paulie left his car. The car is gone. Paulie and Chris go for each other's throats, then break up laughing. In bed back at the student health center, Meadow cries about Jackie as Caitlin tells her he's a real bore.

At dawn, Paulie shoots his makeshift shoe, alerting Tony and Bacala to their whereabouts. "Thank fuckin' God," Chris exclaims. Paulie makes an executive decision not to look for Valery. As they drive home in Tony's Suburban, Tony tells Paulie if "this cocksucker ever crawls out from under a rock," it's entirely Paulie's problem. Again with Melfi, Tony bemoans Gloria's meat-throwing ways. Melfi: "Depressive...unstable, impossible to please...remind you of any other woman?" Tony thinks, but he doesn't get it.

Amour Fou

Teleplay by
Frank Renzulli.
Story by
David Chase.
Directed by
Tim Van Patten.

Tony has a dramatic showdown with Gloria, Carmela struggles with her health, both mental and physical, and Jackie, Jr. leads an ill-fated raid on a mobbed-up card game.
Touring an art museum in Manhattan, Meadow announces to her mom that the Jackie, Jr. affair is "so over." An emotional Carmela breaks down in front of a beatific baby Jesus portrait. Gloria tries to lure Tony back to her in a parking lot. Melfi calls their mixed-up affair an *"amour fou,"* or crazy love. Tony tries to bribe Melfi to tell him more about Gloria. Melfi hints at Gloria's obvious dark side, but Tony sees only her deep, black, seductive eyes, like a Spanish painting by "Goyim."

As Jackie, Jr. and Dino try to impress Ralphie, Gloria tells her family problems to Tony in a motel room and hopes that maybe a truck will go by and she'll "get plastered onto a grille." Jackie, Jr. pulls a gun on some troublemakers and almost gets caught by Chris. Gloria – *Fatal Attraction*-style – strikes up a "friendship" with Carmela. Ralphie tells Jackie, Jr. how Jackie, Sr. and Tony, years ago, showed their *stugots* by holding up a card game run by "O. G." Feech Lamanna. Ralph himself couldn't make the heist – he had the clap.

While Carmela cries over a dog food commercial, Gloria finds her tires slit and goes ballistic, blaming Tony's "immigrant alcoholic probably HIV-laden slut" of an ex-squeeze, Irina. Gloria perks up when Tony said he once beat up Irina. Jackie, Jr. announces to his bud Dino that he thinks Ralph is "a fuckin' secret fag" and it's time to rob a card game, just like his dad.

Carmela confesses to a Kenyan priest named Father Obosi that her whole life is a lie – she's made "a mockery of God" – and maybe has ovarian cancer or is pregnant. The priest advises her to cool it, to "learn to live on what the good part [of Tony] earns." Carmela's response: "The Church has changed so much."

As Carmela tells Tony that "the Queen of Mean" is no longer dating Jackie, Jr., Gloria calls to pitch her on the new E-320. Two seconds later Tony is down at Globe Motors, telling her that if she goes near Carmela again, "I'll cut your fuckin' head off."

After a trip to Dr. Rotelli, Carmela announces to friends that she's in perfect health. During another Gloria tearfest, Tony realizes he's known her his whole life. She's a "fuckin' bottomless black hole," just like Livia. She threatens to tell Carmela and/or Meadow and he loses it. "Go ahead, kill me now!" Gloria screams, with Tony's hands around her neck. Tony walks away.

High on crank and wearing ski masks, Jackie, Jr., Dino, and Carlo stick up Eugene Pontecorvo's card game. Both Christopher and Furio are there. As Sunshine the dealer warns them that "victory has a hundred fathers but defeat is an orphan," Albert Barese comes out of the john and chaos ensues. Jackie, Jr. shoots Sunshine, then Christopher wastes Carlo, then Jackie, Jr. shoots Furio in the thigh. By the time Jackie, Jr. and Dino hit the street, Matush the driver is long gone. Jackie, Jr. grabs a car and takes off, leaving poor Dino to face Chris and Albert, execution style.

Dr. Freid is called away from an erectile dysfunction commercial to tend to Furio's wounds. Chris is ready to whack Jackie, Jr., but Tony says no; Chris calls him a hypocrite. At dawn, Ralph tells Tony that he wants to give Jackie, Jr. a pass. Tony says, "I'm sure you'll do the right thing," leaving Ralph staring into space. Melfi tells Tony what he already realizes: Gloria is Livia in a tight skirt. Patsy Parisi takes Gloria on a test drive and scares the crap out of her. Ralph tells Ro that Jackie, Jr. has a drug problem, Tony returns home to Carmela, Patsy picks up some stuffed shells, and life goes on.

The Army of One

In the season closer, AJ gets expelled from Verbum Dei and faces military school. Jackie, Jr. makes a last plea to Tony before Ralph has him killed. Meadow struggles with confusion and grief, and Junior sings a haunting song, "Core 'ngrato."

AJ and Egon break into a teacher's desk while Jackie, Jr. hides out with a black friend of a friend in the seedy Boonton Housing Project, or the "Boontown Holiday Inn."

Written by David Chase & Lawrence Konner. Directed by John Patterson.

Paulie Walnuts shows his beloved mom, Nucci, "the queen," around the Green Grove Retirement Home; the price tag is 40 g's. Carmela laments Jackie, Jr.'s fate. At the Vince Lombardi Rest Stop, Ralph and Paulie bitterly argue over splitting 100 grand from a heist in Morristown.

A frantic Jackie, Jr. calls Tony, who tells him to work it out with Ralphie. As Ralph drops off 300 g's of Esplanade bribes, Tony tells him Jackie, Jr. called and that it's Ralph's problem. "Chain of command is very important in our thing." Principal Cincotta corners AJ and Egon with evidence of the break-in: DNA from their urine. Agent Cubitoso and colleagues, miffed that Junior beat the Big C, assign greenhorn agent Deborah Cicerone to become Adriana's new best friend.

Jackie, Jr. loses another chess match to the little girl he's staying with. He walks outside and is whacked by Vito. Vito walks in on Ralph as he is arguing with Jackie's mom about car repairs. Preparing for the Superbowl book, Paulie and Tony trade notes about pain-in-the-butt Ralph when Carmela calls – AJ has been expelled. At home, a livid Tony, clearly bothered by the whole Jackie, Jr. situation, wants AJ to go to military school. That night, Carmela gets the call about Jackie, Jr. As she goes to Ro, AJ calls Meadow at school. All Tony wants for his kids, he tells Melfi, is to "get far away from me."

While Carmela tries to convince a distraught Meadow that Jackie, Jr. was not killed by "boogeymen with Italian names," AJ meets Major Zwingli at the Hudson Military Institute. Zwingli outlines "a blueprint for total self-discipline," then tells Carmela and Tony that he'll turn AJ into "an army of one." Back home, Carmela tells Tony that she refuses to send AJ "to that place."

Season 3

THE Sopranos

At Jackie, Jr.'s wake, Meadow collapses, Janice peddles her devotional music, and Tony is wracked with guilt. Later, Carmela tells him that they'll try it his way. At a sit-down, Tony gives Paulie only 12 of Ralph's 100 grand, which perturbs him mightily. FBI mole Deborah, now Danielle, hits it off with Adriana at Versace. AJ parades his goofy new mil-

itary look before his parents, cries about going, then collapses in another panic attack. There goes military school, Tony tells Melfi. "He's got that putrid rotten fucking Soprano gene!"

At Jackie, Jr.'s interment, with traffic roaring in the background, the local cops bust Silvio and Christopher for "promoting gambling" as both Paulie and Junior take off. Later, at Rosalie's, Meadow and Kelli, Jackie Jr.'s sister, argue about family business after Kelli claims Jackie, Jr. was killed "by a fat fuck in see-through socks."

At a post-interment affair at Nuovo Vesuvio, Tony and Junior commiserate and Paulie complains to Johnny Sack about getting screwed by Tony – "Tony fundamentally don't respect the elderly." Driving over, Meadow tells Carmela that Jackie, Jr.'s parents failed him. Chris and Silvio return from their brief incarceration as Junior, full of vino, begins to sing an old Neapolitan love song, "Co-re...core 'ngrato." All but Carmela and Meadow seem moved. Meadow, drunk, begins pitching rolls at Junior, then runs out of the restaurant, telling Tony, "This is bullshit!" Tony returns and tears stream down many faces as the Soprano community listens to Junior's sad song. Adriana asks Gabriella, "What's that mean, 'core 'ngrato'?" Gabby tells her: "Ungrateful heart."

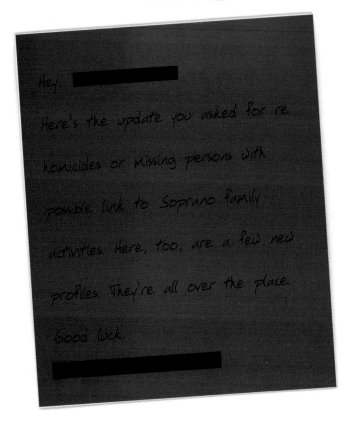

Hey, ████████

Here's the update you asked for re

homicides or missing persons with

possible link to Soprano family

activities. Here, too, are a few new

profiles. They're all over the place.

Good luck.

████████

VICTIM #17: MUSTANG SALLY INTILE
Local punk, long arrest sheet for assault,
extortion, drugs, car theft, D & D,
usual shit. Kind of guy who would mangle
a hot-dog guy over too many onions.
Killed in Staten Island house along with
Carlos (see below), allegedly by Robert
"Bacala" Baccilieri, Sr., longtime
DiMeo/Soprano soldier (again, see below).
Raison d'être: Sally allegedly beat one
Bryan Spatafore into vegetable state with
a golf putter. Over a girl, we think.
No charges were filed, but Bryan
is the brother of Vito Spatafore, part
of the late Gigi Cestone's crew. Baccilieri
was Sally's godfather. Connect the dots.

Like killing a rabid dog

VICTIM #18: CARLOS
Friend of Intile, Puerto Rican, about
40, last name unknown at this time,
another neighborhood tough guy and
sometime drug pusher. Killed in same
place - reputedly, his girlfriend's house
- and same shootout as Sally. We
believe he was simply in the wrong
place at the wrong time. Sally
needed a hideout; Carlos was stupid
enough to provide one.

Another dead jamook

Should've stayed in Florida

VICTIM #19: ROBERT
"BACALA" BACCILIERI, SR.
Longtime DiMeo/Soprano operative,
68, father of Bobby "Bacala" Baccilieri,
Jr., also in the family and right-hand
man to titular boss, Corrado Soprano,
Jr. Long record for gambling, extortion,
loansharking, etc. Believed to be
permanently retired in Miami, dying of
lung cancer (lifelong smoker), but
apparently called upon to clip Mustang
Sally et al. Died of massive stroke
while driving on Staten Island shortly
after shootout. Why would they send a
sick old man to do their
dirty work? The mob works in
mysterious ways.

Sad, sad business

VICTIM #20: TRACEE
A 20-year-old stripper at the Bada
Bing Club, last name unknown. According
to co-workers, a high school dropout
and mother of 2-year-old son, named
Danny. Disappeared last fall, whereabouts
unknown but believed dead. By all
accounts an excellent mother and
provider, co-workers say disappearance
completely out of character. Same
co-workers say she was a girlfriend or
"goomar" of Soprano captain Ralph
Cifaretto and allegedly pregnant with his
child. Cifaretto a well-known sadistic
prick - maybe Tracee was leaning on
him and he leaned back.

Drew a bad hand

VICTIM #21: SUNSHINE
Longtime area card dealer, last name and
personal history unknown, well respected at
his job, dealer of choice for Soprano-run
games. Known to deal "executive games,"
i.e., the real high rollers like Frank Sinatra,
Jr., et al. Something of a goombah
philosopher; called "Sunshine" because he
always looked like he had the weight of
world on his shoulders. Killed during routine
Saturday night game at J. Basile Electrical
Contracting, West Orange. Game believed run
by one Eugene Pontecorvo, reporting to
Ralph Cifaretto. Shot point-blank in
apparent robbery.

VICTIM #22: CARLO RENZI
Local wiseguy wannabe, 25, no adult
record but known associate of
troublemakers like Dino Zerilli and
Jackie Aprile, Jr. Also believed to be
involved in pushing Ecstasy at area clubs
like the Lollipop, aka Crazy Horse.
High probability that he was a
shotgun-toting accomplice in the
Pontecorvo debacle. Shot, as they say,
right between the eyes.

What were these guys thinking?

So young, so stupid

VICTIM #23: DINO ZERILLI
Friend of Renzi, close friend of Aprile,
Jr., college dropout, suspect in many area
crimes, convicted for drug trafficking,
served short sentence for selling X. Killed
execution-style, multiple shots to the head
and body, on street in front of card
game location, i.e., hung out to dry by
accomplices. Like Renzi, autopsy revealed
large dose of meth in bloodstream. Hey,
speed kills.

VICTIM #24: GIACOMO
"JACKIE" MICHAEL APRILE, JR
Son of former DiMeo/Soprano
boss, Jackie Aprile, Sr., best friend
of Tony Soprano. College student
at Rutgers until a month before
murder, cheated on test, then
flunked out. Killed in Boonton
Projects in what police report
called a drug deal gone awry. Not
so sure. We believe Jackie, Jr. was
hiding out in projects after the
Pontecorvo robbery and they found
him. Order had to come from Ralph
Cifaretto, who just happens to live
with kid's mom, Rosalie Aprile. Kid
also known to be dating Tony
Soprano's daughter, Meadow. Ralph
couldn't order hit without Tony's
okay, so in essence Tony killed his
best friend's kid. What a dark universe.

A drug hit?

RALPH CIFARETTO

Ralph Cifaretto, age 44, is the captain of the Soprano crew once run by the late Gigi Cestone and before that Richie Aprile, now disappeared and believed dead. After Aprile vanished, Cifaretto magically reappeared from a lengthy vacation in Miami; by all accounts he's a sly opportunist and skilled at playing one associate against another. He grew up in the area and went to school two years ahead of Tony Soprano. He dropped out of high school reportedly to take care of his ailing mother, but the rumor is that he quit to avoid prosecution in the mysterious drowning death of a girlfriend. He's currently a suspect in the disappearance of stripper Tracee, a former goomar. Formerly married with two known sons, he is now living with Rosalie Aprile, widow of ex-boss Jackie Aprile and mother of the late Jackie Aprile, Jr. Considered by all to be an exceptionally good earner in extortion, carting, and the recently announced Riverfront Esplanade building project.

WEAKNESSES: Extremely short fuse and affinity for mayhem. Also, he has a dyspeptic sense of humor and is actively disliked by many Soprano associates, not the least of whom is Tony himself.

BOBBY "BACALA" BACCILIERI, JR.

Bobby "Bacala" Baccilieri, age unknown, is a very trusted soldier in the family, reporting directly to titular boss Corrado "Junior" Soprano. Married with children, he's by all accounts an extremely shy, soft-spoken, sensitive man, a kind of 300+ lb. "Gentle Giant," the total opposite of someone like Ralph Cifaretto. He functions full-time as Junior's "goombah-de-camp" during Junior's house arrest for health problems. Bacala is the son of Robert Baccilieri, Sr., a lifelong Soprano associate who recently died of a massive stroke after what police believe was a double hit approved by Tony Soprano. Bacala, Jr. is certainly capable of malice, but you wouldn't know it if you met him at a bar. He's the kind of guy you'd ask to play Santa Claus if he wasn't too shy to accept.

WEAKNESSES: Inability to stay cool under pressure and given to loss of emotional control. He is loyal to the core, but in the right state of emotional confusion, he might inadvertently reveal family secrets.

JOHN "JOHNNY SACK" SACRIMONI

Johnny Sack, a longtime business ally of the DiMeo/Soprano family, works largely out of our district. He is New York based and, we believe, reports to a Carmine Lupertazzi, but we are unsure of the exact New York family connection. Sack's wife, Ginny, is a former professional dancer but now suffers from a weight problem. Sack appears to be an emissary between the Sopranos and New York and is believed involved with Tony Soprano, Ralph Cifaretto, and others in industrywide corruption activities surrounding the announced Riverfront Esplanade project and the Museum of Science and Trucking. The Sacks recently purchased a palatial estate in Essex County but still maintain a residence in New York. Is Sack moving in on traditional Soprano territory? Time will tell.

WEAKNESSES: Hard to spot any. A supremely skilled and shrewd operator, adept at exploiting the Sopranos without offending them. His Achilles' heel could be his wife. Obesity invites diabetes and other health problems. If she's sick, he'll probably want to be with her and not up the river, which may be grounds for cooperation.

OFFICE MEMORANDUM

UNITED STATES GOVERNMENT

TO: ALL PERSONNEL
FR: █████████
RE: HAVE YOU SEEN THIS MAN?

Missing: Ralph Cifaretto, age 45, West Orange, NJ, a captain in NJ DiMeo/Soprano crime family. Last contact at West Orange home on █████████████████ via phone call with Aqueduct horse trainer Lois Pettit re the death by fire of Cifaretto-owned horse, name: Pie-O-My. The mob line is that he went into the program. Truth: negative. If alive, either in the wind or placed in hiding by boss Tony Soprano or others. Stakeouts at home, Morris Plains Med Center where son is recovering from brain damage, homes of ex-girlfriends Rosalie Aprile and Janice Soprano, and usual Soprano haunts. Also Miami. Cifaretto is armed, dangerous, and borderline wacko.

Any information concerning the whereabouts of Ralph Cifaretto, please contact agent █████████ at the Newark office.

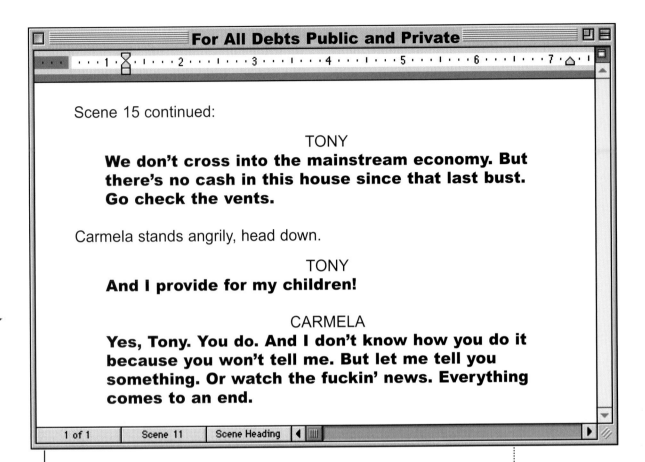

Scene 15 continued:

> TONY
>
> **We don't cross into the mainstream economy. But there's no cash in this house since that last bust. Go check the vents.**

Carmela stands angrily, head down.

> TONY
>
> **And I provide for my children!**

> CARMELA
>
> **Yes, Tony. You do. And I don't know how you do it because you won't tell me. But let me tell you something. Or watch the fuckin' news. Everything comes to an end.**

| 1 of 1 | Scene 11 | Scene Heading |

For All Debts Public and Private

Written by David Chase. Directed by Allen Coulter.

In a post-9/11 world, Carmela is worried about money and security, Junior is worried about his trial, Bacala is worried about Nostradamus, and Tony is worried about everything. As Tony hides cash, Chris kills a newly retired cop and Junior gets bamboozled by an undercover nurse.

Carmela starts the day by reading to a bored AJ that in Italy, "influence peddling is not a crime," as Tony takes his morning stroll to retrieve the paper. Across town Special Agent Deborah Ciccerone-Waldrup, a.k.a. "Danielle Ciccolella," primps for another rendezvous with Adriana. A begrudging Chris drives Tony to meet Junior at Dr. Shreck's while Uncle Junior flirts with a fetching nurse 40 years younger. His trial about to start, Junior needs money—"The fuckin' lawyers are taking my internal organs." Tony balks. Carmela sees Angie Bonpensiero at the market hawking kielbasa and she freaks. Chris comes home to Adriana and her good friend "Danielle," then shoots up and whines about a petulant Tony. While Tony tries to watch *Rio Bravo*, Carmela hassles him about future finances. "I'm talking about some simple estate planning,

Tony, that's all." Later a frustrated Tony attacks Georgie the barkeep for wasting ice, then tells a gathering of capos that he's "depressed and ashamed" about "the zero growth in this family's receipts."

Tony stashes some cash in the pool house, then suffers through a dinner with bigmouthed Ralph, a depressed Ro, and deadly dull grandpa Hugh: "I was stationed in Nova Scotia but I'd caught diverticulitis..." Adriana pops up with "Danielle," and while Danielle is shown around Tony's home, Janice snorts coke and goes down on Ralphie in the bathroom. Zellman gives Tony a real estate idea while Junior coos at the nurse and decides to move Bobby Bacala up a notch. Tony hides more dough in the duck feed as Paulie Walnuts, in an orange jumpsuit, calls Johnny Sack from a Youngstown, Ohio, jail. He got picked up on a gun charge while driving out to Dean Martin's home in Steubenville. Tony has an Esplanade confab with Carmine and some Icelandic stewardesses. He suddenly grabs Chris, drags him to a Clifton restaurant, and points out retired cop Barry Haydu, the man who Tony says killed Chris's dad, Dickie Moltisanti. Chris gets the picture as Tony splits with Bacala. Meanwhile, Junior finds out about a mole at Dr. Schreck's — the nurse.

Chris ambushes Haydu at his beach house. Haydu denies all knowledge of the Dickie hit and says Chris is being set up. Chris kills him anyway. Tony and Bacala have a long late-night chat about Nostradamus and Notre Dame. "I always thought: okay, hunchback of Notre Dame. But you also got a quarterback and a halfback of Notre Dame..." They arrive at Junior's, where they console a sad and distraught Junior about the nurse/informant. "Young cooze smiled at me and birds started chirping." Tony, in a two-faced gesture, agrees to buy some of Junior's distressed real estate to feed him some cash. With Melfi, Tony says that if he wants to live to be ninety, he has to rely on family in the business, i.e., Christopher. Chris visits his mom and leaves her with her Bailey's and Haydu's last $20 bill.

*Written by
Terence Winter
and David Chase.
Directed by
John Patterson.*

No-Show

Chris becomes an acting capo and blows it, Meadow decides to go to Europe and visits a New Age therapist, Adriana is brought in by the FBI and loses her lunch, and Tony must stomach the unpleasant fact that his sister is shacking up with Ralphie.

Undercover agent "Danielle" makes plans with Adriana. When Meadow wakes up at two in the afternoon, Carmela raises the roof about her lazy, jobless state all summer. Meadow's defense is "twelve credits two semesters in a row" and Jackie, Jr.'s death. After Carmela points out that Meadow's reading load is Mary Higgins Clark, friend Misty arrives and they hit the pool. Furio announces to Carmela that he's buying a house in Nutley.

At a big bash, Ralph pops a fateful joke: "Hey, speakin' of 98 pounds, I heard Ginny Sack is gettin' a 95-pound mole taken off her ass!" It gets a huge laugh. Little Paulie and

Patsy bicker with Ralph over free carpentry jobs for Paulie. Silvio settles it, then announces that Chris is being made acting capo, much to Patsy's chagrin. At the Crazy Horse, Adriana confesses to Danielle that she may be unable to conceive. Chris arrives with coke and an emerald bracelet for Adriana. As Tony walks in on Janice and her new beau Ralph watching *Faces of Death*, Little Paulie visits Paulie in Youngstown and repeats the Ginny Sack joke. Paulie doesn't laugh.

At the job site, Chris, a "no show," visits with the boys who are "no works" and gives Patsy a nod to steal high-priced fiber-optic cable. Tony tells Melfi about the Carmela-Meadow schism; Melfi sympathizes with Meadow and suggests a shrink, Dr. Wendi Kobler, for the grief-stricken coed. Meadow drops a bombshell on her mom: She's taking the year off, going to Europe with Misty. Tony yells at Chris about the cable theft while Ralph waxes to Vito about Janice's "earthy quality." Tony's reaction to Meadow's trip: "There is no fuckin' way she's going to Europe."

Chris shoots up, tells Adriana that Danielle is a dyke, then wails on Patsy about the stolen cable. Meadow says her trip is all about hanging out with Dogma and "the restorative nature of travel." Tony flip-flops and gives his consent; Carmela steams, then decides to call Dr. Wendi Kobler. Meadow and Dr. Kobler tuck legs together. After asking Meadow if her parents ever molested her, "Wendi" tells her to "blow off their self-esteem issues" and go abroad.

Silvio worries about Patsy feeling "marginalized" (and really means himself) as Chris tries to strike up a threesome with Adriana and Danielle, then sweet talks a teary Ade by blaming it on Danielle. Silvio approves another theft at the site. Janice thinks Tony is trying to sabotage her happiness with Ralph. Danielle/Deborah gets the f-off message from Adriana. The FBI decides it's time to bring Adriana in.

On the golf course, Esplanade contractor Jack Massarone whines to Tony about the new theft of floor tiles. Down at the site, Chris attacks Patsy for disobeying his orders. Patsy blames Silvio, then smashes the skull of a fellow laborer. After Tony hears that "Wendi" approved the Europe trip, he wants to "take Melfi's head and crush it like a fucking walnut"; Carmela feels "battered." When Meadow refers to Tony as "Mr. Mob Boss," Tony reacts with rage. "You got something you want to say to me?" Meadow blinks

first, but still claims she's leaving. Tony: "I'm warning you—do not do it."

The FBI brings Adriana into a room and offers her a way out—not a wire, not testimony, just information. The price for saying no? A coke charge worth 25 years in prison. After Agent Harris reminds her that she brought Deborah into Tony's home "during Sunday dinner," Adriana lets loose with an *Exorcist*-size stream of vomit. Deborah doesn't blink as she sees puke dripping down Adriana's new bracelet.

In his basement, Tony accuses Silvio of defying him re the tile incident. "You're gettin' to be a very strange man in your old age." They reach a rap-

prochement, and Silvio cuts him in on the take. Ralphie cuts his toenails in Janice's bed as Meadow, back at school, signs up for "Morality, Self, and Society." Tony and Carmela share a final moment of mutual guilt.

Christopher

Teleplay by Michael Imperioli. Story by Michael Imperioli and Maria Laurino. Directed by Tim Van Patten.

Columbus Day excites ethnic passions; Tony and friends defend their Italian hero as activist Del Redclay et al. rip him to shreds. Karen Baccilieri dies in a car crash, breaking Bobby's heart, and Janice shifts her mercurial affections from a kinky Ralph to a grieving Bacala.

The boys down at the Pork Store, wasting time betting on out-of-state license plates, are apoplectic over planned Native American protests of their beloved Columbus Day. Bacala sums up their feelings about them: "I wouldn't mind sitting on my ass all day smoking mushrooms and collecting a government check." Silvio calls it "anti-Italian discrimination." Furio, on the other hand, doesn't like Columbus. Why? He was from Genoa.

Carmela and the other wives work out at the Flamingo Fitness Center, sign on to a luncheon down at the church, and discuss Furio's ponytail. Janice, deep in the covers under Ralph during sex, calls him "Mama's little tramp." Paulie phones Johnny Sack and relays the Ginny joke. Johnny busts Tony's chops about the under-the-table deal on Frelinghuysen Ave. A chummy Carmela and Furio watch *Montel* as Del Redclay and Phil Di Notti debate whether Columbus was the Great One or "a genocidal colonial general." Tony walks in, looking a "little moosha-moosh" because of Uncle Jun's trial. Down at federal court, Junior whines about phone charges on his legal bills while his life is being adjudicated.

Concetta Longo-Murphy, the ladies luncheon speaker at Saints Peter and Paul, rails about the gangster image of Italians, a slap in Carmela's face. Father Phil tries to soften the point, but Gabby, ready to "cut him a new one," tells him to remember who pays for his church. All hell breaks loose at a Columbus Park protest when Patsy rips down a "murderer" effigy of Columbus while Little Paulie gets hit with a thrown bottle and Artie with a milkshake. Carmela and friends say good-bye to Karen Baccilieri in the church parking lot. Bacala is stuck in traffic, not knowing that his wife has just been killed in a car wreck up ahead. Carmela hears the awful news from Gabby.

As the news of Karen's death spreads, Tony promises Silvio he'll do something about the Columbus protests; he calls Zellman, who claims that his "hands are tied on this one." Janice meets with her own therapist, earth mother Sandy Shaw, where Janice says her problem with men stems from her childhood, when she was "shamed and ridiculed for being artistic." Ralph drops by Rutgers to assault Professor Redclay with a poster of Iron Eyes Cody, "a second-generation Sigilian' from Louisiana named Espera DeCorti!" Redclay's graduate assistant tells him it's bunk.

Carmela and Tony react bitterly to the news that AJ, reading Howard Zinn's *A People's History of the United States*, has a teacher who thinks Columbus is a war criminal like Slobodan Milosevic. Tony: "In this house Christopher Columbus is a hero! End of story!" As Ralph buys the racehorse Pie-O-My, Hesh weighs in on the controversy by kicking a Cuban off his property for comparing Columbus to Hitler, then agrees to put Tony in touch with "a big Mohonk."

At the funeral home, Bacala, the only one of the Soprano crew without a goomar, is devastated by the loss of his wife. The women mourn while Johnny Sack gives Ralph the cold shoulder, and Tony wonders who's feeding information to Johnny and Carmine. Later Ralph tells Rosalie that he can't handle her pain and leaves.

While Carmela comforts Bobby Bacala, an insensitive Junior calls up and wonders if he's going to take him to court the next day. Speaking of sensitive, Ralph grinds against Janice and announces that "now there can be no guilt, no fear, just sex." At Nuovo Vesuvio, Tony meets Chief Doug Smith, casino owner and big talker who promises Tony that there will be no more protests. Bacala breaks down in front of Janice—"I should've been there to help her...my sweet Karen. My sweet girl." Janice is deeply moved. Chief Doug calls Tony to say that he struck out with Redclay, while Sandy the shrink tells Janice she must "speak the truth" to Ralph, then dump him. Janice gets it: "Somehow I have to move away from darkness and toward light."

At Chief Doug's Indian casino, Tony announces his grandmother was in the "Fugahwe" tribe, i.e., lost nomads who were always saying "Where the Fugahwe?" Melfi and her ex-husband, Richard, watch the protests unfold. With a new prospect in sight, Janice shoves Ralph down the stairs and tells him to get out. Tony is pissed that Chief Doug only wanted an in to Frankie Valli and sums up the whole Columbus question in an argument with Silvio on the ride home. "Where's our self-esteem?" he asks. "It don't come from Columbus or the Godfather or fuckin' Chef Boyardee!" Silvio is not convinced but clearly beaten.

Written by
Terence Winter.
Directed by Jack Bender.

The Weight

Johnny Sack is ready to kill Ralphie over dissing his wife, and Tony calls in some decrepit old gangsters from Rhode Island to kill Johnny. Meadow volunteers at a poverty law center while Furio throws a housewarming party and dances even further into Carmela's heart.

Outside of a Mulberry Street hangout, Johnny Sack, still fixated on the Ginny joke, pummels a Ralphie crew member, Donny K, then urinates on his head. As Johnny heads home to his beloved Ginny, Tony suffers through cousin Brian Cammarata's spiel on "a growth-oriented relocation of your assets," then hears about the Donny K beating. Tony berates Johnny about this senseless act; Johnny blames it all on Ralph's sick joke about his wife's weight problem. "That woman is my life." Tony asks Johnny to hear Ralphie out; Johnny promises to send Donny's mom something nice.

Furio drinks coffee with Carmela and announces that "I make a party for the housewarm." Meadow sparks to a South Bronx Poverty Law Center speech at school while Tony and crew spin conspiracy theories about "who's writing the family gossip column" and feeding it to Johnny Sack. Chris: "Silvio talking to Johnny? You never know, T." Melfi talks to Dr. Elliot Kupferberg about the erratic behavior of her son, Jason. Ralph returns from Florida and is pressed by Tony to placate Johnny. Ralph tells Johnny he didn't make the joke, then apologizes for making the joke, undercutting his whole defense. Johnny asks Carmine to sanction a hit on Ralph for "violating my wife's honor." Carmine, not surprisingly, says no.

Tony drops by school to annoy Meadow about "defendin' fare beaters" down at the poverty center and bumps into Elliot Kupferberg in the parking lot. Tony and Ralph have a sit-down with Carmine and Johnny but Johnny walks out. Tony and Carmela argue

over who between them equates love with money. On speakerphone, Junior tries to settle the fat joke issue, but in the face of Johnny's recalcitrance, everyone gets mad. Carmine tells Johnny, "Get the fuck over it," then later calls Tony to tell him in mobspeak that Johnny is expendable. Tony sends Ralph back to Miami, then consults with Junior about disappearing Johnny. Junior suggests ancient hit man Lou DiMaggio and the Atwell Avenue Boys in Providence. They call him DiMaggio "after the cops found Lenny and his wife with their heads bashed in by a baseball bat."

In Providence, Chris and Silvio explain the hit to a sightless Lou and his ghoulish, sans-a-belt wearing crew and make a quick exit. At home, Johnny Sack has a short chat with soldier Joe Peeps about wasting Ralph in Miami, then leaves his home. Carmela drags AJ over to Furio's new house.

Having forgotten his jacket, Johnny returns home to find Ginny in the basement, gorging on Twix bars and Fig Newtons. Ginny: "I was having low blood sugar." He blows up, then embraces her, sobbing. At Miami's Del Ray Hotel, Ralph is about to get whacked in the elevator when Joe Peeps calls it off via cell phone.

At Furio's housewarming, AJ locks Bobby, Jr. in the garage while Furio dances a sensuous tango-cum-flamenco with Carmela. Melfi confesses to Kupferberg that she still feels guilty about her rape. Johnny Sack announces he is ready to accept Ralph's apology, and Tony calls off Lou and the boys. Later in the bedroom, Tony offers up flowers and a new dress to Carmela, then proceeds to make love to her as she stares at the ceiling, her mind still dancing with Furio.

Pie-O-My

Written by Robin Green & Mitchell Burgess. Directed by Henry J. Bronchtein.

The Feds get cozy with Adriana, Janice tries to resuscitate a brokenhearted Bacala, and Tony falls in love with a beautiful racehorse, Pie-O-My, and makes a late-night trip to the stables to save her.

Alternative band No Soap Radio wraps its set at Crazy Horse as Tony and Silvio drop by; a paranoid Adriana thinks she hears Tony say something about "an FBI informant." Tony splits and Silvio joins Chris and Furio in the cellar to literally beat the piss out of Joey Cogo. As Janice watches JoJo Palmice make nice to Bobby Bacala next door, Adriana gets a call from Agent Deborah to meet the Feds at a distant bakery. Janice barges in on JoJo and Bacala in his kitchen, then acts like Mother Teresa as Bobby falls apart at the sight of Karen's last baked ziti. At the bakery, a distraught Ade is grilled by Agents Harris and Deborah and by new agent Robyn Sanseverino about Chris's movements and missing mobsters Big Pussy and Uncle Richie, neither in the Program. Deborah splits, leaving Ade in Robyn's hands.

Tony turns down Carmela's request for $10K to buy stock, then pockets a wad of cash from a birdfeed bag. Tony, his accountant, Ginsberg, Silvio, and others join Ralph at the track stables as he shows off his horse, Pie-O-My, trained by Lois Pettit and about to race. Janice slips JoJo's

chicken marsala to Junior as the old man gripes about Murf's driving—"...like a little old lady. Gas, brake, gas, brake." Accountant Ginsberg advises Tony not to set up an irrevocable trust, then Pie-O-My comes from way back in a race to win. As Inez Munoz, Ralph's maid and Pie-O-My's paper owner, gets her picture snapped, Ralph passes out money and champagne in the winner's circle, and Tony goes home and counts out his take to Carmela. He agrees to sign all the estate papers but not the main document, the family trust. Carmela is not happy.

Adriana fakes the flu to avoid dinner with Tony. A motherly Janice fixes someone else's casserole for Bacala and the kids, then tells Bobby she had "both barrels of a shotgun" in her mouth when her husband left, but carried on for the sake of son Harpo, and now Bacala has to do the same. The next race for Pie-O-My is a stakes race, and Ralph asks Tony how to run it. As Ralph, Tony, and cousin Brian the broker watch, the horse wins straight up. Ralph feeds Tony's wallet, due to his "horse wisdom." Tony is now ready to give Carmela the stock money, but it's too late. Down at Dorley's Lounge, Bacala is back at work, strong-arming a local shop steward.

As Chris wanders in at dawn, Adriana fries him eggs and pleads that they should quit this life and take off together, which Chris dismisses as "fuckin' negative shit." Ralph and crew decide to use Crazy Horse as a clubhouse, and Fat Vito breaks a chair. Back from court, Junior grumbles about his courtroom sketch rendering on TV. Bacala walks in, says he's back on the case, and sings Janice's praises. Adriana complains to Chris about the gangsters hanging around the club, then goes down in Vito's broken chair. Bobby joins Junior in court as Junior stares down the courtroom sketch artist. Under pressure, Ade gives the Feds a small tidbit that Patsy buys suits in White Plains. Back home, Bobby is still not ready to eat Karen's last ziti.

After a business confab with Tony at the Crazy Horse, Ralph gets a late-night call from Inez that the horse is sick and the vets won't intervene unless Ralph pays his bill. Tony gets the call and takes off to help the horse. Adriana shoots up as Tony pays the vet, then sits on a feed bucket next to Pie-O-My as the horse lies quietly in her stall.

Everybody Hurts

Written by Michael Imperioli. Directed by Steve Buscemi.

Tony tells Chris he's the man, Artie makes a bad loan and tries to kill himself, Tony becomes enraged upon hearing that Gloria did kill herself, and AJ discovers that his girlfriend Devin is richer than Croesus's daughter.

Nodding out with Adriana, Chris gets an urgent call from Tony. AJ's friends, including girlfriend Devin Pillsbury, pepper him with questions about his dad. At a late-night rendezvous, Tony tells Chris that he needs to limit his exposure and will start giving orders through Chris. "You're going to take this family into the twenty-first century." AJ takes his "crew" by the Pork Store, confusing it with the Bada Bing. In the bedroom, Carmela conjures up a potential blind date for a lonely Furio, then casually drops the news that Gloria Trillo committed suicide: "Hung herself." Tony reels. At Nuovo Vesuvio, Artie is approached by Jean-Philippe, brother of hostess Elodi, for "a bridge loan" of $50K for the North American rights to Domaine Vezelay Armagnac, "the new vodka." Artie says yes for a 7.5 percent fee. Charmaine tells Artie to get Tony to pay his $6K tab.

While Tony inquires about Gloria down at Globe Motors, Ralph turns down Artie's loan request, because Ralph won't be able to hurt Artie if he reneges. Tony assaults Melfi about Gloria—"Why the fuck didn't you help her?"—then turns the blame on himself. At Artie's bachelor pad, Tony is upset that Artie went to Ralph first—"What am I, a toxic person?"—then insists on loaning his old friend the $50K. That night Tony has a disturbing dream in which Gloria serves him dinner wearing a six-foot-long scarf around

her neck. Plaster flakes fall from the ceiling into his drink and Gloria begins to remove the scarf. He wakes up, shaken.

In the presence of cousin Brian, Tony happily signs the Soprano family living trust papers, much to Carmela's relief, then offers Brian a deal on suits. Artie hands the loan money to Jean-Philippe. Lovebirds AJ and Devin are interrupted by Carmela, so they take off to the city in a Town Car. They end up at the poverty center where Meadow works in the South Bronx, and she refuses to loan them her apartment. They then drive around Manhattan, weighing the differences between the rich and the poor. Artie is getting

worried—Jean-Philippe is avoiding him.

At the health club, Adriana tells Carmela that she and Chris can't make the Billy Joel concert. Tony treats Janice to dinner at Nuovo Vesuvio to ask her about dealing with suicide. In the bathroom, he advises Artie "to get your arms around this thing" regarding Jean-Philippe. Artie practices talking tough in a mirror, then confronts Jean-Philippe, who says the money's gone and he's not paying it back. They fight and Jean-Philippe rips out Artie's earring and kicks him out. AJ takes a drive up to Devin's *Godfather*-like mansion. Artie gulps down a bottle of Armagnac, takes a handful of pills to kill himself, then interrupts Tony's lovemaking to announce his demise. Tony calls 911. Admiring the family Picassos, AJ feels stupid comparing his wealth to Devin's, but she doesn't care—she likes him.

In the ER, Tony agrees to assume the $50K debt in exchange for the cancellation of his $6K tab at the restaurant. Artie accuses Tony of seeing "twenty moves down the road" and maneuvering for free food. Tony, disgusted, makes up a mugging cover story for Artie's attempted suicide and leaves.

After the Billy Joel concert, Tony regales his dinner guests at Nuovo Vesuvio about the night he decided to marry Carmela, while Carmela watches Furio and his date coo. Brian, in a new Tony-connected suit, toasts his host. Tony tells Melfi the Artie story, then says he'll make a donation to the suicide hotline in Gloria's

name and "the hell with both of 'em." As Furio knocks on Jean-Philippe's door, AJ's friends crown him "the Pillsbury dough boy."

Watching Too Much Television

Teleplay by Terence Winter and Nick Santora. Story by David Chase & Robin Green & Mitchell Burgess & Terence Winter. Directed by John Patterson.

Paulie is back from prison but not happy with how he's being treated by Tony. Tony hooks up Zellman and a Newark insider to pull off a lucrative HUD scam. After much hand-wringing, Chris pops the question to Adriana, and Tony belt-whips Zellman for banging Irina.

"Whadaya hear, whadaya say?" Paulie announces to his cronies at the Bing after four months in a Youngstown jail. Silvio plays Paulie's favorite Frank tune, "Nancy (With the Laughing Face)." As Tony hands him a fistful of cash, Paulie whines about not getting "a boost" while incarcerated. Across town, a light goes off in Adriana's head as she watches a rerun of *Murder One*. After Tony awakens him from an all-nighter, Brian fills Tony and Ralph in on a real estate scam he cooked up in college involving HUD, a non-profit front man, and distressed ghetto property. Tony and Ralph are all ears.

Taking a group schvitz, Assemblyman Zellman introduces Tony and Ralph to his old University of Michigan buddy, urban activist Maurice Tiffen. Out front, Furio calls Carmela to flirt. While Ralph and Maurice plot out the HUD sting, Zellman tells Tony that he's banging Irina. Tony: "I wish you nothing but the best, Ron." Dr. Fried gets the HUD ball rolling by buying property at 25 Garside in Newark to sell to Maurice at an inflated price.

Adriana's new best friend, FBI agent Robyn, accosts her in a card store, where Ade hints of marriage to Chris. Tony takes AJ on a nostalgic trip to the old neighborhood to see the church his great-grandfather helped build. He imparts some sage advice: "Buy land. 'Cause God ain't makin' any more of it." As he points out the row houses involved in the HUD deal,

Angelo the crack merchant and his wasted sister Mecomia tell them to keep their "cracker ass" off their block.

Cubitoso and his FBI team gather and decide it may be to their advantage if Adriana marries Chris. Maurice gets the money from HUD to pay Dr. Fried and Tony drops by Zellman's to complain about the crack squatters who are in the way of $7K worth of copper piping. Unfortunately, Irina is with Zellman.

Adriana suggests to Chris that they get married, then delivers the heartbreaking news that years ago her uterus was pierced. "Both of them?" he asks. He then calls her "damaged goods" and storms out. Tony and Silvio advise Chris to get married so that he doesn't end up like Uncle Junior or worse, Paulie. While Chris shoots up yet again, Zellman leans on Maurice about offing the crackheads. Melfi chides Tony for his unacceptable behavior after the Gloria news. Tony's comeback is that he has been controlling his anger and anyway, he was still mad about "that half-assed adolescent shrink" that she recommended for Meadow. A wasted Chris returns to a tearful Ade and sets a date. "Soon, next month." Carmela is the first person Ade tells. "I'm getting married!"

Down on Garside Street, a group of Maurice's young vigilantes lay waste to the crackheads with Uzis and baseball bats, shooting Angelo in the groin. Dr. Fried gets the $1.3 mil for the property from Maurice, thanks to his HUD loan, and cousin Brian gets a $15K Patek Philippe for his grand scheme. Carmela has a strange front door encounter with a smitten Furio. Paulie whines to Johnny Sack that Tony is treating him "like the ugly girl at the dance" and spills the beans about the HUD scam. Zellman drops by the property to watch Tony extract copper pipe. Adriana buys a $2,800 wedding dress, then turns to Stan Gurman at 1-800-LAW-4-YOU to hear that she is still vulnerable to forced testimony.

As Silvio splits the proceeds with all HUD parties at the Bing, Tony toasts the federal government, and Maurice and Zellman share regrets about becoming low-rent sell-outs. "The revolution got sold." At a guidette bridal shower, a distracted Adriana gets a cappuccino maker from Janice and a toaster oven from Gabby. Tony drops by Zellman's and belt-whips him for screwing his old girlfriend. So much for his anger management program.

Mergers and Acquisitions

Tony gets a hot new goomar, Valentina, who tells him about Ralph's sick side; Paulie moves Nucci into Green Grove, where she is dissed by old friends; and Carmela discovers a telltale fingernail and steals grudge money from Tony's stash.

Furio returns to Naples to see his dying father. After talking colostomy bags with Paulie, Tony barks orders to a groggy Chris, who takes notes on a pillowcase. Tony and Carmela join cousin Brian and his wife for dinner at Nuovo Vesuvio, where Brian almost leaks the HUD scam and Carmela sees that Brian is now part of Tony's circle.

At a church diaper drive, Carmela complains to Rosalie about Tony's way with money, though he did go halfway on the trust. Tony watches Pie-O-My getting shoed as Ralph arrives with new girlfriend, Valentina La Paz, a woman whose idea of fun is getting Ralph

Teleplay by Lawrence Konner. Story by David Chase & Robin Green & Mitchell Burgess & Terence Winter. Directed by Daniel Attias.

to step in a pile of manure. While Ralph hoses down his shoes, Valentina suggests a horse painting and Tony eyes the half-Italian, half-Cuban beauty. Tony: "...a dangerous combination."

Paulie moves his mom into Green Grove, which she considers "a palazzo." Old pals Cookie Cirillo and Minn' Matrone pop up and as Nucci darts into the WC, they tell Paulie

that she can't sit with them in the dining room. Tony tries out his new monster media room, then gets bored and meets Valentina at a studio to order up a painting of Pie-O-My and himself. He pays the $6,500 in cash and moments later is both banging Valentina and suffering one of her jokes, the trick salt shaker bit. Afterward, he buys a diamond pin to blow her off. At Green Grove, Cookie disses Nucci over a game of blackjack. Later Tony pulls a prank on Carmela—a glass of cold water in the shower—that falls flat.

Paulie pays a visit to Cookie's son, high school principal Charles Cirillo, to ask him to intercede on Nucci's behalf. Carmela finds Valentina's lost fingernail in Tony's wash. Tony is yelling at Silvio and Chris about a business screwup in North Amboy when in walks Ralph and Valentina. In the back, Valentina returns the "consolation prize" pin to Tony and asks why he's dumping her. Tony: "I don't like to be where Ralph Cifaretto has been." Valentina tells him no worry, Ralph is "some kind of freak." At home Carmela tries to smash open the duck feeder and fails.

The next day Valentina follows up with graphic details about Ralph's peccadilloes: hot candle wax, rubbing him with a cheese grater, etc. "Ralph is loco." Tony asks Melfi about a freak like Ralph. She explains the condition of "paraphilia" in which pain and humiliation is a form of sexual release. Tony wonders that if a guy acts like that, is a girl really his girlfriend? Melfi won't answer.

While Tony showers, Carmela steals his keys, opens the feeder, and helps herself to the cash. Nucci is now bedridden over her social rejection. "They keep making me eat alone." At his father's funeral in Naples, Furio confides in his uncle Maurizio about his love for "the don's wife." Maurizio's reply: "The only way you can have her is if you kill the man." At home Carmela zones out, imagining a dance of love with Furio. Ralph brags about his exploits with

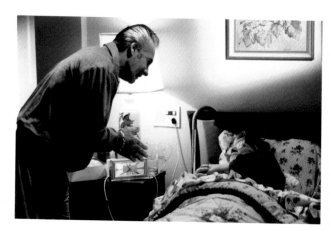

Valentina while Tony asks about his mother. Back at Green Grove, described by the director as "high school with wheelchairs," she tells Paulie that Nucci is a crybaby, a tattletale, and doesn't always put her teeth in.

Tony agrees to meet with Valentina. To send a message to Cookie that she should be nicer to Nucci, Benny and Little Paulie chase her son Charles through the halls of Bergen North High. Valentina announces her split from Ralph, then stomps out after Tony blows her off again. Carmela opens up brokerage accounts all over town. Tony engages in what Janice considers an "insulting" conversation about Ralph's sex habits, but for $3K she tells all. Tony jumps back in bed with Valentina. At home he discovers the missing money. Charles and his wife tell Cookie to shape up or move out. As Tony dresses the next morning, he sees the lost nail in plain sight. At breakfast, he asks if anyone's been in the backyard. As he hangs back, arms crossed, Carmela asks, "You sure, Tony, there's not something you want to talk about?" Tony: "No. Like what?"

Whoever Did This

Written by
Robin Green
& Mitchell Burgess.
Directed by
Tim Van Patten.

Junior takes a hard fall and develops a crazy act. Ralph's son is injured by an arrow, sending Ralph into a spiritual tailspin. A suspicious fire kills Pie-O-My, leading an irate Tony to confront and ultimately kill Ralph. Tony and Chris cut up Ralph and bury the remains.

Grousing about missing the early bird special after another long day in court, Junior is distracted by a foxy reporter, gets hit in the head with a sound boom, and tumbles down the courthouse steps. Tony takes Carmela to the stables to meet Lois the trainer and Pie-O-My, or "Lady Pie," whom Carmela pronounces "magnificent." Dr. Wong at Saint Erasmus tells Tony that Junior's concussion could have played into already-existing dementia. Ralph, sure that it was Paulie who ratted him out regarding "Shamu's fat ass," makes a crank call to Nucci to tell her Paulie was caught pleasuring a Cub Scout, with "a small rodent in his rectal passage."

Visiting a recovered Junior, Tony says the magic word: mistrial. While playing in the park with his friend, Ralph's son, Justin, is struck by an arrow in the chest, cutting off oxygen to his brain. At Morris Plains Medical Center, Ralph, supposedly in charge of Justin, is confronted by his ex-wife, Ronnie, and her husband, Dennis. A wrestling match ensues, Tony breaks it up, Ralph breaks down. At the other hospital, lawyer Melvoin details the dementia game. "All you gotta do is act oobatz," says Tony to Junior. In Jason's room, Ralph and Rosalie Aprile make up over the boy's comatose body.

Eating at Nuovo Vesuvio, Carmela and Rosalie agree that both Ralph and Artie should go see Father Phil. Being prepped by Bobby back home, Junior is not happy having to play "a 'shcumpari," or drooling idiot. The one-legged Svetlana arrives with Branca, a nurse for Junior. At the door Svetlana disses the leg-stealing Janice: "You are boring woman." Ralph confesses to Father Phil that his son is paying for Ralph's own sins. Phil tells him "to get yourself right with God." Ralph seems deeply

affected by the priest's prayer.

At breakfast Carmela tells Tony that Ralph set up a scholarship in Jackie, Jr.'s name and asked Rosalie to marry him. Tony wrestles with AJ, then watches Ralph break down again at the Bing, mentioning in passing that he's now dating Valentina. Paulie enters as Ralph leaves, enraged about the crank call he's sure that Ralph made to Nucci, now suffering from nervous bowel syndrome. If he finds proof, Paulie says, "He's a fuckin' corpse." Back at Junior's, Melvoin and Agent Grasso watch as a Dr. Zalutsky tests the old man's grasp of reality; Junior, contrary to his own assessment, is not a good actor.

Tony, sleeping with Valentina, gets a call from trainer Lois that there was a stable fire and Pie had to be destroyed because of burns. Tony goes to the track, hears about the fire's cause, and sees the dead horse as it's being dragged away. Tony then drops by Ralph's place to tell him. Ralph: "What sick fuck would do that on purpose?" As Ralph scrambles eggs, Tony alludes to the fact that they just took out a $200K policy on the horse. He then asks Ralph about a local firebug, Corky Ianucci. Ralph says Pie was going downhill, and Tony realizes that Ralph "cooked the horse alive." As Ralph screams, "It's a fuckin' animal!" Tony attacks. In a vicious brawl, Tony has Ralph in a choke hold and Ralph sprays his face with Raid. Ralph tries to break free but can't. Tony chokes him and bangs his head against the floor until Ralph dies. Tony vomits in the sink.

As Chris shoots up, the phone rings. At Tony's beckoning, he staggers into the murder scene. Tony harangues him about his drug problem, then tells him to get a mop and "get him draining." Tony bathes his eyes in Visine. Chris reaches to cut Ralph's head off and pulls off his wig. When they've finished hacking up the body, they watch a little TV and Tony admonishes Chris that "you can't be high on skag and have children." They take Ralph's severed head and hands, stick them in a bowling bag, and head for the quarry.

At the quarry's edge, they throw Ralph's torso in the water, and Chris says, "I hear you, T," regarding the drugs. They hotwire a back hoe and with Tony maneuvering the levers, dig a deep hole in a farmer's field. In goes the telltale bowling bag. Back at the Bing, Tony showers, then nods off from exhaustion. At dawn, with FBI agents watching, Junior wanders outside in his pajamas, ostensibly doing his crazy act but scaring himself in the end.

Tony awakens, wanders through the empty club, and exits into the glaring light of day.

The Strong, Silent Type

Chris sits on Adriana's dog, then gets jacked by junkies and punches his fiancée, all leading to a group intervention and a trip to rehab. Tony plays "the sad clown" over Pie-O-My's death and ends up sleeping with tough gal Svetlana. Furio returns to his unrequited love dance with Carmela. Paulie ends up with a retouched horse painting.

Written by Terence Winter and Robin Green & Mitchell Burgess. Story by David Chase. Directed by Alan Taylor.

Watching *The Little Rascals*, Christopher shoots up for breakfast and sits on Adriana's adorable dog, Cosette. In anticipation of Furio's return, Carmela gets a youthful haircut, to Tony's dismay. "Omigod!" Adriana screams when she discovers her dead dog under her comatose fiancé. She rightfully blames it on Chris's "smack...lifestyle."

The boys shoot pool as Tony feigns another call to Ralph's house. Chris walks in with the painting of Tony and Pie-O-My. Tony unwraps it, quickly exits, then tells Silvio to burn it. As Furio takes a cab from the airport, Albert tells Silvio and Patsy over dinner that he thinks Tony killed Ralph. Furio and Carmela greet awkwardly; Furio cries in the car while Carmela is crushed that he didn't bring her a present from Italy. Tony tells Melfi that the picture of Pie-O-My threw him for a loop, but for the sake of all, he's got to be "the sad

clown," a description that doesn't mesh with the hot-headed wall puncher she's come to know. Tony's solution: more Prozac. Melfi points out Tony's inordinate affection for animals. Tony sees the dead horse and Ralph's brain-damaged son, Jason, as indicative of "what kind of fuckin' toilet world we live in." Then: "My wife prays to God. What kind of God does this shit?"

Agent Robyn pesters Adriana for info, then suggests an intervention regarding Chris's drug problem. Paulie and Silvio wait around for no-show Chris. Meanwhile Chris is in Perth Amboy getting beaten up and dispossessed of his Range Rover and other valuables by punk dope dealers. At dinner, Carmela worries about her mother's skin condition while Tony is preoccupied with Ralph's son and his dead horse. Chris's

skag friend Eddie drags Chris home to Adriana. Ade kicks Eddie out; Chris punches Ade for putting him "on some mailing list for junkies." Paulie saves the horse painting from the ash heap. Ade runs to Carmela and Tony and tells them the whole sad story of Chris's behavior.

Paulie proudly hangs the painting in his house. Carmela drags AJ to an impromptu visit with Furio, where he gives her a bottle of 35-year-old vinegar. Furio confesses he now feels like a man without a country. Tony bumps into one-legged Svetlana at Junior's, where they share a bottle of wine and talk about her remarkable attitude. "There are worse things," says Svetlana. The painting of the boss starts to make Paulie nervous. Rosalie tells Carmela that if she hasn't already slept with Furio, don't. Tony hits upon the name of ex-juicer Dominic Tieri to help with Chris. At Silvio's house, Dominic fills Tony, Adriana, and others in on a formal intervention, or in the parlance, a "carefrontation."

In a brief encounter at the pier, Johnny Sack tries to squeeze Tony regarding the HUD scam; Tony walks away. Paulie asks the portrait artist to replace Tony with Napoleon. Tony announces to a gathering of capos that "it was New York" who offed Ralph, but won't take action until there is a thorough probe. At the big intervention, Adriana starts the ball rolling by announcing that Chris both killed Cosette and can "no longer function as a man." Tony: "I oughta suffocate you, you little prick!" and "I know what it's like to lose a pet." After Paulie tells Chris he's weak and out of control and Chris calls his own mother a whore, Paulie smacks him in the head, leading to a general stomping of Chris by the whole crew.

As Chris gets treated for a hairline skull fracture, Tony reads him the riot act: He's on his way to rehab. "You're goin' in, you're stayin' in." Tony shares a drink with Svetlana, where she nails whiny Americans—"You expect nothing bad ever to happen when the rest of the world expects only bad to happen"—and tells Tony that he is big, strong, and full of life. Passion quickly ensues.

Chris checks in to the Eleuthera House rehab center ("A Place for New Beginnings"). After lovemaking, Svetlana tells Tony it would be too much trouble to continue a relationship. That night, with Carmela out of town, Tony eats alone, a sadder Furio eats alone, and Paulie admires his new, less threatening painting with Tony in full American Revolutionary garb.

Calling All Cars

*Teleplay by
David Chase
& Robin Green
& Mitchell Burgess
and David Flebotte.
Story by David Chase
& Robin Green
& Mitchell Burgess
& Terence Winter.
Directed by
Tim Van Patten.*

Tony has a worm-headed Ralphie dream, a major problem with a recalcitrant Carmine, and continued frustration on the couch. Bobby Bacala, fixated on his dead wife, is coached back to reality by Janice. AJ plays a cruel trick on Bobby's kids, Junior's crazy act is thrown out of court, and in a shocking gesture, Tony walks out on Melfi after four tempestuous years.

An eerie visage: a bald Ralph with a caterpillar on the back of his head. Next to him is a long-haired Carmela driving an old Cadillac like Tony's dad's. In the backseat we see Tony, then Gloria Trillo, then Svetlana, then a butterfly on Ralph's head. It's a dream. Tony wakes up, sweating. With Melfi, he tries to understand this creepy nightmare. "We never seem to get anywhere—kind of like this therapy." Melfi sees a reconciliation going on, centering on Carmela, the driver. Tony says his dad would never let a woman drive his car. Fed up with psychobabble, Tony vents about his poor impulse control. "It leads me to make mistakes at my work." After four years of therapy, he's pissed.

Bacala's daughter, Sophia, discovers a birthday cake for her dead mom in the back of his car. Bacala buries the cake at the gravesite. At a sit-down, Tony again snubs Johnny and Carmine regarding the HUD scam, then walks out at the mention of Ralph. That evening, Janice confronts Bobby about the cake. Bacala says it was their fourteenth anniversary. Janice says "grieving is a process." Tony calls Johnny, makes a lowball offer, and Johnny says, "Not acceptable." Carmine sends a goomba after Vic the appraiser. Sophia tells Bobby, Jr. that she's scared of their mom's ghost and can sometimes smell her hair. He acts tough, then hides under the covers. In a private chat, Johnny tells Paulie that "there could be a change" regarding Tony and that "Carmine won't forget you."

Tony runs into Junior's nurse Branca as he tries to talk about "Plan B" (corrupting a juror) to a worried and distracted Uncle Junior. Janice drops by Carmela's to weasel an invitation to a dinner thrown for Bobby and the kids, though she's worried she's seen as "the harpy coming between him and his dead idealized wife." Tony's appraiser Vic is worked over by Johnny's boys. Tony decides not to go ballistic, then, outside of Paulie's hearing range, asks Silvio to get Beansie to set up a meeting with Little Carmine, Carmine's son in Miami. At the dinner for Bacala, AJ cracks up Bobby, Jr. with his goofy one-liners while Tony gets a call from Beansie that the Miami sit-down is on. Post-meal, AJ and girlfriend Devin are forced to play with Bobby, Jr. and sister Sophia. They decide on the Ouija board. Tony suggests to Silvio that Paulie is the leak. AJ spooks the kids by turning off the lights and conjuring up the faux spirit of seaborne "Captain Jacobus" in a séance, complete with wet sponge. Carmela et al. are mortified by AJ's idea of fun.

Janice tells Bacala that he is guilty of "morbid clinging." Svetlana calls to thank

Tony for the diamond brooch and say good-bye. Tony confesses to Melfi that Svetlana thought he was "high maintenance" and returns to the theme that therapy is a waste of time. "All this fucking self-knowledge. What the fuck's it gotten me?" His verdict: "Pain. Truth—I'm just a fat fuckin' crook from north Jersey." Melfi pleads with him to continue his quest for "what you're really after in your very brief time on this earth," but Tony's had enough. He kisses her on the cheek, then walks out for good. A stunned Melfi calls Kupferberg. "Guess who's no longer a patient of mine? Calling all cars."

The conniving Janice anonymously emails Bobby, Jr. and his sister to go to the Ouija board in their house. Tony arrives in Miami. In federal court, Judge Runions flatly rejects Junior's bogus crazy act and orders the trial resumed. Bacala calls Janice, tells her that the kids are trying to contact their mother. Per Janice's plan, he feels guilty. In a bid to get Bacala to move on, Janice pulls Karen's last ziti from the freezer. Bacala nods okay.

After Beansie and three comely lasses depart, Tony and a dimwitted Little Carmine thrash out the problem. Little Carmine promises to intercede. As Bacala takes a bite of his dead wife's ziti, Tony returns to dreamland. He's now an immigrant Italian laborer approaching a farmhouse. He knocks. "Hello, hello, I'm-a here for masoning." He sees a shrouded figure descending the staircase. He awakens in Miami, again sweating and afraid, then stumbles to the balcony and the dreamy tropical beauty of south Florida.

Eloise

A lovesick Furio takes off for Naples, Tony's problems with Carmine escalate into a work stoppage, Carmela is vehement that Billy Budd isn't gay, one of Junior's jurors is intimidated, and Paulie robs and kills an old lady for cash.

"Corrado Soprano is not some harmless old man," says Junior's prosecutor in his summation, "but a killer who orders up murder like you and I order up coffee." As AJ starts to read his rewritten *Billy Budd* piece for school, Carmela is distracted by Furio. Tony enters with a trip to Paradise Island from which Carmela begs off. In the car, Tony tells the lovesick Furio that "she can be a moody bitch." Little Carmine meets up with his dad and Johnny on the golf course to deal with the Tony debacle but gets nowhere. Carmine thinks of the Sopranos as a "glorified crew." Carmela gives Furio decorating tips for his mother's cottage, then they make a date for Color Tile. "You're a very special woman," he tells her.

While Nucci's friend Minn' pulls her car into the VFW parking lot and Nucci and Cookie rattle on about Julius LaRosa, Minn' smashes into another car. At the Deerpark Casino, Tony stays late to drink and carouse. Paulie arrives at the ER to chastise Minn' and take over the driving chores. "This is my ma we're talkin' about." Carmela arrives at

Written by Terence Winter. Directed by James Hayman.

THE SOPRANOS

Meadow's apartment to hear roommate Colin's mom rave about Meadow's maturity. Meadow comes in, complains about boyfriend Finn. "Some men have to move at their own pace," says Mom.

A drunken Tony and a drunker cousin Brian helicopter back from the casino, after Brian upchucks on the runway and Furio almost pushes Tony into a swirling blade. The next morning, Furio is not around and Tony is too hung over to care. Meadow calls Carmela to invite the folks for dinner. Later, at Carmine's soon-to-open Venezia Ristorante, Johnny again asks for a usurer's fee for HUD and again Tony walks. Carmela finds out at church that Furio has put his house on the market, and then Tony confirms that "the stupid fuckin' zip moved back to Italy." Carmela is devastated. While Meadow introduces her parents to boyfriend Finn and to roommates Alex and Colin, Little Paulie and crew trash Carmine's restaurant. During a post-meal chat about *Billy Budd*, a contentious Carmela thinks the idea that he is gay is just "this nonsense" pervading American life, despite what Leslie Fiedler says.

As Carmine inspects the damage, Silvio tells Paulie that "certain people are startin' to wonder where your heart is"; Paulie fumes and announces that "nobody knows what the future holds." Carmela cracks up over the loss of Furio while Paulie lunches with the old ladies; he finds out that Minn' keeps all of her money in cash when he retrieves some Parker House rolls from her doggy bag for his mom. On orders from Carmine, Dave Fusco, business agent, Local 42, shuts down the Esplanade II construction site.

At a convenience store, Soprano juror Danny Scalercio brushes elbows with Eugene Pontecorvo and is admonished to "do the right thing." Meadow calls her mom to invite her to lunch at the Plaza as Tony sits tight re the shutdown. The Plaza tête-à-tête quickly descends into an argument about Billy Budd, love, and mutual belittling. Paulie approaches Carmine at a wedding to talk turkey and Carmine doesn't know him from Adam. At home, Carmela tells Tony regarding Meadow that "if I never see her again, that would be just fine."

Meadow extracts from AJ that Furio might have something to do with her mother's strange mood. Minn' Matrone discovers Paulie in her house, freaks out, starts to set off her emergency necklace, then after an extended tussle with her intruder, succumbs to suffocation by pillow. Paulie turns around and hands the money to Tony as a fat

payment. Tony tells Meadow to ease up on her mom, that she may feel "unfulfilled." Johnny tells Tony that Carmine won't bend and though he's healthy, "if something were to happen to him, God forbid..." Tony gets the message.

Tony and Carmela have one last bedroom conversation about their daughter. "She hates my guts," says Carmela. Tony: "She's becomin' a wonderful woman, Carm. Smart, beautiful, independent...Isn't that what you dreamed about?" Carmela: "Yes."

Whitecaps

*Written by
Robin Green
& Mitchell Burgess
and David Chase.
Directed by
John Patterson.*

Tony wrangles a deal for a luxury beach house. Carmela gets a shocking call from Irina and rages at Tony to leave. Tony sets up a hit on Carmine, then calls it off. The beach house owner won't return Tony's deposit, so Dean Martin moves in offshore. Junior wins a mistrial, and after a furious final argument with Carmela, Tony agrees to leave home for good.

The finale of season four begins with Carmela on Dr. Cusamano's examining table and Tony receiving word that Chris is out of rehab and looking good. Dr. Cusamano concludes that Carmela's problem is probably a viral syndrome, maybe mono, aggravated by stress. Tony takes a detour on the way home, surprising Carmela with a seaside "caviar wish" of a house called Whitecaps. It costs $1.45 mil, *if* they can get it. "It's for the family," Tony says.

Judge Runions asks the hung jury in Junior's trial to go back in and try to reach a verdict. Over take-out Chinese, Carmela is wishy-washy about the beach house, but an excited AJ is fined $3 for saying the f-word. In bed, she changes her tune, thinks the house might be a good investment. Tony reunites with a clean and sober Chris, then after some hard bargaining, agrees to off Carmine for Johnny. Chris suggests some black guys for the job.

Tony presses owner Alan Sapinsly about the beach house and Sapinsly abruptly blows off the first in line, the Kims, contract or no contract. Carmela gets the call: they got it. The whole family is in ecstasy as they walk around the place. Tony and Carmela kiss sweetly on the beach. Chris meets with hit men Credenzo and Stanley and hands them a plan and an envelope.

Back home, AJ answers the phone. It's a drunken Irina. She tells Carmela that not only has she slept with Tony, so has her one-legged cousin. "It's so absurd—why would I make it up?" she says. Tony comes home to golf clubs in the driveway and a raging wife. "The Russian called—your son answered the telephone!" In the bedroom, Carmela is inconsolable. "Don't you touch me. Ever again." Tony vehemently denies the Svetlana tryst, fingernail aside, and accuses Carmela of stealing $40K from the bird feeder. Carmela asks, "What does she have that I don't have?," then begs him to leave.

Tony goes looking for Irina and finds Svetlana. She tells him Irina was mad about the Zellman incident, that he couldn't perform after the belt whipping. Svetlana, a child of divorce herself, consoles Tony: "You're a strong guy, you'll be all right." Tony goes to the beach house to crash. In a parking garage, FBI agent Robyn meets with Adriana and the ice starts to melt. The next morning Tony tells Sapinsly the deal is off but the tough-talking lawyer refuses to negate the contract. His wife, Trish, is rightfully concerned.

Johnny Sack tells Tony that Carmine is ready to settle. Carmine backs down to a 15 percent take on the HUD deal. Meadow tells Carmela that their entire family life is "all predicated on bullshit," then asks, "How could you eat shit from him for all those years?" Paulie suggests that Tony kick *her* out. Sapinsly calls, says he's releasing Tony from the deal but keeping the $200K deposit. Tony defies Carmela and moves back into the media room, complete with plastic inflatable bed. Chris gets the signal to call off the hit, then pays off the two hit men right before he has them wasted.

As Tony floats in the pool, Carmela comes out to bust his balls about the theater seats on the lawn, then about not being "the least bit loving." The argument continues in the media room. "Carmela, who the fuck did you think I was when you married me, huh?" "You don't really hear me, do you?" she replies. "You think for me it's all about things." After she confesses her year-long crush on Furio, Tony raises his fist to strike her, then drives it into the wall, repeatedly. When he brings up Svetlana—"she's had to fight and struggle"—Carmela has had enough. "You fucking hypocrite," she says, and walks out.

Tony calls Melfi, then hangs up. Junior's jury is still hopelessly deadlocked because one juror, Danny Scalercio, won't budge, so the judge declares a mistrial. AJ tells Tony he wants to move into the media room with him; Tony nixes the idea. The celebration at Junior's begins by Bacala ordering a couple of pies and giggling with Janice. A delightful dinner party at the Sapinslys' is rudely interrupted by an ear-shattering Dean ("...direct from the bar") Martin doing his Vegas act on a speaker system coming from Tony's boat, *The Stugots*, just offshore. "Fuckin' goomba trash," Sapinsly whines.

Tony tells Johnny that the hit is off: "Whacking a boss is bad for business." Johnny, "left holding my cock," ends the chat with a ritual hug and a glare. Tony announces to the whole family that he is moving out. Meadow is crushed. Carmela and AJ watch as the Suburban pulls out of the drive. The Sapinslys sip cognac on the deck. A booming Dean Martin carries on: "I don't drink anymore. I freeze it now and eat it like a Popsicle..." Trish screams, "Give him his money!"

As Dean sings, the season ends.

Whitecaps

Scene 48 continued:

CARMELA

You know what, Tony? What's done is done--we are where we are--and it's for the best--but just for the record or it might even interest you to know--I actually might have gone on, with your cheating and your bullshit . . . if your attitude around here had been the least bit loving, cooperative . . . interested . . .

TONY

(toweling off)

Whose idea was Whitecaps?

CARMELA

A bigger version of an emerald ring. So you can keep up with your other life.

TONY

You don't know me at all.

CARMELA

I know you better than anybody. Even your friends. That's probably why you hate me.

TONY

(smirking)

Hate you?

1 of 1 Scene 11 Scene Heading

To ███████

Per your request, here's an

additional list of deaths and/or MIAs

connected to the Sopranos. There may be

more, of course. Who knows?

███████

Retired for life

VICTIM #25: BARRY ANDREW HAYDU
Retired Clifton detective lieutenant, 32 years
on force, died on the night of his retirement
party. Location: Mantoloking beachfront bachelor
pad. Body found with revolver at side and
handcuff on right wrist. High alcohol level.
Strange scene — banister broken, head shot
off of stuffed marlin, no money in wallet.
Suicide? Soprano link — Haydu possibly long-
term mole for mob and may or may not be
implicated in late '70s death of associate
Richard "Dickie" Moltisanti, father of current
made soldier Christopher Moltisanti.

VICTIM #26: KAREN BACCILIERI

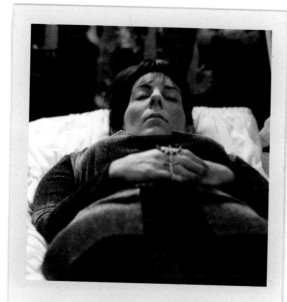

A pure accident

Wife of newly crowned Soprano capo, Robert "Bacala" Baccilieri, Jr., of Junior Soprano crew. Mrs. Bacala died of injuries sustained in an auto accident on Pompton Avenue in Cedar Grove, apparently hit on driver's side by a senior citizen. No evidence of foul play. Ironically, husband, subject Bacala, was only a few blocks back in traffic at the time of the accident. Besides Bacala, she leaves two children, Bobby, Jr., age 11, and Sophia, age 9. Thug though he is, Bacala apparently is deeply shaken by her loss. NOTE: Nickname "Bacala" means "salted cod fish" in Italian. Origin of nickname of subject believed to refer to his flat affect.

VICTIM #27: PIE-O-MY

Insurance scam?

Promising two-year-old race horse principally owned by Inez Munoz, maid of prominent Sopranos capo Ralph Cifaretto, recently disappeared (see below). Horse put down by trainer Lois Pettit after suffering extensive burns from a stable fire of unknown origin. Arson a possibility, say fire investigators. Tony Soprano also had either a financial and/or an emotional interest in this horse and was seen on location shortly after death occurred. According to eyewitnesses, he observed the carcass and left quickly.

VICTIM #28: RALPH CIFARETTO
A big MIA. Major earner/psychopath
(Riverfront Esplanade, etc.), Cifaretto, 46,
missing since the day after above-referenced
horse, Pie-O-My, succumbed. May just be a
coincidence — many hated this guy. Enemies
include: "Johnny Sack" Sacrimoni, New York,
apparently apoplectic over fat joke directed at
hefty wife; Paulie Walnuts, something to do with
a crank call to his mother; all the strippers at
the Bada Bing, since Ralph is rumored to have
beaten one to death; Rosalie Aprile, whom he
dumped to hook up with Janice Soprano;
Janice Soprano, who kicked him out shortly
thereafter; etc. Father of one son, Justin, 12,
recently severely injured in bow-and-arrow mishap.
Why would the man walk away from a sick son
and a lucrative career?

Nice guy

How low can you go?

VICTIM #29: MINERVA "MINN" MATRONE
A senior citizen, age 79, suffocated in an
apparent nighttime home invasion gone awry in
her Nutley home. Routine homicide except for
this — victim was good friends with Marianucci
Gualtieri, mother of "Paulie Walnuts" Gualtieri.
In fact, Paulie was seen in the company of
Mrs. Matrone, his mother, and another oldster,
Cookie Cirillo, attending The Producers in NY
just days before break-in. According to close
friends, Mrs. Matrone kept a lot of cash around
the house. Theory: Could a Soprano have decided to help himself?

VICTIM #30: STANLEY JOHNSON
African-American, late 20s,
sometime-resident of MLK Projects,
Newark, a known crack and heroin
dealer and occasional bone breaker.
Killed execution-style in a Passaic
River parking lot. Probable cause:
drug deal gone very bad. Sopranos
link: believed to be a key heroin
source for Chris Moltisanti when he
was an addict.

What a waste

Ditto.

VICTIM #31: CREDENZIO CURTIS
Partner of Stanley Johnson, also African-
American, drug dealer, and all-purpose
thug. Driver of the car both men were
killed in at parking lot. No drugs or
money found on either. These guys were set
up but they're savvy businessmen — would've
had gun-toting backup if this were a conventional deal. Something funny here. Given
the professionalism involved — at least
three gunmen — mob could be a party.

CARMINE LUPERTAZZI

Carmine Lupertazzi, age mid-70s, legendary OC figure, Brooklyn based, boss status in a major New
York crime family, but hard evidence is scant. A
contemporary of Junior Soprano, Carmine goes back
to the old days, is a stickler for protocol,
respect, and especially payments upstream. Wife,
Violet; a daughter; and one son active in organization, Carmine, Jr., based in Miami and generally not
deemed leadership material (TS once called him
"Brainless the Second"). Underboss "Johnny Sack"
Sacrimoni heavily involved in construction activities, including in New Jersey, with Sopranos.
Carmine has wavering respect for Sopranos, considers them "a glorified crew." Constant money
disputes with TS involving Esplanade project, other
large-scale scams. Sack caught in the middle, pla-
cating Carmine while keeping Tony from blowing up.
E.g., in a recent tug-of-war over a lowly
real estate appraiser, Carmine's new
restaurant in Brooklyn was vandalized.
Undoubtedly Tony's work. It's a volatile
relationship and someday someone's going
to get hurt.

WEAKNESSES: old, relatively healthy
but sometimes addled, thinks his son is
much smarter than he actually is, and
when push comes to shoot, is extremely
rigid and unbending. As the OC world
changes, Carmine will probably get left
behind.

ASSEMBLYMAN RONALD ZELLMAN

Ronald "Ron" Zellman, NJ State Assemblyman for district that includes alleged Sopranos activities such as the Riverfront Esplanade project. Zellman is not under active investigation at this time but he bears watching. Raised in Newark, a graduate of the University of Michigan, he was a '60s activist who decided to "work within the system." Divorced, with two young daughters, reputedly a tireless "pothole fixer" for his district, and moves in many circles. Business friends include contractor Jack Massarone, local activist Maurice Tiffen, and, we think, Tony Soprano. He frequents known Soprano hangouts like the Bada Bing, but plays his cards very close to the chest, i.e., didn't back Italian hotheads in Columbus Day protests. If he does favors for TS, he's bound to slip up at some point and we'll be there.

WEAKNESSES: Like most pols, likes the ladies. Also, doesn't seem to have the "stugots" to run with the mob. If we caught him in a Marion Barry–type sting, he'd sing like a coked-out canary.

PROFILE: THE FBI WORKING GROUP

ASSIGNED TO THE SOPRANOS

FRANK CUBITOSO, Bureau chief, North New Jersey office, principal decision maker in ongoing Soprano investigation. Savvy veteran more than up to the task of tracking down this outfit.

DWIGHT D. HARRIS, Special Agent, Newark, been on the Sopranos squad since 1996. Operational point man on most Sopranos activities post-CW 16, i.e., the S.E.T. project at TS home, etc. On first-name basis with Tony, et al.

DEBORAH CICCERONE-WALDRUP, Special Agent, Newark, first major undercover assignment to befriend Adriana La Cerva. As streetwise "Danielle Ciccolella," of "Lilac Personal Shopping," very effective in infiltrating Adriana's world, even TS's home in North Caldwell. Four months undercover before falling out with La Cerva. Married to Agent Mike Waldrup, one son, six months.

ROBYN SANSEVERINO, agent brought in to run CW Adriana La Cerva after agency threatened La Cerva with indictment (cocaine trafficking) and reassigned Agent Ciccerone-Waldrup. Currently La Cerva's principal contact. Very good at winning over CWs.

Cosette

We Love You   1999–2002

THE SOPRANOS CAST AND CREW—Seasons One Through Three

Created by DAVID CHASE

Executive Producer DAVID CHASE
Executive Producer BRAD GREY
Executive Producers ROBIN GREEN &
MITCHELL BURGESS
Co-Executive Producer ILENE S. LANDRESS
Co-Executive Producer–
Seasons 1 & 2 FRANK RENZULLI
Supervising Producer TERENCE WINTER
Producer MARTIN BRUESTLE
Producer HENRY J. BRONCHTEIN
Producer–Seasons 1 & 2 ALLEN COULTER
Producer–Seasons 2 & 3 TODD A. KESSLER
Associate Producer–
Seasons 1 & 2 GREGG GLICKMAN
Associate Producer–Season 3 GIANNA MARIA SMART
Executive Story Editor–Season 1 JASON CAHILL

Series Cast JAMES GANDOLFINI
LORRAINE BRACCO
EDIE FALCO
MICHAEL IMPERIOLI
DOMINIC CHIANESE
VINCENT PASTORE
STEVEN VAN ZANDT
TONY SIRICO
JAMIE-LYNN SIGLER
ROBERT ILER
AIDA TURTURRO
DREA DE MATTEO
DAVID PROVAL
JOHN VENTIMIGLIA
FEDERICO CASTELLUCCIO
STEVEN R. SCHIRRIPA
KATHERINE NARDUCCI
ROBERT FUNARO
and NANCY MARCHAND
and JOE PANTOLIANO
Also Starring JERRY ADLER

Stunt Coordinator PETE BUCOSSI
Casting GEORGIANNE WALKEN &
SHEILA JAFFE
Casting Associate–
Seasons 1 & 2 MARY CLAY BOLAND
Casting Associate–Season 3 MEREDITH TUCKER
Directors of Photography ALIK SAKHAROV
PHIL ABRAHAM
Production Designer–Pilot EDWARD PISONI
Production Designer–Season 1 DEAN TAUCHER
Production Designer–
Seasons 2 & 3 BOB SHAW
Costume Designer–Pilot ANE CRABTREE
Costume Designer–Series JULIET POLCSA
Editor–Pilot JOANNA CAPPUCCILLI
Editors–Series SIDNEY WOLINSKY, A.C.E.
CONRAD GONZALEZ
WILLIAM B. STICH, A.C.E.
Music Editor KATHRYN DAYAK
Unit Production Manager–Pilot ALYSSE BEZAHLER
Unit Production Managers HENRY J. BRONCHTEIN
SCOTT HORNBACHER
ILENE S. LANDRESS
Unit Production Manager–
Season 1 BART WENRICH
1st Assistant Directors MICHAEL DECASPER
MARK McGANN
RANDY BARBEE
2nd Assistant Directors KRISTIN BERNSTEIN
JEFFREY T. BERNSTEIN
MICHELLE L. KEISER
LISA M. ROWE
SCOTT SCHAEFFER
2nd 2nd Assistant Directors JENNIFER TRUELOVE
DYLAN K. MASSIN
MATTHEW SIRIANNI
NOREEN CHELEDEN

Camera Operator BILL COLEMAN
Script Supervisor CHRISTINE GEE LOWREY
Production Supervisor–
Season 1 LORI DOUGLAS
Production Coordinator HANS GRAFFUNDER
Asst. Production Coordinator STEVE KORNACKI
Asst. Production Coordinator CHRIS COLLINS
Production Sound Mixer MATHEW PRICE, C.A.S.
Gaffers KEVIN JANICELLI
JOHN L. OATES
Key Grip–Season 1 JIM McMILLAN
Key Grip–Seasons 2 & 3 DENNIS GAMIELLO
Dolly Grip–Seasons 2 & 3 ED LOWRY
Key Rigging Grip–
Seasons 2 & 3 LOUIS PETRAGLIA
Art Director–Pilot DIANN DUTHIE
Art Director–Season 1 HARRY DARROW
Art Director–Seasons 2 & 3 SCOTT MURPHY
Set Decorator–Pilot JESSICA LANIER
Set Decorator–Series JANET SHAW
Leadman GERARD PINEO
Property Master ANTHONY J. DIMEO
Associate Costume Designer LAUREN PRESS
KIM WILCOX
Wardrobe Supervisors GAIL FITZGIBBONS
KEVIN FAHERTY
Key Make-Up Artist KYMBRA CALLAGHAN
Key Hair Stylist MEL McKINNEY
Scenic Charge MICHAEL ZANSKY
On Set Scenic JAMES COVINGTON
Construction Coordinator GARY GRILL
Key Construction Grip CHRIS MARZULLI
Assistant to David Chase JULIE ROSS
Writers Assistant–Season 1 ETHAN GOLDMAN
Writers Assistant–
Seasons 2 & 3 FELICIA B. LIPCHIK
Production Accountant–
Seasons 1 & 2 LYNDA VAN DAMM
Production Accountant–
Season 3 SALVATORE CARINO
Unit Manager/ CHARLES MILLER /
Location Manager–Pilot BILL BARVIN
Location Manager–Series MARK KAMINE
Assistant Location Managers JASON L. MINTER
REGINA HEYMAN
Transportation Captain JIM LEAVEY
Transportation Co-Captain HARRY J. LEAVEY
Extras Casting GRANT WILFLEY CASTING
Extras Casting Associate ANNA MANISCALCO
Caterer PREMIERE CATERING–
MIKE HERNANDEZ
Craft Service DEBBIE FEARON
Supervising Sound Editors ANNA MACKENZIE
BILL ANGAROLA, M.P.S.E.
RAY SPIESS, M.P.S.E.
Re-Recording Sound Mixers KEVIN PATRICK BURNS
TODD ORR
RON EVANS
TOM PERRY
ADAM SAWELSON
FRED TATOR, C.A.S.
ADR Mixers PAUL ZYDEL
ROBERT DESCHAINE, C.A.S.

Special Thanks To:
The New Jersey Film Commission
and The People of New Jersey
New York City Mayor's Office
for Film, Theater, and Broadcasting
Green Hill Retirement Home
Harrison Board of Education

Filmed at Silvercup Studios and on location in New Jersey

This list represents only ⅓ of the crew of *The Sopranos*.

THE SOPRANOS CAST AND CREW—Season Four

Created by	DAVID CHASE
Executive Producer	DAVID CHASE
Executive Producer	BRAD GREY
Executive Producer	ROBIN GREEN &
	MITCHELL BURGESS
Executive Producer	ILENE S. LANDRESS
Co-Executive Producer	TERENCE WINTER
Producer	HENRY J. BRONCHTEIN
Producer	MARTIN BRUESTLE
Co-Producer	GIANNA SMART
Co-Producer	ANN HOLM
Associate Producer	SCOTT HORNBACHER
Associate Producer	JULIE ROSS
Series Cast	JAMES GANDOLFINI
	LORRAINE BRACCO
	EDIE FALCO
	MICHAEL IMPERIOLI
	DOMINIC CHIANESE
	STEVEN VAN ZANDT
	TONY SIRICO
	JAMIE-LYNN SIGLER
	ROBERT ILER
	AIDA TURTURRO
	DREA DE MATTEO
	JOHN VENTIMIGLIA
	FEDERICO CASTELLUCCIO
	STEVEN R. SCHIRRIPA
	KATHERINE NARDUCCI
	VINCENT CURATOLA
	and JOE PANTOLIANO
Stunt Coordinator	PETE BUCOSSI
Casting	GEORGIANNE WALKEN
	& SHEILA JAFFE
Casting Associate	MEREDITH TUCKER
Casting Assistant	KATHLEEN BACKEL
Director of Photography	ALIK SAKHAROV
Director of Photography	PHIL ABRAHAM
Production Designer	BOB SHAW
Costume Designer	JULIET POLCSA
Editors	SIDNEY WOLINSKY, A.C.E.
	CONRAD GONZALEZ
	WILLIAM B. STICH, A.C.E.
Music Editor	KATHRYN DAYAK
Unit Production Managers	HENRY J. BRONCHTEIN
	SCOTT HORNBACHER
	ILENE S. LANDRESS
1st Assistant Directors	MICHAEL DeCASPER
	MARK McGANN
	RANDY BARBEE
2nd Assistant Directors	KRISTIN BERNSTEIN
	MICHAEL SMITH
	NOREEN CHELEDEN
2nd 2nd Assistant Director	JOHN SILVESTRI
Camera Operator	BILL COLEMAN
Script Supervisor	CHRISTINE GEE-LOWREY
Production Supervisor	HANS GRAFFUNDER
Asst. Production Coordinators	STEVE KORNACKI
	CHRIS COLLINS
Assistant to Producer	JENNIFER G. FISTERE
Production Auditor	SALVATORE CARINO
1st Assistant Auditors	KYLE O'BRIEN
	DEIDRE SCHROWANG
Payroll Auditor	TOSHA HAWKINS
2nd Assistant Auditors	TONY CYPRES
	CHAUENCY REESE
Production Sound Mixer	MATHEW PRICE, C.A.S.
Boom Operator	PAUL KORONKIEWICZ
Gaffers	KEVIN JANICELLI
	JOHN OATES

Best Boy Electrics	TOM PERCARPIO
	THOMAS ANDERSON
Electricians	PETER KOOLA
	BEN NOBLE
	JOSEPH M. ORI
	ROBERT A. FALCONE
	ROBERTO JIMENEZ
Key Grip	DENNIS GAMIELLO
Dolly Grip	EDWARD LOWRY
Key Rigging Grip	LOUIS PETRAGLIA
Best Boy Grip	AARON DAWLEY
Grips	JOHN LOWRY
	LOUIS SABAT
	KEVIN LOWRY
	ANTHONY GAMIELLO
	PHILIP PURIFICATO
Art Director	SCOTT MURPHY
Set Decorator	JANET SHAW
Assistant Set Decorator	JENNIFER STARKE
Leadman	GERARD PINEO
On Set Dresser	JEFFREY M. MARCHETTI
Set Dressers	JAMES J. ARCHER
	TROY R. ADEE
	VINCENT OROFINO
	ERIC STEPPER
	THOMAS J. HEAPS
	JOHN BASILE
	ERIC METZGER
Property Master	DIANA BURTON
Assistant Property Masters	RENA DeANGELO
	ANTHONY BALDASARE
Associate Costume Designers	LAUREN PRESS
	LORRAINE CALVERT
Wardrobe Supervisors	GAIL FITZGIBBONS
	ELIZABETH FELDBAUER
Costumers	JOSEPH LA CORTE
	BARBARA KRAUTHAMER
Tailor	MILDRED DEL RIO
Key Make-Up Artist	KYMBRA CALLAGHAN
Make-Up Artist	STEPHEN KELLEY
Key Hair Stylist	VICTOR DeNICOLA, JR.
Hair Stylist	DALE BROWNELL
Scenic Charge	MICHAEL ZANSKY
On Set Scenics	JAMES HOFF
	ANNE HAYWOOD
Construction Coordinator	GARY GRILL
Key Construction Grip	CHRIS MARZULLI
Writers Assistant	FELICIA LIPCHIK
Location Manager	MARK KAMINE
Assistant Location Managers	JASON L. MINTER
	REGINA HEYMAN
Location Scouts	ZORAN BLAZEVIC
	SANDRA VANNUCCHI
	JAMES COSPER
	CLARE LORD
	DAVID CHAMBERS
Locations Coordinator	JESSICA ARCHER
Transportation Captain	JIM LEAVEY
Transportation Co-Captain	HARRY J. LEAVEY
Extras Casting	GRANT WILFLEY CASTING
Extras Casting Associate	ANNA MANISCALCO
Caterer	PREMIERE CATERING
Chef	MICHAEL HERNANDEZ
Craft Service	DAWN WOLF
Supervising Sound Editors	ANNA MACKENZIE
	WILLIAM ANGAROLA, M.P.S.E.
Re-Recording Sound Mixers	KEVIN PATRICK BURNS
	TODD ORR
ADR Mixers	PAUL ZYDEL, M.P.S.E.
	GREG STEELE

THE SOPRANOS SELECTED GUEST STARS*

Season I

Character	Actor
Giacomo "Jackie" Aprile	MICHAEL RISPOLI
Detective Vin Makazian	JOHN HEARD
Dick Barone	JOE LISI
Brendan Filone	ANTHONY DESANDO
Mikey Palmice	AL SAPIENZA
Georgie	FRANK SANTORELLI
Irina Peltsin	OKSANA LADA
Shlomo Teittleman	CHUCK LOW
Ariel	NED EISENBERG
Dr. Bruce Cusamano	ROBERT LUPONE
Jean Cusamano	SAUNDRA SANTIAGO
Rosalie Aprile	SHARON ANGELA
John "Johnny Sack" Sacrimoni	VINCENT CURATOLA
Father Phil	PAUL SCHULZE
"Larry Boy" Barese	TONY DARROW
Raymond Curto	GEORGE LOROS
James "Little Jimmy" Altieri	JOE BADALUCCO, JR.
Fred Peters	TONY RAY ROSSI
Young Livia Soprano	LAILA ROBINS
Giovanni "Johnny Boy" Soprano	JOSEPH SIRAVO
Young Junior Soprano	ROCCO SISTO
Attorney Melvoin	RICHARD PORTNOW
Richard La Penna	RICHARD ROMANUS
Bobbi Sanfillipo	ROBYN PETERSON
Jason La Penna	WILL McCORMACK
Agent Harris	MATT SERVITTO
Agent Grasso	FRANK PANDO
Frank Cubitoso	FRANK PELLEGRINO
Massive Genius	BOKEEM WOODBINE
Madam Debby	KAREN SILLAS
Miss Giaculo	CANDY TRABUCCO
Isabella	MARIA GRAZIA CUCINOTTA

Season II

Character	Actor
Neil Mink	DAVID MARGULIES
Matt Bevilaqua	LILLO BRANCATO, JR.
Sean Gismonte	CHRIS TARDIO
Barbara Giglione	NICOLE BURDETTE
Mary DeAngelis	SUZANNE SHEPHERD
Hugh DeAngelis	TOM ALDREDGE
Gigi Cestone	JOHN FIORE
Skip Lipari	LOUIS LOMBARDI, JR.
Reverend Herman James, Sr.	BILL COBBS
Reverend James, Jr.	GREGALAN WILLIAMS
Dr. Elliot Kupferberg	PETER BOGDANOVICH
Peter "Beansie" Gaeta	PAUL HERMAN
Dr. Douglas Schreck	MATTHEW SUSSMAN
Angie Bonpensiero	TONI KALEM
Gabriella Dante	MAUREEN VAN ZANDT
Joanne Moltisanti	MARIANNE LEONE
Annalisa Zucca	SOFIA MILOS
Zi Vittorio	VITTORIO DUSE
David Scatino	ROBERT PATRICK
Himself	FRANK SINATRA, JR.
Sunshine	PAUL MAZURSKY
Vito Spatafore	JOSEPH R. GANNASCOLI
Dr. Ira Fried	LEWIS J. STADLEN
Amy Safir	ALICIA WITT
Himself	JON FAVREAU
Herself	JANEANE GAROFALO
Herself	SANDRA BERNHARD
Vic Musto	JOE PENNY
Jack Massarone	ROBERT DESIDERIO
Bobby Zanone	VITO ANTUOFERMO, SR.
Svetlana Kirilenko	ALLA KLIOUKA
Albert Barese	RICHARD MALDONE
Donny K.	RAYMOND FRANZA
Giacomo "Jackie" Aprile, Jr.	JASON CERBONE
Patsy/Philly Parisi	DAN GRIMALDI

Season III

Character	Actor
Noah Tannenbaum	PATRICK TULLY
Assemblyman Zellman	PETER RIEGERT
Caitlin Rucker	ARI GRAYNOR
Benny Fazio	MAX CASELLA
Eugene Pontecorvo	ROBERT FUNARO
Little Paulie Germani	CARL CAPOTORTO
Dino Zerilli	ANDREW DAVOLI
Bobby "Bacala" Baccilieri, Sr.	BURT YOUNG
Officer Leon Wilmore	CHARLES S. DUTTON
Tracee	ARIEL KILEY
Dr. John Kennedy	SAM McMURRAY
Gloria Trillo	ANNABELLA SCIORRA
Aaron Arkaway	TURK PIPKIN
Slava Malevsky	FRANK CIORNEI
Valery	VITALI BAGANOV
Ginny Sack	DENISE BORINO
Nucci Gualtieri	FRANCES ESEMPLARE
Father Obosi	ISSACH DE BANKOLE
Agent Deborah Ciccerone	LOLA GLAUDINI
Major Carl Zwingli	TOBIN BELL

Season IV

Character	Actor
Lt. Barry Haydu	TOM MASON
Carmine Lupertazzi	TONY LIP
Bobby Baccilieri, Jr.	ANGELO MASSAGLI
Sophia Baccilieri	LEXIE SPERDUTO
Dr. Wendi Kobler	LINDA LAVIN
Carlo Gervasi	ARTHUR NASCARELLA
Dr. Sandy Shaw	JOYCE VAN PATTEN
Professor Longo-Murphy	ROMA MAFFIA
Karen Baccilieri	CHRISTINE PEDI
Himself	MONTEL WILLIAMS
Brian Cammarata	MATTHEW DEL NEGRO
Agent Robyn Sanseverino	KAREN YOUNG
Prosecutor	DAN CASTLEMAN
Judge Whitney R. Runions	RANDY BARBEE
Joe Peeps	JOE MARUZZO
Jean-Philippe Colbert	JEAN-HUGUES ANGLADE
Devin Pillsbury	JESSICA DUNPHY
Finn DeTrolio	WILL JANOWITZ
Lois Pettit	MANON HALLIBURTON
Elodi Colbert	MURIELLE ARDEN
Valentina La Paz	LESLIE BEGA
Cookie Cirillo	ANNA BERGER
Minn' Matrone	FRAN ANTHONY
Marty Schwartz	JERRY GRAYSON
Maurice Tiffen	VONDIE CURTIS HALL
Dominic Palladino	ELIAS KOTEAS
Little Carmine Lupertazzi	RAY ABRUZZO
Beppy Scerbo	JOE PUCILLO
Alan Sapinsly	BRUCE ALTMAN

*Actors are listed under the season in which they first appear.

Allen Rucker is a writer and television journalist. He cofounded
the video group TVTV and has written numerous award-winning
TV specials and documentaries. His published work includes the
New York Times #1 bestseller *The Sopranos Family Cookbook*, and
two books of satire, *The History of White People in America* and *A
Paler Shade of White*, both coauthored with the comedian Martin
Mull. He also teaches in the School of Cinema-TV at the University
of Southern California and lives in Los Angeles.